KANSAS CITY'S MONTGALL AVENUE

KANSAS CITY'S MONTGALL AVENUE

BLACK LEADERS AND THE STREET THEY CALLED HOME

MARGIE CARR

 UNIVERSITY PRESS OF KANSAS

© 2023 by the University Press of Kansas

All rights reserved

Published by the University Press of Kansas (Lawrence, Kansas 66045), which was organized by the Kansas Board of Regents and is operated and funded by Emporia State University, Fort Hays State University, Kansas State University, Pittsburg State University, the University of Kansas, and Wichita State University.

Library of Congress Cataloging-in-Publication Data available.

Library of Congress Control Number: 2023905925

Title: Kansas City's Montgall Avenue / by Margie Carr

ISBN 978-0-7006-3467-5 (paperback : alk. paper)

ISBN 978-0-7006-3468-2 (ebook)

British Library Cataloguing-in-Publication Data is available.

Printed in the United States of America

10 9 8 7 6 5 4 3 2 1

The paper used in this publication is acid free and meets the minimum requirements of the American National Standard for Permanence of Paper for Printed Library Materials Z39.48–1992.

CONTENTS

PREFACE

When Ninth Street Baptist Church, a historic Black church in Lawrence, Kansas, was celebrating its 150th anniversary in 2013, I wrote a story about it for our local newspaper.[1] While researching details about the church's past, I stumbled across an oral history from a woman who remembered hearing scholar and civil rights leader W. E. B. Du Bois speak at one of the church's well-known Sunday afternoon forums.[2] Hoping to pinpoint a date for this lecture, I decided to peruse Du Bois's papers at the University of Massachusetts at Amherst, which are available online. This search led me to the magnificent Montgall Avenue in Kansas City, Missouri. In the Du Bois collection, I found a number of letters to the scholar from the 2400 block of this remarkable street. The correspondence came from different households and different decades.

One letter was from a World War I veteran, Homer Roberts (2453 Montgall Avenue), who had heard that the scholar was working on a project about Black soldiers' service in the war. As a member of the 325th Field Signal Battalion, "the first man enlisted therein,"[3] Roberts offered Du Bois his assistance on the project. Another short note was written by Clark University professor William Crogman, who had known Du Bois from his days in Georgia. Crogman had invited the former Atlanta resident to visit his daughter's home on Montgall (2447) after one of his speaking engagements in Kansas City. And there was a long letter from Anna Holland Jones (2444) from November 1911. Du Bois and Jones were friends, and she began her letter by reminding him of his recent visit to her home. She then went into detail about how she and the other Black families on the street had been targeted in attacks that had escalated to the point of dynamite. She asked Du Bois whether he could summon the support of his newly formed civil rights organization, the National Association for the Advancement of Colored People (NAACP), to assist them in their fight against the violence.

West side of Montgall Avenue in 1911. *Crisis*, February 1912.

Digging into the lives of Anna Jones, William Crogman, and Homer Roberts, I was overwhelmed by what I learned about their lives and accomplishments. More research about their neighbors, some of whom will be familiar to students of Kansas City history, such as Chester Franklin (2447 Montgall) and Lucile Bluford (2444 Montgall), convinced me that I should share not only their stories but also the story of the evolution and devolution of Montgall Avenue itself.

I grew up in suburban Kansas City, in an area that had racially re-strictive housing covenants. I was aware of this as a youngster and thought it was unfair, but at the time, residential segregation felt like distant history and had little personal meaning or significance for me. It was an abstract concept with nameless, faceless victims, and it lacked the drama that made other forms of discrimination more compelling.

In school I was taught about the White men who built Kansas City. We took class trips to the Nelson Art Gallery, which was con-structed on land donated by newspaper publisher and editor William Rockhill Nelson. We studied the architecture in the historic Country Club Plaza, designed and created by Jesse Clyde Nichols, the same man who created my childhood neighborhood in Fairway. We also

East side of Montgall Avenue in 1911. *Crisis*, February 1912.

researched the lives of successful entrepreneurs, some of whom made their money off the backs of slaves. Studying these businessmen, I believed that I was learning the complete story of the most important leaders in my hometown. I had no concept of the Kansas City that existed east of Troost Avenue, the city's Black/White dividing line, and no knowledge of the parallel world that was built by Black America during the "separate but equal" era of Jim Crow, which continued well past the civil rights era. The closest I got to this other world was around Halloween in the 1980s when I, along with thousands of other teenagers and young adults, visited "Dr. Deadly's Haunted Hospital" at 1826 Forest Avenue in Kansas City, Missouri. Only in the research for this book did I learn that this "haunted hospital" was the former Wheatley-Provident Hospital, the tragic remains of the institution started by John E. Perry, the physician who lived at 2451 Montgall for more than five decades. I find my lack of knowledge about these important men and women sadly unfortunate, and I want to share this information as broadly as possible.

A close examination of this street is in no way a complete study of Kansas City's African American community. But no study of the city's Black community, or of Kansas City, is complete without the story of the men and women of Montgall Avenue. And perhaps no story of the Black experience in twentieth-century America is complete without an understanding of the evolution of a street in the heartland that was home to many of the city's Black professional class.

ACKNOWLEDGMENTS

When it takes ten years to research and write a book, you come across a lot of people who made the journey possible. I am in debt to the librarians and archivists I've met over the years from the Black Archives of Mid-America, the Missouri Valley Special Collections at the Kansas City Public Library, the Kansas City branch of the State Historical Society of Missouri, the Kansas Historical Society, and the Spencer Research Library at the University of Kansas. You do the good work to preserve the stories that tell us who we are. Thank you for helping researchers find them.

In addition, there are individuals without whom this book would not have been possible, and I wish to highlight them—some posthumously. Interviews and conversations with the men and women of Montgall helped shape this book. Thank you to Guion Bluford, Renée Cochée, Danny Herndon, Retha Lindsey, Columbus Neal, Paul Pittman, Rozelia Russell, and Errol Warren. You were generous with your time and your experiences. There is one Montgall resident above all the others, though, who made this work possible. I owe a tremendous debt to Gwendolyn Calderon, who lived a lot of the history in this book. Thank you for sharing so much of your life. You are the heart of this story, and I am grateful that I can call you my friend.

Others also guided me over the years, including Bill Tuttle, whose knowledge is boundless. From the start, he convinced me that what I had discovered was worth pursuing. Michael Sweeney was another enthusiastic and generous supporter who shared resources and opened doors for me. I only hope that I can pay your generosity forward.

Working on this book, I gained new appreciation for the neighbors I have had in my life, from Canterbury, to Cypress Point, to Stratford. My Canterbury neighbors were a positive influence during my childhood, like the Cypress Point folks were to my children. Thank you all—especially my former neighbor and friend, Margaret Severson, who read early drafts and offered brilliant advice. Bill Worley and Juli Warren Ward, and especially Charles Coulter, helped me clarify thoughts and made my words more accurate and precise.

Thank you to the good people at the University Press of Kansas, especially Joyce Harrison, who encouraged and supported me every step of the way.

My friends have been incredibly supportive over the years as I carried on about this project. I don't dare try to list you all because I would, undoubtedly, forget someone. I am grateful for the support I have received from all of you: coworkers, my book club, mosaics group, the "moonies," and especially the Tuesday night bowling team. You are more than friends—you are family.

Finally, I want to acknowledge my family. Dad left me his love of history, and Mom gave me her love of writing. My children, Amla, Charlie, and Mary, put up with a lot of my distractions over the years. I love you more than you know. What a privilege it is for me to be your mom. And finally, there was Jim, who made all the best parts of my life possible.

INTRODUCTION

Today, two nondescript rows of century-old homes stand on the 2400 block of Montgall Avenue in Kansas City, Missouri. The street is showing its age, and many of the homes are in need of repair: gutters dip from roofs, front porches sag, and weeds sprout through the buckled sidewalks. The house at 2444 Montgall is empty, and plywood covers its doors and windows. In the area surrounding Montgall now, empty storefronts stand like skeletons, and the only commercial activity is at a few gas stations and liquor stores sprinkled throughout the neighborhood. In the summer of 2004 serial killer Terry Blair stalked the area and placed his victims' bodies in its vacant buildings and detached garages. Other, more recent headlines continue the troubled narrative: "Large KC House Fire Might Involve Meth Lab," "Suspect Critical after Shot by KC Officer," "Police Find Victim's Body on Sidewalk of KC Neighborhood."[1] Today this inner-city street is the epitome of urban blight.

But this neighborhood hasn't always been defined by bleak headlines. As the twentieth century began, owning a home on Montgall symbolized a level of achievement, a fulfillment of the American dream and a promise of hope for a brighter future. "So T. C. Unthank has bought him a house way out on Montgall," Lewis Wood, editor of one of Kansas City's weekly Black newspapers, wrote admiringly. The editor went on to compare this move to Civil War general Ulysses S. Grant's final assault on the Confederacy. "Old General Grant has begun his march toward Richmond and the rebels are all moving!"[2] Thomas Unthank, a prominent African American physician, was, as Wood suggested, part of a charge into a new housing development in the center of the city's White middle-class neighborhoods. It was a move that pushed the housing limits of Kansas City's Black community just as the city's racial lines were beginning to crystallize.

During the first half of the twentieth century, the 2400 block of Montgall Avenue was a "Black island," as the *Kansas City Call*'s long-time editor, Lucile Bluford, called it—an enclave of African American families living amid the larger majority.³ It was home to some of the most accomplished men and women in Kansas City's history, many of whom were committed to improving the living and working conditions of African Americans in the face of unimaginable barriers.

Montgall Avenue's story provides a vessel and a context for the larger story of the African American experience in twentieth-century America. The street is a microcosm of the changing face of discrimination in the twentieth century as it transformed from a middle-class, integrated community to the neglected, blighted place it is today. At the turn of the twentieth century, when the houses on the block were emerging from the midwestern prairie, there were no rules about where African Americans could live. Black families settled alongside immigrants from Russia and Europe.⁴ As the European immigrants assimilated into American culture, they became part of the ruling majority. At the same time, people of color continued to fight attitudes and stereotypes of the day. These attitudes hardened into discriminatory policies that settled over the city and the country like concrete. And like concrete, they could only be chiseled away.

Americans have been taught to view racism in twentieth century America as primarily a southern problem, one that can be understood with a quick study of sharecropping, the fallacy of the separate but equal principle, and some knowledge of discrete yet horrifying events: the murder of Emmett Till, the use of attack dogs against peaceful protestors, the charred remains of lynched Black men. It is a view of America that African Americans have experienced terrible injustices but there is a steady forward movement, and all Americans can feel good about this progress. This narrative is enhanced with rich biographies of heroic men and women who triumphed over racism in order to achieve great things. Looking at this book from that level, as a series of biographies about men and women who led and served Kansas City's Black community, leaves one with a hopeful outlook about the progress of Black Americans. But there is more to the story of the African American experience in twentieth-century America. A study of the rise and fall of the place that these individuals called home paints a more complete—and more disturbing—picture of the role that race continues to play in America's story.

Very rarely have White Americans been asked to consider the devastating consequences of deep-seated attitudes toward people of color, beliefs held by the ruling class, which understands that the best way to govern disparate groups is through compromise and appeasement, deals that have repeatedly used Black people as bargaining chips. Consider this: Montgall Avenue is named after Kansas Citian Rufus Montgall, a slave owner who was allowed to keep his slaves during the Civil War because his state elected to remain in the Union rather than joining the Confederacy. Montgall Avenue is located in a state known for the 1820 Missouri Compromise, which allowed the United States to expand while maintaining a balance of power among free states and slave states, slave states that counted a person of color as only three-fifths of a person, the result of a compromise made by a previous generation.

The deterioration of Montgall Avenue to its condition today did not occur overnight or in a vacuum. Through the lens of history, though, we can see patterns as they play out again and again. In 1903 W. E. B. Du Bois predicted that the problem of the twentieth century would be the problem of the color line.[5] His prescient observation is no more evident than with the story of Montgall when its earliest Black residents faced harassment, threats, and even dynamite, all designed to get them to move. They didn't, and the street became an enclave of African Americans situated in the middle of a larger Jewish community.

At the height of the discriminatory policies of Jim Crow, the men and women of Montgall, like the spokes of a wheel, reached out into Kansas City's Black community through the institutions they built and maintained. These included the *Call*, Lincoln High School, Wheatley-Provident Hospital, General Hospital #2, the Paseo YMCA, Home Seekers Savings and Loan, and the Niles Home for Negro Children. Together these institutions provided the foundation for educational, economic, and social supports for the Black community at a time when Black Kansas Citians could not attend public schools with White students, were not treated in the city's most up-to-date hospital, could not visit the popular amusement park, Fairyland, or play golf or swim at the city's facilities in Swope Park. Black Kansas Citians were barred from most hotels, were not allowed to try on clothes in the downtown department stores, and could not eat in most of the city's restaurants.

In addition to building and directing the city's segregated institutions, Montgall residents taught their children to believe in the American dream. They told them that thrift and hard work were the most effective weapons to fight racism. Their children learned that if they were patient and played by the (White) rules, then eventually discrimination would disappear. These leaders could not have foreseen how White Americans would change the rules in ways that devastated the residents of Montgall Avenue. At the dawn of the twentieth century, academic scholarship was focused on racial differences, and those defined as "Negro" were thought to be inferior to Caucasians in every way—physically, intellectually, and morally. Kansas City's White leaders, many of whom had migrated from the South, were primed to accept these beliefs and turn them into policy. These men were eager to establish themselves atop the social order in a metropolis that was still catching its breath from the changes brought by industrialization and the arrival of thousands of Europeans. Montgall's earliest Black homeowners fought these stereotypes vigorously, and their protests illustrate the variety of ways in which the Black community dealt with the discriminatory laws of Jim Crow, a fight that ended successfully in the courts but not in the hearts and minds of many White Americans.

Most overt talk about "Negro inferiority" faded away by the middle of the twentieth century, but other harmful attitudes about race persisted. Specifically, many believed that there was an inverse relationship between African Americans and home values and that the only way for a neighborhood to maintain its home value was to be all White. These attitudes seeped into and directed government policy, and in 1933 the federal government formed the Home Owners Loan

Corporation (HOLC), which devised a rating system to assess the creditworthiness of homeowners across the country. Streets inhabited solely by Whites were given the highest ranking, and the blocks where only Black people lived earned the lowest. Integrated neighborhoods, like the area around Montgall, were seen as unstable because they were viewed as "in transition"—and as transitioning the wrong way. In the early 1940s, when Kansas City's "security rankings" were published, the 2400 block of Montgall received the lowest score because its residents were all Black. As far as the federal government was concerned, the men and women on Montgall were some of the least creditworthy people in the country. At the same time that millions of White Americans learned that it would be a lot easier to invest in a home through a federally insured mortgage program, Black homeowners saw the value of their homes, their most valuable assets, evaporate after banks stopped investing in these neighborhoods. In addition, the federal government provided tax incentives for homeownership, a significant government transfer program that is frequently overlooked in contemporary political discourse.

After World War II, new housing developments provided spacious homes and state-of- the-art schools for the city's White community, but restrictive covenants barred Montgall Avenue's families from moving into such places. Montgall residents watched as White people fled the area surrounding their street and poorer Black families moved in, families that had been deprived of adequate housing for decades. On street after street, profit-hungry real estate professionals initiated "block-busting" campaigns to move White families into new housing developments and farther and farther away from the city core.

Montgall was once home to many African American migrants from other states, especially teachers, who found it a safe haven from which to launch or build their adult careers. But for today's residents the neighborhood is a trap. Many of the children who grew up on Montgall in the 1920s and 1930s left the street—and the city—for successful careers.

Those who stayed had a different experience. Consider the stories of two families who moved to Montgall in the early twentieth century and lived in two homes, 2449 and 2444. Arthur and Marguerite Pittman migrated to Kansas City after Arthur took a job at Lincoln High School. They raised four children on Montgall Avenue, and two of their sons attended out-of-state universities and flourished as veterinarians, one for the horses at Ak-Sar-Ben race track in Omaha, Nebraska, and the other in Los Angeles. The youngest Pittman, Paul, remained in his childhood home throughout his life. In the 1970s thieves broke into his home at 2449 Montgall while he was at work. They took the brass chandelier and sconces that hung in his dining room and stole Adirondack chairs that his father had built. In 1976 they set fire to his detached garage. His insurance company dropped his policy. He lived the rest of his life without having homeowner's insurance.

Like Arthur Pittman, John Bluford moved to Montgall Avenue after accepting a job at Lincoln High School. He and his second wife raised three children in the home at 2444 Montgall. After graduating from college, Bluford's youngest son, Guion, moved to Philadelphia and became an engineer. His son, also named Guion, became an astronaut. In 1983 the young Guion was the first African American to reach outer space aboard the space shuttle Challenger. He went on to fly in three more space shuttle missions. Back in Kansas City, as his nephew was making his way through the ranks at NASA, sixty-seven-year-old John Bluford was arrested after a routine traffic stop not far from Montgall. Bluford left police custody permanently disabled. John Bluford returned to his childhood home for a time where his sister, Lucile, and a neighbor took turns caring for him.

This book seeks to paint a more complete picture of the Montgall residents who may be familiar to students of Kansas City history, such as *Call* editors Lucile Bluford (2444) and Chester Franklin (2447). It also introduces residents who are lesser known but who also played a significant role in the city's history, such as Anna Holland Jones, John Edward Perry, and Hugh Oliver Cook, among others. This book tells a larger story too, one that encompasses the African American experience in twentieth-century America. Tracing the rise and fall of

Montgall Avenue makes this bigger story painfully clear, illustrating how the laws and policies established by a majority White leadership presented obstacle after obstacle to Black Americans and systematically weighed them down with disadvantages, all while making investments and offering support to other groups as they assimilated into American society.

How the Book Is Organized

Chapter 1 of this book focuses on Rufus Montgall, a pioneer who owned the land where the street was built. He lived during a remarkable period of Kansas City's history, when it grew from a small outpost into an industrial giant. When he died in 1887, Kansas City was somewhat integrated as Blacks and Whites shared neighborhoods and streets. But Montgall's own attitudes foretold how Kansas City's African American community would be treated after his death.

After chapter 1, the book is organized chronologically and by addresses and the homeowners who occupied individual homes. Chapters 2–5 cover the early years, roughly 1904 to 1919, and the lives of Hugh Oliver Cook and Myrtle Foster Cook, Anna Holland Jones, Frances Jackson, and Hezekiah Walden. They were teachers charged with educating and lifting the children of freed Black men and women from poverty. These homeowners were anchors both for Montgall and for Kansas City's larger African American community.

Part 2 (chapters 6–11) covers roughly 1920–1941, as Jim Crow rules became more entrenched in Kansas City and discrimination morphed from personal attitudes to institutional policy. These chapters tell the stories of John Edward Perry, Chester Franklin, and Homer Roberts, among others. Unlike Jones and the Cooks, who had middle-class upbringings, were well educated, and saw it as their life mission to "lift up the race," these individuals were more self-made. Their mission was to further their own careers, although that usually meant helping others in the Black community in the process.

Part 3 (chapters 12–15) focuses on later time periods: 1941, 1942–1954, 1955–1967, and 1968–1998, with a special focus on Lucile

Bluford, who was on the front lines as Jim Crow policies—but also her street—began to dissolve. These chapters tell the stories of those who grew up on Montgall and were taught to work hard and play by the rules but found that these skills did not translate well to life on the diminished street.

At one point in time there were sixteen houses along Montgall Avenue between Twenty-Fourth Terrace and Twenty-Fifth Street. Today, eleven remain, one of which has been boarded up for nearly twenty years. Montgall Avenue stands as a symbol for racial discrimination in twentieth-century America, a brutal reminder for a city and a country that are still struggling with their devastating racial history.

PART 1

THE FOUNDATION OF
A COMMUNITY
MONTGALL AVENUE
FROM 1904 TO 1919

2436 Montgall: Hugh Oliver and Myrtle Foster Cook
2444 Montgall: Anna Holland Jones
2442 Montgall: Hezekiah Walden
2434 Montgall: Frances and Charles Jackson,
   Carolyn Brydie, and Gwendolyn Calderon

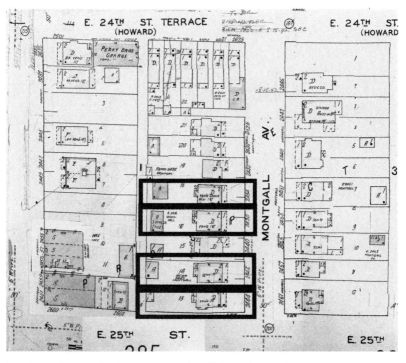

The Foundation of a Community—detail from the *Sanborn Map, Kansas City, Vol. 3, 1909–1950*, p. 360. Bold outlines added to indicate the homes of Montgall's pioneers. Missouri Valley Special Collections, Kansas City Public Library, Kansas City, Missouri.

His principles were so high, his conduct so manly and his sterling worth so manifest that no man had more friends than Rufus Montgall.
    Carrie Westlake Whitney, *Kansas City, Missouri: Its History and Its People,* vol. 2, *1908*

RUFUS MONTGALL
THE MAN BEHIND THE STREET

1

Rufus Montgall, the White man for whom Montgall Avenue is named, is a forgotten leader of the city's past, but he is someone who represents the complicated relationship between Black and White Kansas Citians. Montgall was part of a southern tide of migrants moving to the area in the 1840s, many of whom came from the same county in Kentucky as Montgall, Shelby County. Also from Shelby County, Kentucky, were lumberman R. A. Long, farming and real estate developer John Wornall, and the grandparents of future president Harry Truman.[1] Rufus Montgall's presence explains, in part, why Kansas City was known for its "Southern exposure,"[2] an outlook that has left a residue on the street that bears his name.

✳ Rufus and Nancy Montgall arrived in what would become Kansas City in 1840. With a population of less than seven hundred, it was more an outpost, a stopping-off place for those who understood that their futures lay farther west—in Oregon, Santa Fe, and California. Although its location at the crux of two great rivers seemed to make the city's future inevitable, the high bluffs along the Missouri River made settlement difficult.[3] These conditions led many migrants to choose other settlements along the Missouri to plant their stakes, places like Independence and Saint Joseph, Missouri; Leavenworth, Kansas; and even the more interior town of Westport, Missouri.

Rufus Montgall settled south of the city proper, along Brush Creek, and for seventeen years he, his wife, Nancy, and at least one slave cleared the forested acreage and worked the farm, "transforming the land into rich and fertile fields."[4] It is not known how many slaves, if any, accompanied the Montgalls on their journey from Kentucky to Missouri, but Missouri's 1860 registry of slave owners identifies Rufus Montgall as the owner of a sixteen-year-old Black male.[5] Although too young to have made the 1840 journey, this young man could have been the offspring of someone who did. Or perhaps Montgall purchased him at one of the slave auctions in Westport. Montgall's neighbor, fellow Kentuckian John Wornall (whose legacy was also secured with the naming of a street), used slave labor to grow his business, which provided food and other sundries to migrants heading west.

The area's largest slave owner of the time, Jabez Smith, arrived in Independence from Virginia in 1843. He settled into his new Missouri life with over three hundred Black men, women, and children, all of whom were chattel, according to state law.[6] Slave owners like Rufus Montgall would have been aware of the Black codes that dictated the treatment of slaves in Missouri, codes that dated back to the 1700s when the region was controlled by the French. Under these codes, slave children assumed the status of their mothers. If the woman was free, her children were also considered free, even if the children's father was enslaved. If a child was born to an enslaved woman, he or she became the property of the mother's master. Slaves could not testify against their masters or serve as witnesses in court trials, unless no White witnesses were found, and slaves were not allowed to bring charges in a civil case. Those who resisted an owner's orders were to be whipped thirty-nine times. Slaves who raised their hands to White people, except in cases of self-defense, were also to be punished at the discretion of the justice of the peace. The Louisiana French even developed their own especially barbaric system for dealing with runaways. If a slave ran once, he would be branded with a fleur-de-lis on his shoulder and have his ears cut off. If he ran a second time, his hamstrings would be cut; a third offense led to death.[7] Although it is not known whether Wornall, Montgall, or Smith resorted to any of these heinous practices, the proximity to free territories would surely have made the slave owners anxious about the possibility of runaways.

As Montgall's farm prospered, others chiseled the bluffs along the Missouri River, preparing a foundation for what eventually became downtown Kansas City, Missouri. In 1850 Rufus and Nancy welcomed their son, William, and they continued at the farm for seven more years before moving into town to the corner of Nineteenth Street and Agnes Avenue. What prompted the Montgalls' move is not known, but it could have been a response to growing violence in the countryside. In 1854 Congress passed the Kansas-Nebraska Act, a decision that brought the most strident advocates on both sides of the slave issue to the area. On May 21, 1856, Lawrence, Kansas, an abolitionist stronghold about forty miles west of Montgall's first home, was ransacked by pro-slavery activists. Three days later, abolitionist John Brown and his sons killed five pro-slavery settlers along the Pottawatomie Creek, south of the Montgalls' farm. As southern states began to declare their independence from the Union, Montgall and every other Missourian were forced to choose which side to support in the escalating conflict.

In 1861 pro-Confederate raiders seized a federal arsenal in nearby Liberty, Missouri. Soon after, militiamen marched into the area from Independence and stole weapons from one of the largest warehouses on the levee. For a time, it looked as if the region had fallen to pro-Confederate forces. Voters, however, had elected a pro-Union mayor in 1861, Robert Van Horn, who organized several local militias that drove the pro-Confederates from the area, with help from federal troops from Leavenworth.[8] Although Rufus Montgall was a slave owner, he joined the Union effort and became a militia leader just two months before the battle of Westport, the last major Confederate offensive west of the Mississippi.[9]

It is doubtful that a sudden wave of conscience hit Montgall when he joined the fight to preserve the Union, and when it came to his feelings about Black/White relations, he was probably more aligned with Confederate sympathizers than with the abolitionist cause. Although there is no record of his personal beliefs, one can infer something about his convictions through his political affiliations. An early history of Kansas City indicates that he was originally aligned with the Whig Party. After the war, he did not align with the Republican Party, the party of Lincoln, but instead became a "stanch [sic] democrat,"[10] a party on the rise after the end of Reconstruction, especially among southern leaders committed to passing Jim Crow legislation (see chapter 3).

Living on a farm southwest of town, Montgall watched as thousands of migrants traveled through the area to their western destinations. This position gave him a firsthand understanding of the role that commerce played in the area's economy. Another enterprise that was making men wealthy was real estate, something that Montgall engaged in just as the violence over slavery swept onto the national stage. In 1861, the same year that shots were fired on Fort Sumter and Confederate-leaning guerrillas seized the armory on the Kansas City levee, Montgall paid John Lockridge $1,200 for fifteen acres, land that was annexed to Kansas City in 1875.[11] This property was eventually plotted and sold as individual lots for homes on the street that would bear his name.

After the war ended, Kansas City leaders took on a more regional battle, one for a major infrastructure project that would ensure the future of their municipality. If the Town of Kansas could secure funding for a railroad bridge before its neighbors in Leavenworth, Independence, and Saint Joseph did, the city would become a critical link in bringing the cattle and grain producers from the South and West to the markets of the North and East. A bridge would transform the Town of Kansas into a bona fide city and a major player in the nation's economy, rewarding those who had had the foresight to invest in it. The leaders' efforts paid off, and Kansas City was selected as the site of the Hannibal Bridge. The bridge, which opened in 1869, transformed the settlement as thousands poured into the area.

In 1870 Kirkland and Charles Armour arrived with their uncle to open Armour Meatpacking, and before long, the area was home to the biggest names in meatpacking, including the three other giants of the day, Swift, Cudahy, and Wilson. Other industrialists and businessmen arrived as well, including August Meyer, who opened a smelting plant that employed a thousand men on the Kansas side of the state line. William Volker came from Germany by way of Chicago. He purchased a languishing frame-making business and transformed it into a linoleum and window-shade giant. The thirty-nine-year-old future editor of the *Kansas City Star*, William Rockhill Nelson, arrived as well, eager to escape the obscurity in his more-cultivated hometown in Indiana.[12]

Even as industries were flourishing after the opening of the Hannibal Bridge, Kansas City was "Cow Town" to the rest of the country, a rough-and-tumble, Wild West kind of place. This reputation wasn't totally undeserved given the distinct smell emanating from the stockyards and meatpacking plants. Most of the streets were unpaved, and the only time that dust wasn't a problem was after a rain, when it turned to mud so thick it could halt a carriage in its tracks. After shepherding cattle and sheep through city streets to the stockyards, cowboys could visit Annie Chambers's bordello at the northwest corner of Third and Main, or one of the dozen saloons on "Battle Row," a block of Main Street so rowdy that it had its own police contingent.[13] One visitor to Kansas City at the time noted that she could not imagine a "more unpleasant place."[14]

A large group of free African Americans arrived in Kansas City to work on the Hannibal Bridge. Like the millions of European immigrants who arrived in the United States after the Civil War, the freed slaves believed that hard work was a necessary first step, a sacrifice so that later generations would get a piece of the American pie. The men who came to work on the bridge formed a community along the river known as Hell's Half Acre, an aptly named slum in the West Bottoms. Most of these migrants would leave as soon as they could afford to.[15]

More freed slaves, the Exodusters, came in the 1870s, drawn to the area where their hero, John Brown, had made a name for himself.

Black families from rural Missouri also arrived so that their children could receive an education, albeit a separate one because Missouri state law made it a criminal offense for Whites and Blacks to attend school together. In addition to the African Americans, thousands of European immigrants poured into the city where word had spread that "there was a job for every man."[16]

The new arrivals tended to live in fairly distinct areas of town, constrained by proximity to their work and drawn by the support of others who shared their heritage. In addition to the settlement in the river bottoms, a community of African Americans lived in the North End, where they shared space with Irish immigrants and new arrivals from Italy. Black people with more means could be found in the Church Hill neighborhood, which sprang up along Tenth Street between Charlotte and Troost and so named because of the two churches in the area, Allen Chapel AME and Second Baptist. German settlers lived farther south, on land that would eventually become Union Station and Hospital Hill. Although various ethnic neighborhoods emerged as immigrants settled into the growing city, there was no uniform pattern of segregation. People generally lived where they could afford to, and it was not uncommon for Blacks and Whites to be found on the same block. Newspapers even carried stories of interracial marriage, especially between German/African American couples.[17]

The more-integrated environment occurred, not because White Americans were able to look past skin color to see the humanity of people of color, but because Kansas City, like many cities in the North and Midwest after the Civil War, had not yet figured out how Whites and large numbers of free Blacks were going to coexist.[18] Most African Americans still lived in the South, and although Reconstruction briefly brought federal troops and the Freedmen's Bureau to ensure their rights as US citizens—equal access to schools, the courts, and the voting booths—by 1877 that assistance was gone. In another compromise, the federal government pulled its troops out, leaving the former slave-owning oligarchy to restore order the only way they knew, through a social and political system that subjugated Black people. Democrats regained control of state houses throughout the South and passed legislation that separated the former slaves and brought them under White control, such as a Georgia law that made it illegal for Blacks and Whites to occupy the same train car; a Florida law that made it illegal for Whites and a person of color to marry; and an Alabama order that made it illegal for Black and White people to eat in the same restaurant.[19]

Kansas City's leaders in the 1870s and 1880s were barely keeping up with the daily challenges that industrialization brought, but once they did catch their breath, they, like much of the country, looked to their southern brethren for guidance on what most White Americans referred to as "the Negro problem." As the century ended, they adopted southern norms: not only the Jim Crow laws and customs that excluded people of color from hotels and other places of business, but also more subtle expectations about Black and White people's behavior. For example, Black men and women were to call White people "sir" or "ma'am," while they could be addressed by their first names; Black men and women entered White people's homes not by the front door, but through the back; and Black men were expected to tip their hats and give White women a wide berth on sidewalks.[20]

Rufus Montgall lived through great changes in Kansas City's history, arriving at a time when the area was known more for those moving through than for those who stayed, but he wasn't a transient. He remained, as did others from his Kentucky home. Less well-known than other leaders of the day, he fought alongside them during the Civil War—on the right side of history, most likely more motivated by economic self-interest than by any sense of justice. Like these other men, Montgall would gain if industry came to the region. Industry did arrive after the opening of the Hannibal Bridge, and Montgall did gain, but the growth ushered in new sets of problems, such as how to handle a more class-based society and how to clean up their increasingly polluted municipality. These problems would be addressed by the next generation of White leaders. The new leaders commemorated their predecessors with monuments and other honors. They named a street after Rufus Montgall. The history of this street shows what happens when society allows its judgment and norms to be based on skin color alone.

I think that I am safe in saying that the American people have arrived at the stage where they are willing to say that the Negro is essentially human and can be educated, that he should be the chief agent for his own education, and that the education of Negroes, as of whites, should be compulsory.

Asa Martin, Teacher, Westport High School, Kansas City, Missouri, 1913 master's thesis

2436 MONTGALL AVENUE
HUGH OLIVER AND
MYRTLE FOSTER COOK

2

The home at 2436 Montgall Avenue belonged to one of the most important families in Kansas City history. Hugh Oliver Cook lived at 2436 Montgall Avenue for forty years, from 1904 to 1943, and as a Lincoln High School teacher and later its principal, it would be difficult to overestimate the influence he had on Kansas City's Black community. He moved into his new home in 1904 with his wife, Daisy, two young sons, Hugh Jr. and Hartwell, and an adopted daughter, Chloe. It was an integrated street when the Cooks arrived: Boris and Anna Kittis, born in Russia, lived at 2428 Montgall with their daughters Ida and Matilda. Adam Hildebrand, German-born, lived at 2430 with his wife and son; and two doors down from the Cooks, at 2432, lived Irish-born Richard Mayberry and his wife Emma.[1]

Later residents of Montgall believed that Cook was able to purchase his home because he was light-skinned, and that it was only after seeing Daisy that the seller realized he had sold the new home to an African American family. The story continues that the Cooks' move encouraged other Black families to move to the street, and, before long, the street became entirely Black.[2] It is a believable story, one that, years later, Lucile Bluford and other residents of Montgall accepted as truth, and one that exemplifies a Jim Crow mentality in which the only way that White and Black families could live on the same block

Hugh Oliver Cook. 1926 Lincoln High School yearbook, Thatcher Family
Collection, Kansas Collection, RH MS 1250, Kenneth Spencer Research
Library, University of Kansas Libraries.

would be if a mistake were made. Although something like this could
have happened, this conclusion isn't supported by many of the facts.

The problem with this account is that the newly built home on
Montgall was advertised in a Black newspaper. In the 1904 advertisement the asking price for the "elegant, 6-room modern brick and
frame" home was $3,500, $500 down and the "balance to suit."[3] When
Hugh Oliver Cook responded to this advertisement and moved to

Myrtle Foster Cook. *Lifting as They Climb*, ed. Elizabeth
Lindsay Davis (Washington, DC: National Association
of Colored Women, 1933).

Montgall, the street was in a middle-class, integrated neighborhood
in the American heartland, truly a melting pot of Black families living
among first- and second-generation immigrants.[4]

While Cook lived on the street, he lost his wife Daisy, raised two
biological and numerous adopted children, served in a world war,
and cofounded Kansas City's Paseo YMCA. Cook and his second wife,

FOR SALE.

1716 Lydia, price $1,450; $250 cash, balance to suit.. John Rone, 708 E. 17th street.

1420 E. 17th St., price $1,350; $250 cash, balance to suit. John Rone, 708 E. 17th street.

1412 Highland, price $1,650; $250 cash, balance to suit. John Rone, 708 E. 17th street.

New house, 2436 Montgall. Elegant 6 room modern brick and frame; price $3,500; $500 cash, balance to suit. John Rone, 708 E. 17th street.

1331-3-5-7-9 Kensington. Price, $1,350 each; cash, $150, balance to suit. John Rone, 708 E. 17th street.

Ad for 2436 Montgall Avenue. *Rising Son*, June 24, 1904 (emphasis added).

Myrtle, were active in the NAACP and founded the Home Seekers Savings and Loan.[5] They were also integrally involved with the Urban League, the Missouri State Association of Negro Teachers, the Research Academy, Alpha Phi Alpha fraternity, the Women's League, and the Book Lover's Club. Yet H. O. Cook's role in these institutions was secondary to the one that consumed his life: his work at Lincoln High School, bedrock of the city's African American community and the only high school for Black youths in greater Kansas City, Missouri. Lincoln High School had an outsized influence on the destiny of its students.[6]

Except for a brief absence to serve in World War I, Cook was at Lincoln for forty-two years, arriving in 1901 as a math and psychology instructor. He was promoted to assistant principal before his service in the First World War, and in 1922 he became principal. Cook was with Lincoln at the historic high school's three locations. In 1906 the school moved from its original building at Eleventh and Campbell

Streets to Nineteenth Street and Tracy Avenue, and in 1935 it relocated to its current home at Twenty-First Street and Woodland Avenue. Cook led Lincoln High through its transition from an elite school with a faculty of six to a large institution of more than thirty instructors who adapted to the needs of a diverse and growing community.

Known as "Ollie," Cook was born October 31, 1873, in Washington, DC, on the campus of Howard University, the second of three boys born to Howard law professor John Hartwell Cook and Isabel Petero Cook, a sewing instructor. The boys did not have an easy childhood, according to the eldest brother, musician Will Marion Cook.[7] After their father died from tuberculosis in 1879, the family collapsed as the children were separated. For a time in the late 1880s, Ollie and his mother lived in Kansas City, Kansas, after she was hired to teach sewing. His brothers were sent to other family members.

Ollie's older brother, Will Marion Cook, became a renowned violinist and composer best known for his collaborations with poet Paul Laurence Dunbar and his work with vaudeville performers Bert Williams and George Nash Walker. The musician was also known for his violent outbursts and "uncontrolled passions," a reputation that could be summed up in a story once told by Duke Ellington. In 1895, after Cook's performance at Carnegie Hall, a critic wrote that he was the "greatest Negro violinist." After publication, Cook paid the journalist a visit. He informed the reviewer that he was not the greatest Negro violinist, but rather the greatest violinist. Period. He then took out his violin and smashed it on the critic's desk. It is said that he never picked up the instrument again.[8]

If a difficult childhood contributed to his older brother's tempestuous behavior, those same circumstances seemed to have had the opposite effect on Ollie, who, according to the *Call*, "never allow[ed] himself to become bitter over the prejudices and discriminations which Negroes face[d] in Kansas City."[9]

The Cooks' warmth and generosity to children, both in and out of Lincoln, were legendary in Kansas City's African American community. Myrtle Cook reported that in the early days of their marriage, her husband would call to tell her that he was bringing home a child who needed a place to stay. The child might stay for a week, a year, or several years. "He was welcome at the Cooks' until he could stand on his own feet."

Over the years, the couple supported dozens of children. Some were adopted, and others were helped financially through high school or college. Leonard Reed was one such youth. After high school, Reed left Kansas City and became a regular at the Cotton Club and the Apollo in New York City, performing as the "Shim Sham Shimmy Man" and enjoying a long career as an entertainer and producer in Harlem.[10] In his later years, he acknowledged the important role that the Cooks played in his life when they brought him into their Montgall home.

Clearly, Cook had a soft spot for youth, and we can only speculate whether that compassion had its roots in his difficult childhood. The only hint he provided was a cryptic statement he made to a *Call* reporter indicating that he understood children because he "remembered his own childhood days."

After graduating from Cornell University, Ollie and his first wife, Daisy Lee Jackson, settled in Huntsville, Alabama, where he taught at the Normal A&M College. The couple remained there for several years until the overt racism permeating the area proved too much. Describing to the *Call* what led him to Kansas City, Cook told the story of how, after presenting his fifty-five-dollar paycheck to an Alabama bank teller, the teller responded, "you n—are making too much money over at that college." Cook decided "then and there that Alabama was no place for him." Not long after, he accepted a position at Lincoln.

Ollie and Daisy originally settled in the Church Hill neighborhood, and in 1904 they moved into one of the new homes on the 2400 block of Montgall. At the time of the move, the couple had two biological sons, Hugh Oliver and Hartwell, and an adopted daughter, Chloe. Daisy was educated and was a founding member of the Book Lovers Club. She may well have devoted her life to improving conditions for other African Americans, as Hugh Oliver's second wife did, but in August 1914 Daisy died from tuberculosis in their Montgall home.[11] A few years later Ollie married a colleague from Lincoln, Myrtle Foster Todd.

The Cooks may have been able to escape one kind of terror when they left the South, but no Black American could escape other forms of racism pulsing through the country at the turn of the twentieth century, and their effects proved more far-reaching and, ultimately, more destructive, for they came from those with a lot more influence than a bank teller.

In 1910 Howard W. Odum, who would go on to become the first president of the American Sociological Society, published his doctoral dissertation, which outlined how schools for Black students should operate, a work that became a sourcebook on the subject. In *The Social and Mental Traits of the Negro*, Odum asserted that most Blacks were incapable of abstract thought. "As a rule, after negro children become older than ten or twelve years, their development is physical rather than mental; whatever mental ability in the child gave promise of worth to be recognized in later years is crowded out by the coarser physical growth."[12] When Blacks did get an education, Odum argued, they were

> not a force for good in the community but for evil . . . [because] they feel that manual labor is beneath their dignity; they are fitted to do no other. They sneer at the idea of work, and they thus spread dissatisfaction among the members of their race. They imitate the whites and believe themselves thereby similar to them. They love only the show of apparent results and do not care for the details of attainment.[13]

Howard Odum was not alone with his attitudes that Black people were inferior to those classified as Caucasian. Rather, he was part of a larger group of influential men who preached White supremacy, including the chief statistician at Prudential Life Insurance, German-born Frederick Hoffman. Hoffman's book, *Race Traits and Tendencies of the American Negro*, spread toxic ideas about skin color. Studying the marginalized Black population in the post-Reconstruction South, Hoffman found that African Americans experienced higher rates of disease, incarceration, alcoholism, and suicide than their White

counterparts. Ignoring the environmental conditions and the historical trauma from slavery that the Black population endured, Hoffman
concluded that "physiological peculiarities" between the races led to
the different outcomes. For Hoffman, this was all the proof needed
to argue for White supremacy. "The Aryan race is possessed of all the
essential characteristics that make for success in the struggle for the
higher life, in contrast with other races which lack in either one or
the other of the determining qualities," he wrote.[14] For Odum, Hoffman, and others who espoused these beliefs, skin color was a way to
attribute all kinds of differences, from intellectual capacity, to disease susceptibility, to criminal proclivity. For these scholars, Anglo-
Saxons were at the top of the social order and represented the pinnacle of civilization.

Howard Odum's approach to the racial differences was to propose
a different curriculum for Black students, one that clearly delineated
the differences between right and wrong "in order to eradicate the
criminal tendencies." He also supported using different textbooks
for Black and White students with messages about Black inferiority
so that African Americans would always see themselves as "lesser
than whites." Black students who were educated beyond elementary
school, however, could use the same texts as Whites because they "will
most likely be intelligent enough to understand their position."[15]

White high school teacher Asa Martin absorbed these attitudes
and applied them to Kansas City's "Negro" population. He noted that
Blacks were more than three times as likely to die from pneumonia
than Whites and more than five times as likely to die from tuberculosis. Like Hoffman, who predicted that African Americans would eventually become extinct because they would not be able to survive in
modern society, Martin concluded that the higher death rate was a
matter of biological differences. "The Negro has much less power of
resistance in the struggle for life than has the Caucasian," he wrote.
"The high death rate among the Negroes indicates that a rapid process of elimination of those who can not adapt themselves to their
environment is going on among them. This selective process will
tend toward the survival of the more fit elements among the Negroes,

and therefore towards bringing the Negro up to the standard of the Whites."[16]

Wrapped in scholarly legitimacy, these beliefs about Black inferiority became embedded in the psyche of White America, transferred from university professors and scholarly publications to a public school teacher who was then able to transfer these attitudes to his White students at Westport High. By contrast, in Cook's 1925 master's thesis, "A Modern High School Plan for the Negro Children of Kansas City," the Lincoln High School principal avoided any substantive discussion about racial differences. Instead, Cook focused on environment. "Much has been written, some scientific, much that is opinion, to set forth the criminal characteristics of the Negro," he wrote for his (probably all-White) thesis committee at Cornell University in 1925.[17]

If Cook wanted to avoid confrontation during his thesis defense, he clearly did not feel the same constraint within the halls of his school, where students debated issues such as Black migration to northern cities, and whether boys and girls should receive the same education.[18]

In 1901 Cook was one of a handful of instructors at Lincoln when its curriculum was very traditional and offered courses in Latin and oratory. By the time he retired in December 1943, there were scores of teachers, and the curriculum had expanded to include carpentry, auto mechanics, painting, art, and more. "Negro education must shift its emphasis from the classical and the professional to creative industry," Cook wrote (50).

The Lincoln High School principal's approach to education was influenced by the larger reform movement promoted by philosopher and educator John Dewey, who understood that public schools could be effective vehicles for the assimilation of millions of European immigrants. Similarly, Cook maintained that Lincoln should be more relevant to its students. He believed that children between the ages of fourteen and eighteen were at "the most susceptible period of their lives" and therefore needed to stay in school where influences would help them "fix proper standards of self worth" (27).

Delinquency was an ongoing issue with Kansas City youths, and Cook saw how the problem broke along racial lines. Analyzing the retention rates for Black and White students during the 1924–1925 school year, he found a significant difference. Although there was little difference in school attendance for Black and White children aged 7–13 (94.9 percent of Whites and 93.3 percent of Blacks were in school), attendance dropped for Black youths starting at age 14, and this gap widened over the teen years. For students aged 14–15, 85 percent of Whites were in school, but only 77.8 percent of Blacks; for 16- and 17-year-olds, 46.8 percent of Whites were attending school and only 36.1 percent of Blacks; and for young adults aged 18 to 20, Cook found that 15.5 percent of Whites were still in school and only 8.3 percent of Blacks.

The principal understood the role that economics played in luring older students away from school, but he saw an opportunity to entice younger students to stay. To encourage students to remain in school, Cook introduced different classes and brought innovative and engaging instructors to Lincoln, often traveling to other cities in order to recruit them. Joshua Russell was one such teacher. In 1928 Cook persuaded Russell (2434 and later 2461 Montgall) to leave Topeka, Kansas, and teach auto mechanics in Kansas City.[19]

Five years earlier, Cook lured another Topekan to Lincoln High: artist Aaron Douglas, a notable figure from the Harlem Renaissance. Douglas represented attitudes that a new generation of artists and poets offered to American society, people like Langston Hughes and Claude McKay, two writers who focused on racial pride and uninhibited artistic expression. "The world is realizing that the Negro has a deep and instinctive conception of art and art forms; a soul full of both sunshine and sorrow, which is and should be an endless source of material from which artists and composers should draw the most colorful and characteristically expressive works of American art," wrote a Lincoln art club member in 1925, a student no doubt influenced by his high school art teacher.[20]

But Aaron Douglas was not the only racially conscious instructor at Cook's Lincoln High. At the school's 1935 graduation ceremony, students recited the poetry of Phillis Wheatley and Claude McKay. The audience heard Gwendolyn Bennett's "To a Dark Girl," which begins "I love you for your brownness," and they heard the hopeful message from Langston Hughes in his poem, "I, Too."[21]

Decades before the racial pride movement of the 1960s, H. O. Cook and the teachers at Lincoln High School infused pride and a deep sense of self-worth into their students. They also provided them with a means to fight racism. The year that Cook became Lincoln's principal, students organized a Junior NAACP club; one year later, it had a membership of nearly four hundred with Aaron Douglas as its faculty adviser. "Gradually, it is being instilled into the minds of our young people that one of the best ways to help ourselves is to help others, and as we realize that fact, we bend our back to the yoke willingly," wrote student Reginald Franklyn Fisher, class of 1925.[22] Myrtle Cook's pride in Lincoln's Junior NAACP program was evident in a 1925 letter she wrote to Du Bois about the club's membership, which neared five hundred that year: "We hope to have something doing here in the west that will make folk elsewhere open their eyes on Junior possibilities."[23]

Besides expanding Lincoln's curriculum, H. O. Cook put his students' newfound skills to work in the Black community. During the 1919–1920 school year, students plastered the walls at Wendell Phillips School, framed windows and the roof joists for Attucks Elementary, and operated machinery at Wheatley-Provident Hospital. In 1921 and 1922 students improved Dunbar School and created additions to three elementary buildings, Fairmount, Bruce, and Attucks; in 1924 the paint club adorned the walls at the Niles Home for Negro Children and the Crittenden Home for Colored Girls.[24] "The program of studies should embody community activities and community standards, which are, in the last analysis, the major objectives of education," he wrote in his thesis (34).

Cook and Dewey both believed that schools ought to prepare students for their lives of work, but Cook understood that there were fundamental differences between the needs of Kansas City's Black and White populations. In 1912 Kansas City's Board of Public Welfare conducted an investigation of housing conditions for the city's Black community, with Cook doing the legwork. The study brought the educator into the most desperate addresses, and in the report he delivered to city leaders, Cook described what he found. "In all, the work [his study] covered 232 single houses and 59 apartments or tenements containing 2,465 rooms, of these rooms, 334 were without sufficient sunlight and 843 without sufficient ventilation."[25] Cook counted 212 outhouses, none of which were connected to a sewer, and only 151 of the residences had running water in either the house or the yard. The vast majority of the people were without any source of water.

So while Howard Odum promoted a curriculum for children of color designed to address what he saw as their limited intellectual abilities, Cook saw firsthand how many of his students lived and how their environment affected their ability to learn and grow. In his thesis, Cook wrote: "If the labor of the school is to be effective in counteracting the influence of [environmental] conditions, it must organize and maintain a comprehensive health program which both disseminates knowledge, develops proper health habits and creates the desire for pure, wholesome, healthy individual bodies and surroundings" (35).

Cook believed that a primary goal of schools was the promotion of good health, and he designed a curriculum to do just that. His program included instruction and facts about the human body and personal hygiene. He maintained that schools should provide opportunities for physical development and recreation, including games, athletics, and hikes. In addition, he promoted the establishment of medical, dental, and psychological clinics to examine, diagnose, and treat various ailments. "Only through some such program for the health of the individual child and the community can we hope to check the distressing mortality among Negroes of the city," Cook wrote in his thesis (36).

Counteracting environment was an uphill battle for Kansas City's Black teachers considering how city leaders ignored the Black community. "The city takes little interest in any of the Negro districts, except to have them well patrolled by policemen," wrote Asa Martin.

"The streets and walks are poorly kept, and no provision whatever is made for parks, playgrounds, or public baths.... We are putting forth every effort to raise to our standard the foreign element of our population, while we are doing practically nothing for the Negro." Martin's thesis included his own description of living conditions in Kansas City's Black community, much of which, he concluded, was "unfit for human habitation," with no ventilation or light.[26]

As the leader of the city's only high school for Black students, Cook had to choose how to prepare future generations of Black youth for their place in the world: to be fully and equally assimilated into White society, or to be leaders and members of a separate one. He did both, and he led by example.

In 1913 Virginia-born Woodrow Wilson became president, and he appointed two fellow southerners to his cabinet: Postmaster Albert Burelson and Treasury Secretary William McAdoo. Overnight, federal offices, restrooms, and cafeterias—places that Blacks and Whites had previously shared in Washington, DC, and beyond—became segregated. Cook was incensed, and he wrote a widely circulated letter to the president to tell his grievances:[27]

Sir: In as much as the Negro in this country has at all times zealously defended the life and integrity of this Nation and has at no time raised his hand against this government; in as much as he has proven faithful when-ever grave responsibility has been entrusted to him; and in as much as he continues to shoulder the burdens of citizenship with patriotism and enthusiasm:

Be it therefore resolved: We, the colored citizens of the two Kansas Cities, and members of the Kansas City branch of the National Association for the Advancement of Colored People, do earnestly protest against the movement to segregate colored clerks and other workers in the departments at Washington. That: any policy of segregation means humiliation and despair to a race that has proven its worth to share the open door of opportunity and measure strength with any people.

That: any policy of segregation will eventually close the doors of many avenues in industry, trade and the professions, which are beyond question, necessary to the material and moral progress of any people.

That: to crystalize any such unfair and unchristian attitude by legal enactment or official orders is un-American and undemocratic, contrary to the principles and ideals upon which this government was founded.

That: such a policy is a direct contradiction of the assurance made us by our Chief Executive who "pledged a just, fair and equal treatment of his colored fellow citizens."

And be it further resolved: that copies of the above be sent to President Wilson and members of his cabinet, the ministers of Kansas City, and our papers.

Four years after Cook wrote his protest letter, America entered the First World War. When news reached the home front about Black troops who were unable to read or sign their paychecks, and others who were refused service in canteens run by Whites, Cook enlisted. He did not fight, but the forty-five-year-old educator served those who did. He slogged through the front lines and brought cigarettes and cocoa to the men of the 371st Infantry, a racially segregated brigade that, because of its color, was handed off to French leaders. Cook served valiantly, helping victims of mustard gas in the battle of Champagne until he himself was gassed. When he recovered, he rejoined the regiment.[28]

Like many of the Black soldiers serving overseas, Cook felt welcomed by the French. "Conditions here are ideal when it comes to considering how well the Negro is treated and utterly absent any friction between White and colored found in other camps," he wrote.[29] The feelings were mutual, and French commanders were so grateful for Cook's service that he was recommended for the Distinguished Service Cross. He returned home in February 1919 and was met at the train station by many of his Montgall Avenue neighbors, including John E. Perry (2451) and Anna Jones (2444). A celebratory dinner was held in his honor at the Paseo YMCA.[30]

Sensing the opportunities that military service could afford young people of color, three years after he returned from war Cook introduced an ROTC program at Lincoln, where the "boys learn[ed] the essentials of military tactics and adroit maneuvers."[31] Cook again led by example with the founding of a bank within the school, a fund overseen by another Montgall resident, teacher Arthur Pittman (2449). The endeavor mirrored an enterprise he and his second wife, Myrtle Foster Todd, created for the city's larger community.

Myrtle Foster was born in Canada, where her grandfather settled after escaping from slavery. She attended school in Michigan and later moved to Kentucky to work as a missionary and teacher. She met her first husband, Louis G. Todd, a physician, and the two moved to Oklahoma, where he practiced medicine and she taught in a government-run school for African American and Native American children. After Louis Todd's death in 1911, Myrtle moved to Kansas City to head Lincoln's English Department.[32] Not long after Daisy died, Ollie and "M. F.," his affectionate name for her, married.[33] He remained a force within Lincoln, and she became a force outside of it.

On March 24, 1925, the Home Seekers Savings and Loan Association was founded with an impressive sum of $100,000 ($1.47 million in today's money) and a goal, as its name suggests, of helping the Black community acquire home loans. The Cooks acquired the capital through the sale of a thousand shares of stock at $100 each; stockholders from Montgall Avenue included John Bluford, Arthur Pittman, and John E. Perry.[34]

The Cooks' vision for economic self-reliance lasted through the lean years of the Depression, and when the board of directors announced a surplus in 1933, they opted not to take a dividend that year. The *Topeka Plaindealer* noted that the company was a great asset to the community, making "nearly one half million dollars in loans to pay taxes, save homes, pay hospital and doctor bills."[35]

Ollie and Myrtle Cook were pillars in Kansas City's Black community. In addition to the Home Seekers Savings and Loan, Myrtle was a founding member of the Jackson Home for Negro Boys. She also served as founding member of the Paseo YWCA, just as her husband did for the Paseo YMCA.

Ollie Cook did not consider himself particularly political (although he told the *Call* that he leaned toward the Socialist Party), but Myrtle was a staunch Republican and became a leader in the party.[36] During the 1920 presidential campaign, she organized Black women in Jackson County to support Warren Harding, who had verbally supported an anti-lynching bill. (The bill passed the House of Representatives but stalled in the Senate.) During the 1924 presidential campaign, Myrtle Cook was a member of the National Speakers Bureau, charged with traveling the country in support of Calvin Coolidge. In addition, Missouri governor Arthur Hyde appointed her to the state's Negro Educational and Industrial Commission, a position she held for six years. During this time, she supported and petitioned for Black representation at the White House Conference on Child Health and Protection.[37]

Myrtle Foster Cook also rose to prominence in the NAACP in 1923 when she was served as chairman of Women's Defense Fund Committee.[38] Her goal was to raise $100,000 to pay the legal fees for fifty-four members of the Twenty-Fourth Infantry, men who were imprisoned in Leavenworth for their participation in the 1917 Houston riot. The NAACP investigated the conflict—and the conditions that led up to it—and concluded that justice had not been served in these soldiers' cases.

Tragedy struck the Cook household in August 1939 when thirty-seven-year-old Hartwell died. He had been ill with tuberculosis for some time and had returned to Kansas City from New York several years before, perhaps hoping the cleaner midwestern air would help his lungs. Clearly, Ollie and Myrtle hoped so too, for they built a sunroom for him on the back of their home. The cleaner air must have worked for a while, because in the spring of 1935 Hartwell was healthy enough to work with Lincoln students on a show held at Convention Hall. Hartwell even wrote an original song, "Hats Off to Lincoln," which was used as the finale.[39]

Hartwell, just two years old when his father and Daisy moved to Montgall, was a born artist. He spent his childhood singing and dancing, although he never had a lesson in either. After his high school graduation, he moved to New York where his Uncle Will helped him get started in the entertainment industry. He became a featured dancer at the Cotton Club and collaborated with his uncle on a number of songs such as "A Little Piece of Heaven Called Home." He also wrote "Curly Head" and "I'se at Peace with God."[40]

Hartwell was in the final months of his life when Lincoln High students, most likely sensing their principal's grief, wrote a moving tribute to their principal in the yearbook: "To him who is giving his life to Lincoln High, whose perseverance has enabled him to surmount all obstacles, whose integrity has been the cause of Lincoln attaining the high standards, which the school has today, whose strength has guided many classes through their dargest [sic] moments to victory, we the class of thirty-nine, dedicate this volume to our beloved, courageous, and uncompromising principal, Mr. H. O. Cook."[41]

Hugh Oliver and Myrtle Foster Cook left Kansas City in January 1944 and settled in Los Angeles. He died in 1949, followed by Myrtle two years later.

It would be impossible to overestimate the contributions that the Cooks made to the city's African American community with their professional and volunteer affiliations, contributions that the *Call* declared went "hand in hand with the history of the Negro community of Kansas City."[42] Ollie Cook played a transformative role in the history of not only Lincoln High School but also Montgall Avenue, because he brought dozens of young people, teachers, and others to the street. Some of their stories are in the chapters that follow.

When Ollie Cook and his wife, Daisy, arrived on the street in 1904, Montgall was an integrated, middle-class neighborhood, and it looked as if the steady integration of African Americans into White society was possible as long as people like them were leading the charge. Yet, despite their work and advocacy on behalf of Kansas City's Black community, other forces were also at play, such as those led by academics portraying people of color as inferior in every way to those of European descent. As these "White" immigrants assimilated into American society, Montgall's Black residents found themselves increasingly removed from the majority culture and the economic opportunities doled out by its leaders. When Ollie and Myrtle left Kansas City, all of the residents of the 2400 block of Montgall were Black.

The colored women of tomorrow will bring to the larger life of the 20th century, upon which she will enter, a clearer insight, a surer poise, a truer perception of the value of purity of life, strength of personality, and sympathetic helpfulness.

Anna Holland Jones, "A Century's Progress for the American Colored Woman," *Voice of the Negro*, October 1905

3

Anna Holland Jones was a remarkable woman: bright, educated, and capable. She was a leader with a national reputation and was friends with some of the most well-known Black leaders of her time, including W. E. B. Du Bois and suffragist and journalist Josephine St. Pierre Ruffin. Like her neighbors Ollie and Myrtle Cook, she was an educator and believed that education would erase the most harmful stereotypes about her race. And like the Cooks, she was an anchor on Montgall Avenue, moving to the street about the same time that Ollie and Daisy did, and acquiring the brick and wood-clad shirtwaist-style home on the northwest corner of Twenty-Fifth and Montgall. Given the times, Jones's purchase of a new home was itself a remarkable feat, and it is likely that she was the first single Black woman in Kansas City to purchase her own home. Jones's story is the culmination of her family's personal and generational struggles: a tale of hardworking parents who sacrificed so their children would have a better life. But because her family was Black, their American struggle was much more difficult, and their story is not about thriving as much as it is about surviving.

Anna Holland Jones could trace her family tree back to her great-grandfather Charles, who arrived on the American continent before the Revolutionary War. Charles and his brother survived the horrific Middle Passage, and the

Anna Holland Jones. Black Archives of Mid-America.

story goes that when the ship docked, the boys ran. Charles's brother was killed after dogs were sent to find them, but Jones's great-grand-father survived and was sold into bondage to the Jeffreys family of North Carolina.[1] He grew up, married, and had a son named Allen who became a blacksmith, and who was so efficient and skilled that he was able to earn extra money in his free time. As an adult Allen approached George Jeffreys and asked how much his freedom would cost. The answer: $685. Several years later, when he had saved the money, he paid Jeffreys, who ended up keeping both the money and

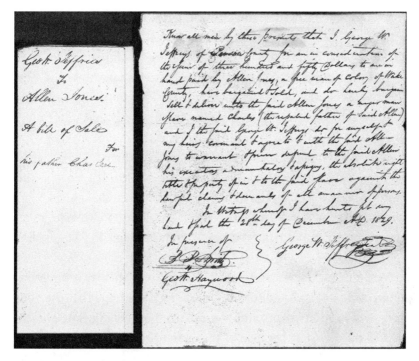

Charles Jones bill of sale. Courtesy of Renée Cochée.

Jones. Jeffreys told him that he could not have possibly earned the cash on his own and that he, as his master, had owned the time and resources required to earn it.[2]

Despite the setback, Jones remained committed to gaining his freedom and began saving again. When he had enough money the second time, he asked a Quaker friend to help with the transaction. The friend agreed, and eventually Jones earned enough money for not only his own freedom but also that of his wife, Temperance, and their son James, who became Anna Jones's father. On December 28, 1829, Allen Jones purchased his last slave—his father, Charles.

Conditions for free Blacks in 1830s North Carolina were precarious at best, because these men and women could not rely on some of the protections that slavery provided. Slaveholders, who were already anxious about the growing abolitionist movement, became more frenzied after Nat Turner's 1831 rebellion, and this anxiety turned into oppression. In 1835 Allen and Charles Jones, as well as every other free Black man in North Carolina, lost the right to vote. By 1840 no Black person could own a weapon of any type without a license.[3]

Despite the mounting oppression, Allen Jones's business and family grew. Several times, with help from Quakers in the Raleigh community, Jones led efforts to build a school for his and other Black children in the area. Each time not only was the school destroyed but Jones was threatened with being tarred and feathered. The situation reached a climax in 1842, after Jones attended an anti-slavery convention in New York and spoke about his experiences in Raleigh. Word about the speech reached back to North Carolina, and when Jones returned, an angry mob dragged him from his home and whipped him repeatedly.

The *Raleigh Register* responded: "We suspect that he is deserving of no sympathy," the editor began, adding: "We hope that the good people of Raleigh will not stop short of the most condign punishment of this outrage, not because of the individual against whom it was perpetrated . . . but for the sake of LAW, which we desire to be upheld against all infractions."[4]

Shortly after, Allen Jones packed up his belongings, including the blood-encrusted clothes he refused to wash, a stark reminder to his descendants of the brutality he endured. The family loaded up their wagon and left North Carolina for good. Accompanying Jones was another family from Raleigh, John and Delilah Copeland and their children, including a nine-year-old son also named John. The senior John Copeland was a carpenter who had gained his freedom after his master died.

Although the travelers intended to settle in Indiana, they changed their minds after they reached Ohio and met a farmer who invited them to attend an abolitionist meeting. There they became convinced that Oberlin, Ohio, offered the best opportunities for their children. The community, thirty-five miles southwest of Cleveland and a haven for runaway slaves, was an important stop on the Underground Railroad and was home to Oberlin College, which had begun admitting Black students.[5]

Allen and Temperance settled into their lives in Ohio, where Allen became a respected member of the community, contributing the ironwork for the First Congregational Church, a structure that still stands. Allen was said to greet those who stopped by his shop with the words, "God bless ye, sir, this is a nice place to eddicate [sic] children in."[6] All five of Allen and Temperance's sons attended Oberlin, including their oldest, Anna Jones's father, James Monroe.

Despite the family's newfound freedoms, Ohio was not the paradise that Jones had predicted. In the 1840s the country underwent what Du Bois called "one of the severest seasons of trial through which the black American has ever passed"[7] as the federal government's attempts to compromise on the slavery question only escalated tensions between the North and South. Blacks could no longer testify in court against Whites, and fines for harboring escaped slaves increased nearly tenfold. More disturbing, however, was the rising number of slavecatchers and kidnappers in the North as southern slave owners sought to recapture runaway slaves, especially after passage of the Fugitive Slave Act in 1850.

James, Allen and Temperance's oldest son, could have been responding to the increased oppression in Ohio when he began attending meetings about establishing a settlement even farther north, across the border in Canada, where government officials promised Black residents that they would be "entitled to all the privileges of the rest of His Majesty's subjects."[8] In 1849, after only six years in Ohio, James Monroe Jones set off to find a new home in Chatham, Ontario, where his group had purchased eight hundred acres. Once settled in their new city, about fifty miles east of Detroit, the migrants built two hundred houses and began cultivating their land.

The Copelands—the family that accompanied the Joneses out of North Carolina—remained in Ohio and became active in the abolitionist movement, especially John Copeland Jr., who became an "Oberlin Rescuer," a member of a group that helped a former slave escape to Canada after slave catchers had caught up with him in Ohio.[9] One year later, the young Copeland accompanied John Brown to Harpers Ferry. Copeland was one of the few men who survived the attack only to be sentenced to death. While awaiting his fate, he wrote touching letters to his family, which cemented his place in American history and made him a hero in the Black community.

As the young Copeland became more committed to the abolitionist cause in America, James "Gunsmith" Jones settled into life in Canada. He married Emily Francis and built a successful metalworking business. He and Emily raised six children: four girls, Anna, Emily Fredericka, and Sophia; and two sons, George and James Jr.

Anna was two years old in 1858 when her father received an invitation:

> My Dear Friend:
> I have called a quiet convention in this place of true friends of freedom. Your attendance is earnestly requested....
> Your friend, John Brown[10]

Brown had come to Chatham to write the constitution for the society he believed would emerge after his attack on Harpers Ferry. Brown was convinced that slaves and free Blacks would join his uprising, just as slaves did in the 1791 Haitian revolt. Chatham was an attractive location because it was home to educated Blacks who were accustomed to self-government. In addition to writing the rules of his new society, Brown also hoped he could gather recruits for his mission. Jones, believing that Brown was on a suicide mission, was not convinced. "One day in my shop I told him how utterly hopeless his plans would be if he persisted in making an attack with the few at his command," Jones later reported (256).

> While I was speaking, Mr. Brown walked to and fro, with his hands behind his back, as was his custom when thinking on his favorite subject. He stopped suddenly and bringing down his right hand with great force, exclaimed: "Did not my Master Jesus Christ come down from Heaven and sacrifice Himself upon the altar for the salvation of the race, and should I, a worm, not worthy to crawl under His feet, refuse to sacrifice myself?" With a look of determination, he resumed his walk. (261)

"In all the conversations I had with him during his stay in Chatham of nearly a month, I never once saw a smile light upon his countenance. He seemed to be always in deep and earnest thought," Anna Jones's father recalled (261). Despite his misgivings, Jones was there when the convention convened on May 8, 1858.

Jones came to believe that Brown intended to sacrifice himself and a few of his followers for the abolitionists' cause, and he began to see Brown's mission as necessary: "to awaken the people from the deep sleep that had settled upon the minds of the Whites of the North." Jones also believed that such an attack would have to come from a White person as the "sacrifice of any number of Negroes would have no effect" (261).

✳ Anna and her sisters grew up to be successful, career-minded women. Sophia attended the University of Toronto, where she hoped to study medicine. After discovering that women were barred from the school's medical program, Sophia transferred to the University of Michigan, where she was one of the first women, Black or White, to earn a medical degree. In 1885 she joined the faculty of Atlanta's Spelman College and helped initiate its first training program for nurses. She followed her older sister Anna to Kansas City, where she established a medical practice for a time.[11] Fredericka also moved to Kansas City and started a private boarding and day school for girls.[12] The *Detroit Plaindealer* described the sisters as having "a strong hereditary vein for woman's suffrage [and] held the thought of matrimony far off in the future." Matrimony was so far off, in fact, that neither Anna, Sophia, nor Fredericka ever married.[13] Anna Jones graduated from Oberlin College in 1875 with an English degree and taught at Wilberforce University before she accepted a job at Lincoln High School. She arrived in Kansas City in 1892.

Anna Jones arrived in a period of heightened anxiety among the White population about the presence of African Americans in the city, a "Rising Black Tide," as an editorialist from the *Kansas City Times* called it.[14] Scholars have attributed this fear to the increased visibility of the African American community.[15] In 1892, the year of Jones's arrival, some of the city's poorest Black residents lived in ramshackle sheds that crept up the hillside from the river bottoms toward the stately homes in the city's Northeast area. This makeshift community became a target for those who sought to beautify the city. That year, the city adopted landscape architect George Kessler's design for Cliff Drive, a meandering, tree-lined road that wound its way up the hillside. This project swept up this community of marginalized residents and crowded them into the already slumlike conditions in the North End and into neighborhoods on the Kansas side of the river. It was the first time—but certainly not the last—that Kansas City would relocate its most vulnerable residents in the name of civic pride.[16]

The city's most conservative element may have felt threatened by the arrival of another Black woman, but one resident greeted Anna Jones's arrival joyfully: Josephine Silone Yates, the most prominent Black woman in the city at the time. Yates was, like Jones, educated and cultured, part of what Du Bois referred to as the "Talented Tenth," a label reserved for the top 10 percent of the African American community, people who would, according to the theory, become the leaders who would lift the entire community. Together, Jones and Yates formed a powerful duo that left an indelible stamp on the city. They were Kansas City's representatives in a national sorority of powerful Black women that included Ida B. Wells, Mary Church Terrell, and Josephine St. Pierre Ruffian, and in 1892 Black women around the country were beginning to pull local networks together to work for temperance, suffrage, and civil rights.[17]

Yates—who was born Josephine Silone in Long Island, New York—was eleven years old in 1863 when she moved to Philadelphia to study under Fanny Jackson Coppin, the prominent educator. She went on to graduate at the top of her class at Rhode Island State Normal School, the first African American student in the school's history. Not long after, she accepted a position as head of the department of natural sciences at Lincoln Institute in Jefferson City, Missouri, a school started after the Civil War by Black soldiers who wanted to help freed slaves. She resigned from the college in 1889 when she married Professor

W. W. Yates, principal of Kansas City's Wendell Phillips Elementary School.[18]

In 1893, months after Jones's arrival, the women established a chapter of the Women's League, with Yates as president and Jones as secretary. They held classes in needlework and sewing. On Saturday mornings "old ladies over fifty" were taught how to read and write their names. By May of that year Yates and Jones had purchased two sewing machines and added dressmaking to their program. They planned to add millinery, hairdressing, and "other industries as soon as practical."[19] This domestic science program was eventually taken over by the Kansas City School District, which continued the program for many years, running it from Garrison School, one of the Black schools in the city's North End.

Jones and Yates were "especially anxious to better the condition of women and girls," and to that aim, they provided gingham dresses to the daughters of a blind woman, and they made sure the children had the proper attire for school and for the winter. The two were also successful in getting another woman's death sentence commuted. Although the details of the woman's conviction are not known, Jones and Yates's investigation led them to believe that "justice to the woman and above all to the womanhood of our race demanded that the sentence should at least be commuted to life imprisonment." They circulated a petition signed by several prominent Kansas Citians, Black and White, and submitted it to the governor, who signed it, which reduced her sentence to fifty years. Unfortunately, the governor's action did not reach jail officials in time, and the woman was executed.[20]

Along with alleviating individual suffering, Jones and Yates engaged in a larger battle over attitudes about women of color that developed and hardened under slavery. Westport High School's Asa Martin summed up these attitudes in his master's thesis. "As a slave, the Negro was sadly deficient morally," he wrote. "The chastity of the female slave was never esteemed of much account, since it was an impediment to her master's wealth."[21] Although acknowledging the incentives to slave owners if their female slaves gave birth, Martin was unable to consider the possibility that these births were the result of sexual assaults. Instead, he concluded that these births were due to Black women's "lustful" and "indecent" natures. The prominent scholar Howard Odum believed that Black women lacked "moral strength."[22] Popular journals were even more blunt in their assessment, and they were able to spread this message of supposed depravity to an even larger audience. For example, *Outlook* magazine declared that African American women had the "brain of a child and the passions of a woman."[23] These attitudes had economic consequences for Black women who were frequently denied factory work, particularly in New England's mills, where owners stressed the need to employ "morally upright and industrious workers."[24] It was attitudes like these—specifically an 1895 assault by Missouri Press Association president James Jacks, who called Black women thieves and prostitutes—that galvanized African American women across the country to form a national network of women of color: the National Association of Colored Women's Clubs (NACWC), founded in 1896. Over its long history, this organization has taken on a number of issues, the most well-known of which was its protest against—quite understandably—the image of a Black woman. In 1923 a southern congressman sought to erect a mammy statue on the National Mall. The NACWC understood that the image of an older Black woman caring for a White baby would reinforce notions of female servitude and suggest that Black women were not invested in their own families and communities. They mobilized and initiated a letter-writing campaign, which had the hoped-for effect: the statue was never built, and the idea for it eventually faded away.[25]

Anna Jones and Josephine Yates, as prominent figures in the NACWC's early days (Yates was the group's second president), helped guide the group as it formulated its position on some of the most important topics of the day, including the use of alcohol. The association also condemned the work of anyone who sought to ridicule the race, which included direct criticism of Thomas Dixon, a best-selling author of the day. Dixon asserted that African Americans were the cause of all of society's ills, and one of his novels, *The Clansmen*, became the basis of D. W. Griffith's 1915 film, *Birth of a Nation* (see chapter 5).

In addition to challenging negative stereotypes, club women spoke up about the spread of Jim Crow. They protested the Sheats Law, legislation in Florida that forbade teaching Blacks and Whites in the same classroom, and they opposed a Louisiana statute that required separate railroad cars for Black and White riders. The issue that the NACWC protested most vehemently, though, was lynching. They condemned mob violence and demanded that anyone who had been accused of a crime receive a fair trial.[26] The women commended Republicans who had denounced lynching in their party's platform and encouraged the Democratic Party to do the same. By 1900 every southern state that was led by Democrats had passed laws to restrict Blacks at the voting booth, whether it was through poll taxes, grandfather clauses, or literacy tests.

This same Democratic Party chose Kansas City to host its national convention in 1900. It was an event better known for what happened before the opening gavel than for what happened after. Ninety days before the convention convened, lightning struck and a fire consumed the building. Newspaper editor William Rockhill Nelson was confident that the hall could be rebuilt, as was his friend, Uriah Spray Epperson, general manager of the Fowler Packing Company Plant. Epperson, a member of the city's Commercial Club, called a special meeting of the group, and within two days he had raised more than $36,000 toward rebuilding the structure.[27] It is not known how he amassed this money, but in today's history books, Epperson is best known for the minstrel show he created: Epperson's Megaphone Mastodon Minstrels, a collection of 125 men complete with canes, tuxedos, top hats—and blackface. This group danced and entertained Kansas City's ruling class in the name of various charitable causes.[28] With or without the help of Epperson's Minstrels, the money and materials for the new convention center came together, and the city welcomed Democratic delegates that summer.

While Kansas City welcomed the Democratic leaders, Anna Jones was a delegate at a different conference. During the summer of 1900, Jones was in London to attend the First Pan-African Congress, a three-day meeting in Westminster Town Hall. Jones was among a prestigious group of people of African descent who met to discuss issues related to colonization, including how to protect the interests of native populations. Among those traveling with her were Bishop Alexander Walters, a leader in the AME Zion church; Anna Cooper; and W. E. B. Du Bois.[29] Walters had emerged as a national voice for African American causes after his stirring speeches about lynchings and the spread of Jim Crow. Anna Cooper, like Jones, held a degree from Oberlin College, taught briefly at Wilberforce, and was a leader in the NACWC.

The Pan-Africanists discussed the importance of instilling cultural pride into African Americans because they believed that this pride would translate into political and economic power. In her conference paper, Jones argued that Black people were "at once spiritual and artistically endowed with traits which needed to be shielded from the highly individualistic and materially obsessed Eurocentric persona."[30] Art and imagery became central themes not only of the conference but of the larger civil rights movement. Du Bois, like other leaders, could see "small cracks in the wall of racism that could, over time, be widened through the production of exemplary racial images."[31]

Du Bois had an opportunity to implement his ideas about imagery at the 1900 Paris World's Fair, where he and Jones headed after leaving London and where Du Bois had co-curated the Negro Exposition. He and Booker T. Washington, founder of Tuskegee Institute, assembled a series of photographs from the all-Black Hampton Institute. The exhibit was designed to illustrate Black people's progress since Emancipation and highlight their contributions to society. Images in this award-winning show were the antithesis of the images that Black people saw of themselves in the United States, demeaning representations rooted in the stereotypical idea of African American inferiority, such as Epperson's Minstrels and other caricatures of Black people with distorted and exaggerated features.[32]

Anna Jones was attuned to how these images influenced her community, and she did what she could to combat them in and out of the classroom. At Lincoln High School she helped form a "very progressive" alliance of female students for the "girls mutual improvement," an outcome achieved through the entertainment of friends, the cultivation of social amenities, and the promotion of literary culture.[33] She continued her positive messaging outside of Lincoln: "There is no inherent inferiority [between Black and White women] which education will not remove," she wrote in 1905. "What education, discipline, and training have done for other races and have already done for ours, they will continue to do, as surely as harvest follows seedtime. Place side by side the writings of Phillis Wheatley and Anne Bradstreet, those of the slave easily surpass those of the first American woman who has won literary fame. Equality of opportunity alone was needed to produce equality of accomplishment."[34]

Despite her efforts, Anna Jones watched as Jim Crow crept into her newly adopted hometown. "Kansas City called itself the 'Heart of America,'" declared Roy Wilkins.

> The claim was partly geographical, partly psychological, a concoction of boosterism and Babbitry that glossed over the fundamental fact that the place was a Jim Crow town right down to its bootstraps. Except for the streetcars, which had somehow escaped the color line, neighborhoods, schools, churches, hospitals, theaters, and just about everything else were as thoroughly segregated as anything in Memphis. In its feelings about race, Kansas City might as well have been Gulfport, Mississippi.[35]

Interestingly, while city streetcars remained integrated throughout the Jim Crow era, one piece of evidence suggests that it was for the benefit not of the city's Black population but rather the city's most powerful. In 1903, as city leaders debated this question, Thomas Corrigan, president of Metropolitan Street Railway Company, argued that integration saved money. "Are the common carriers to be forced to pull a coach across the state for the three or four Negroes to be found on a train? The bill isn't practical any more than it is in its effects on

Anna Jones on porch of 2444 Montgall Avenue, circa 1915. Courtesy of
Renée Cochée.

street car companies," he said.[36] In other words, given the numbers of
Black residents in Kansas City, it would cost streetcar companies too
much money if they had to supply separate cars.

✳ Like most Black middle-class women of the day, Jones measured
womanhood against a European standard, and she believed that the
"highest type of woman" was a lady, one of culture, refinement, and
Christianity. A respectable woman would never be confrontational.
Rather, she should use her "sympathetic touch" when dealing with

others.[37] It was a delicate balance for someone facing injustices due to both her race and her gender, but Jones no doubt believed that she could advance the rights of African Americans and women with reasoned dialogue. It was an approach she used again and again.

Jones contributed a piece to the *Crisis*, the NAACP's quarterly journal, in which she articulated her beliefs about granting women the right to vote. "Of the four great institutions of human uplift—the home, the school, the church, and the State—woman has a direct controlling force in the first three institutions. Since her control in the three is unquestioned, should she not have the legal means—the ballot—to widen and deepen her work?"[38]

For Jones, women's work meant the development of morals and the prevention of vice, and she believed that if women were allowed to vote, they would support the "enactment of laws to secure and regulate sanitation, pure food, prohibition, divorce; the care of the aged and unfortunate, the orphan. All the questions touch in a very direct way the home—the woman's kingdom." Jones argued that women will cast their votes to support "the forces of right."[39]

Jones had a lot of reason to be optimistic. In the years after the Civil War, illiteracy rates for African Americans declined significantly, which offered proof to leaders like Jones that the future was bright for African Americans. The industrial jobs that had brought millions of European immigrants to America's shores and lifted them out of poverty, she thought, would soon be open to Blacks. "The opportunities are increasing," she wrote.

In the new century's rapid growth in commercialism and its consequent wealth all Americans must share. That will mean increase of educational opportunity, another word for refinement in social life, greater intelligence, an uplift of the moral nature, a broadening of the soul's horizon. The higher outlook upon life and its privileges, which is now enjoyed by hundreds will be enjoyed by thousands, and that leavening will change the status of a race.

Referencing King Canute, the Viking warrior who could not control the seas, she continued, "Then with hope we face the future; though

Jones in Douglass School, circa 1918. Black Archives of Mid-America.

there still will be local oppression, injustice, wrongs—they can no more hold down a people with their record of a century, than the commands and chains of the old Danish King could keep back the oncoming tide of the ocean."[40]

Jones wrote this optimistic piece about the future of Black America shortly after her move into a home on Montgall Avenue, a feat that would have inspired anyone, Black or White, about the promise of America. Despite her new home and the hopeful outlook she expressed in *The Voice of the Negro*, she struck a more somber tone in a writing she left for her Lincoln High School students the same year she purchased her home. In the school's 1904 yearbook, she penned a piece that expressed a more realistic vision about how life would likely unfold for them. After encouraging her students not to get lazy during their time off and to read every day, she wrote: "Every vocation, however lowly, can yield something of value. Every domestic task, girls, however menial, may be converted, by the subtle alchemy of mind, from soulless drudgery into soulful work."[41]

In 1919 Anna Jones retired from the Kansas City school district, sold her home at 2444 to John Bluford, and moved to Monrovia,

California, where she bought a small orange grove about twenty-five miles from Los Angeles. Several years later her brothers and sisters joined her. She died in March 1932, but her legacy as a teacher, writer, and feminist lives on—and her home on Montgall Avenue became the home to another strong woman in Kansas City history, Lucile Bluford.

In the block in which I live, five explosions of dynamite have occurred in the past year, causing considerable damage to our homes and much mental uneasiness on the part of our families. The last of these, which happened Saturday Nov. 11, was by far the most destructive of them all, completely wrecking the home of Mr. Hezekiah Walden.

H. O. Cook to Oswald Villard, November 21, 1911

4

Hezekiah Walden moved to Montgall Avenue in 1906. Unlike the Cook family and Anna Jones, whose writings held clues to their personalities, Walden left no written record of his time in Kansas City. As a result, only the most basic facts about him are known. He was born in Virginia just after the Civil War and attended Wayland Seminary, a school established in Washington, DC, for African Americans wanting to enter the ministry, and he eventually found his way to Colby College in Waterville, Maine. Like other Black educators who sought to educate former slaves after the Civil War, Walden headed south in the late 1800s. He moved to Nashville, Tennessee, in 1898, where he headed up the science department at Roger Williams University, an all-Black institution founded in 1866. Walden taught there during a particularly turbulent time that foreshadowed the violence he and his young family would encounter in Kansas City.[1]

In the early 1900s, roughly thirty-five years after its inception, Roger Williams University was in a precarious position. Nashville was growing, and the university's campus was by then situated in an economically desirable area. When White developers began investing in the land around the university, several turned their hungry eyes toward the campus. After legitimate attempts to purchase the university were rejected by school trustees, the violence began. On January 24, 1905, as students attended a prayer session in the school's Centennial Hall, a fire broke out that destroyed the building as well as the school's science library. Roger Williams University limped through the spring semester, when another fire destroyed the women's dormitory in May of that year.[2]

The causes of the fires were never proven, but shortly after the second incident, university officials determined that the institution could no longer continue. Trustees hired a Nashville developer who subdivided and sold off the land. Not long after, Hezekiah Walden arrived in Kansas City, after he was hired to teach physics at Lincoln High School. Unlike the Cook family and others who made Lincoln and Kansas City their long-term home, Walden did not remain on Montgall Avenue, possibly feeling that Kansas City was neither kind nor safe.

An assault on Black voters reached a peak in 1908 when Kansas City's mayor, Thomas Crittenden, proclaimed that the Black vote was as "much for sale as the cattle in the pens at the stock yards."[3] He went on to assert that limiting the Black community's political influence would be a "positive" move. Crittenden would not have been pleased that Hezekiah Walden had settled on Montgall Avenue. After all, most of Kansas City's African American population lived in the city's First and Eighth Wards. The 2400 block of Montgall was in the Tenth Ward. And because most Black men tended to be loyal to the party of Lincoln, the threat of the spread of Republican voters to other wards was not good news for a Democratic mayor.

Mayor Crittenden's tenure was brief, from 1908 to 1910, but other White leaders had similar attitudes, and their actions would only hurt the city's African American community in the years that followed. On May 27, 1911, the Tenth Ward Citizens' Association held a meeting at Posey Hall, at Twenty-Sixth Street and Prospect Avenue, one block south and west of Walden's home.[4] Although "citizens' association" may sound innocuous, its mission was anything but. In the years to come, other neighborhood "improvement" associations like this would be formed: Lindwood, East Side, Northeast, and Greenwood, "all having their origin in opposition to Negroes acquiring homes," Chester Franklin observed several years later.[5]

City prosecutor Floyd Jacobs attended the meeting and told the Posey Hall crowd that he had just returned from a trip through the South, where the White community had to deal with the "Negro problem" on a large scale. Jacobs asserted that the leaders in the southern states, with their large Black populations, knew "how to accomplish many things better than we who live in the North. In all of the principal cities of the Southern states, the negroes are segregated from the Whites. Consequently, there is no deterioration of property as we know it here."[6]

This belief that people of color could be linked to falling property values became a mantra, a way to make discrimination more palatable to White communities in Kansas City and in cities throughout the country. Jacobs contended that he did not make these assertions based on prejudice but rather on *science*—in this case, economics, which held that Black people hurt property values. In saying this he also made it clear that the traditional measures of class in America— education and socioeconomic status—would not apply to the Black residents of Montgall Avenue.

Jacobs made no secret of the southern origins of his ideas, and he spread his beliefs as more and more African Americans moved to Kansas City.[7] In 1900 a typical Black Kansas Citian lived in a primarily White neighborhood, those in which only 13 percent of the residents were Black. In 1910 that number was 22 percent. By 1930 that figure jumped to almost 32 percent.[8]

Traditional analysis of this phenomenon has focused on the macro—broad discussions about the industrialization of cities and the movement of Blacks from the rural South to more urban areas. But there was nothing abstract for the families who lived through these demographic shifts or the sifting out of Black families from predominantly White neighborhoods. In 1911 this demographic trend became very real for the Black families living on the 2400 block of Montgall, as the Cooks, Anna Jones, and Hezekiah Walden suffered through the extreme measures that the White establishment pursued trying to push them out of their homes.

Less than three weeks after the Posey Hall meeting, on June 13, at a special, hastily called meeting of the Kansas City school district's board, member Milton Moore (who had attended the Posey Hall meeting) proposed that the district should fire any "colored person who resides in a neighborhood chiefly inhabited by persons of the white race."[9] Because the meeting did not include the entire board, a final vote was put off. Four days later, at the June 17, 1911, regular meeting, Moore again brought the issue to consideration with Resolution Number 63524:

> Whereas, representations have been frequently made to this Board by patrons of the public schools and tax paying citizens, that colored teachers employed in the public schools have sought and obtained and made their residence in neighborhoods inhabited chiefly by persons of the white race;
>
> And, Whereas, it has come to the knowledge of this Board that the fact of such residence has been productive of much irritation which this Board, without doing injustice to any person, is willing to do All in its power to remove, so far as it may properly act in the matter;
>
> Therefore, Resolved, that this Board declares that it will not, after the first day of August, 1911, be disposed to employ as a teacher in any of the public schools under its control, any colored person who resides in a neighborhood chiefly inhabited by persons of the white race.

The resolution was defeated.[10]

After Moore and his cronies failed to remove the Black residents with the threat of unemployment, more direct—and violent—strategies were used, including a number of dynamite attacks. These culminated in an especially destructive bomb that went off at 2442 Montgall, the home of Hezekiah Walden and his young family.

The attack was so damaging that neither Cook nor Jones could let it go unchallenged, and both reached out for help from W. E. B. Du Bois's newly organized NAACP, a move that showed how sophisticated Montgall's residents were. Although Du Bois was, arguably, the most distinguished African American intellectual of the period, his and the NAACP's place as the primary advocate for civil rights had not yet been settled in 1911, especially considering the popularity of Booker T. Washington's message of accommodation and subordination.

Clearly, Cook, Jones, and the other teachers on Montgall were looking toward the next generation when they placed their trust in the NAACP, sensing that it was the right organization to lead the charge for racial justice. On November 21, 1911, Cook wrote to NAACP cofounder Oswald Villard, who was heading up the agency's legal department:[11]

Dear Sir:

We desire to place before the legal department of the N.A.A.C.P. the case of a group of Negroes of Kansas City, Mo. who have suffered repeated attempts to destroy their property by an organization of men who have demanded that they leave the neighborhood. There are nine Negro families in one block and twelve in the next who have purchased or are in progress of buying their homes, ranging in price from $1500 to $4000. In the block in which I live, five explosions of dynamite have occurred in the past year, causing considerable damage to our homes and much mental uneasiness on the part of our families. The last of these, which happened Saturday Nov. 11, was by far the most destructive of them all, completely wrecking the home of Mr. Hezekiah Walden. At the time Mr. Walden was working in Salt Lake City and his wife, with two small children were alone in the house.

We have again and again appealed to the Mayor and The Chief of Police to give us protection from these crimes, but the detectives have been of no help either in running the perpetrators to earth or in checking further threats and outrages. We feel that we have a clear case against the city in as much as we have all faithfully discharged our duties as citizens, and we are about to retain eminent legal counsel to defend our cause. In addition to this we beg that we may have the assistance of some member of the legal department of the N.A.A.C.P. who will join us in vigorously prosecuting this case.

We fear (as threats have already been issued) that our entire settlement will be dynamited unless active steps are taken to force the city to protect our lives and property. Aside from this, if Negroes are to be driven from one section of a city to another simply because a certain element (many of whom have moved into the neighborhood after the Negroes) demand it, we feel that no place will be left to them except the worse districts, even though they try to be peaceable, honest, and industious [sic] members of the community.

We shall be glad to furnish you any further particulars regarding the situation or its history, and besides such photographs of the house and surroundings as you may consider beneficial to the case. We shall appreciate, also, an early reply.

Very truly yours,

H. O. Cook

2436 Montgall Ave.

In addition to contacting the NAACP's legal department, Cook asked his colleague and neighbor Anna Jones to reach out to Du Bois personally and inform him of the situation. Despite feeling that this type of frank dialogue was out of a proper lady's purview, Jones complied. The letter she composed is one of the most valuable glimpses we have of the incident, providing hints about the myriad forces at play against Kansas City's Black leaders and the terrifying impact they had:[12]

Dear Friend,

Mr. H. O. Cook has asked me to write something of the history of the trouble in our neighborhood concerning which he has had some correspondences with you. I am sorry he imparted the duty upon me. For I think men can do these things with more directness than women. You will recall our neighborhood when you drove out one day when here, when my sister was with me— There are 9 homes owned by colored people at this end of the block....

They [Blacks and Whites] lived in here peacefully till nearly 3 years ago, when the agitation began that some Republican boss had "Africanized" the 10th Ward. Meetings were held in a hall denouncing agents and others who had sold to the col. people, and it was said that they must "go" by fair means or force—that they had depreciated property—etc &tc.

Feelings ran high, and when a place on a neighboring street where no colored had been was sold to a colored man—the throwing of dynamite began. After three attacks on this house, the colored man moved out, and in a few weeks after that, they began trying the same methods in our neighborhood on Montgall.

The attacks seemed to be directed at one house 2nd on the West side owned by a man named Walden, formerly a teacher in the High School. The charges being thrown in the yard back of his house.

Jones went on to describe how the incident was assessed by the insurance company, which did not want to pay for the damage but instead tried to explain it away by calling it a gas explosion. Her letter continued: "The house stands a wreck. . . . Two families have recently received threatening letters, telling them to move out within 30 days—over the signature 'Dynamite.'"

Jones's letter also highlights an interesting wrinkle in the Black community's reaction, and one that hindered the teachings of Cook and Jones, who tried to instill pride into the community. "Public sentiment is very 'wishy-washy' and even many negroes, under the delusion that those out here are trying to get away from the rest of them, are rejoicing over every dynamite explosion. The meetings that started the trouble are not held publicly but it is supposed in some private house & that the throwers of the bombs are hired for the purpose."

＊ There were no more reported attacks immediately after the one that nearly destroyed Walden's home. This attack, however, did succeed to the extent that Hezekiah Walden determined Kansas City was not the place for him or his family. Shortly after the explosion, he moved to Salt Lake City, where he remained until 1917, when he moved closer to his Virginia roots and secured a teaching position at the Bluefield Colored Institute in West Virginia.

Eventually, the immigrant families who lived on Montgall—Boris and Anna Kittis from Russia (2428); Adam and Anna Hildebrand and their son, Lawrence, from Germany (2430); and Irish-born Richard Mayberry (2432)—moved on and sold their homes to Black families. The vacant lots that dotted the east side of the street in 1904, when the Cooks, Jones, and Walden moved in, were sold to other African Americans, including George Gamble (2445), Chester Franklin and Ada Crogman Franklin (2447), Arthur and Marguerite Pittman (2449), John Edward Perry (2451), and Charles Greenstreet (2455). Their stories are in the chapters that follow.

Ollie Cook and Anna Jones were fearless in the face of the dynamite attacks, but they were powerless when it came to the larger struggle against racial injustice. In the years to come, as White families abandoned the entire neighborhood, future residents of Montgall would be as devastated by racism as Hezekiah Walden was in 1911.[13]

We come to-day bearing the olive branch of hope to the boys and girls of Garrison school. What is there for them to hope for in this country, wallowing in the slough of prejudice and rank injustice?

Are we less brave than Garrison, were the times more propitious for the success of his cause than ours? Yet he lived to see the shackles of the slaves broken and the slaves made free citizens. Did he weary because every door was closed in his face? No, he forced them open, not by violence, but by the justice of his cause.

Frances Jackson at the dedication of a portrait of William Lloyd Garrison, namesake of Kansas City's Garrison School, in 1904

5

2434 MONTGALL AVENUE
FRANCES AND CHARLES JACKSON, CAROLYN BRYDIE, AND GWENDOLYN CALDERON

Beyond the fact that Frances Jackson lived at 2434 Montgall, much of her life is a mystery. A 1915 photograph shows a woman staring straight at the camera, head tilted and resting on her hand. She looks strong, confident, smart—all qualities that we can assume she had judging from the limited amount of information that exists. She was born Frances Caswell in 1862, and given that her birth took place in the rural town of Chester, South Carolina, it could be assumed that she was born into slavery, or at least that she was born into the culture of slavery.[1] Yet she was well educated, enough that she became a teacher at Lincoln Institute in Jefferson City, where she taught before settling on Montgall.

Frances' husband, Charles, was born in Ohio, ten years before his wife, and the couple settled in Kansas City sometime around the turn of the century, originally taking up residence near Twelfth Street and Vine. They moved to Montgall Avenue around the same time that the Cooks and Anna Jones did.

The Jacksons lived at 2434 Montgall during the dynamite attacks, and although there is no written evidence of Frances Jackson's response, other evidence suggests that she, like her neighbors, fought back. Four years before her street erupted into violence, Jackson became the city editor for a local Black newspaper, the *Rising Son*.[2]

Six months later the paper ran a scathing editorial about White real estate agents who refused to show African Americans "any house one could call really decent . . . [driving them] out of most all respectable neighborhoods."[3] Several months after that, another pointed editorial appeared, a direct response to a story that had maligned Black homeowners who had purchased homes in predominantly White neighborhoods and was published in another newspaper: "We have always heard a hit dog will howl," began the *Son* editorial, probably written by Jackson.

> Now, esteemed editor of the *Pitchfork* . . . do you not know that the days of Ham are over? Do you not realize that such articles that you write insult the high class white man because you are trying to hurt the self-respecting Negro who would try to lift up his head? Do you not know that the day has come when the Negro, as well as the white man, can interpret the art of Mendelssohn, and commune with the soul of a Wagner, and sigh for a Goethe and a Schiller, or enjoy a Paderewski?[4]

Frances Jackson was not a woman to demur.

Although she did not assume leadership in the National Association of Colored Women's Clubs as her friends Anna Jones and Josephine Yates had, she was a member and was committed to its goals, especially temperance, believing that the city's clubs were a "great evil in our midst allowed to run loose and carry down to ignominious degradation of the young men in their community . . . powerful institutions of vice carrying hundreds of negroes into the vortex of hell's running stream."[5]

Unlike Anna Jones, who was corseted by conventions and eager to pass along the Victorian model of womanhood to her female students, Jackson seemed ahead of her time when it came to assertiveness. Eleven years before Principal Cook chose to ignore the question of the perceived "criminal tendencies" of Black people in his master's thesis, Jackson tackled the issue head on. At a meeting of the NAACP's Kansas City, Kansas, branch, she was part of a panel discussion focused on "Discriminations in the Penal and Correctional Institutions."[6] Although the content of her presentation is not known, the title suggests that she had an appreciation of an aspect of life for Black Americans that is still relevant a hundred years later with the disproportionate number of people of color inhabiting America's jails.

Her fiery personality was on full display in the spring of 1904 when she delivered a speech at Garrison Elementary School, the text of which was printed in the *Rising Son*. The school had just received a portrait of its namesake, abolitionist William Lloyd Garrison, and Jackson spoke at its unveiling. Jackson wanted the students to learn from this White man who had had the courage to advocate for the "down-trodden race."[7]

Jackson wanted the elementary students to appreciate the tenacity of this American hero, even though his words "brought enmity, hatred and all uncharitable upon any one who dared assert that the Blacks had as much right to liberty as the whites."

> Think for a moment what he had to fight against. The church, one would think, would have risen up and in no uncertain tone spoke in behalf of the slave, but did she? No, a thousand times no. She turned her back on Garrison and her minister called him a fanatic, reviled him and helped to persecute him. The state winked at the persecution of him and his followers, the press cried "away with him" and there seemed no place for him to turn for sympathy or help but the mighty arm of the Lord was about him and would not let him fail. He began publishing the Liberator in Boston, and vigorously assaulting slavery in the South and its sympathizers in the North, and nothing daunted or caused him to falter in the course he had chosen.

Although Jackson urged the students at Garrison to fight injustice through peaceful means, she understood the role that violence played in the fight for civil rights, "how bloody footsteps are the way marks of human progress and to whom under God, we owe what is most valuable in our civilization."

Given her NAACP membership and what we know of her leadership within the Black community, Jackson would have supported one of the local chapter's early battles—that of limiting the distribution of D. W. Griffith's divisive film, *Birth of a Nation*, arguably the most dangerous piece of propaganda of the day for the punishing attitudes about Black people that it propagated. It was a battle that Cook and future Montgall Avenue resident and founder of the *Kansas City Call* Chester Franklin took very seriously.

Griffith's film was originally titled *The Clansman* after a Thomas Dixon novel—the same work that had drawn opposition from Anna Jones and the NACWC in 1906 and had drawn criticism from Jackson's newspaper, which understood that it excited "race hatred."[8] *Birth of a Nation* was the first film that attempted to tell a long, complex story with multiple characters and sweeping battle scenes.[9] But more than that, the movie was an attempt to convince audiences of the horrible anguish suffered by White people during the Reconstruction period. And although the film was a piece of fiction, it portrayed itself as fact, especially in its second half, where quotations by President Woodrow Wilson, Dixon's friend from his and Wilson's days at Johns Hopkins, appeared on the screen.[10]

The film presented Black people through a southern lens, starting off with nostalgic images of a genteel Old South that portrayed slaves as childlike characters who, when not happily picking cotton in the fields, could be seen dancing and singing in their cabins. Dixon, Griffith, and others of like mind sought to portray the Civil War as a consequence of meddling interference by northern agitators. In this scenario, after the war ended, the once-happy slaves turned into raging, menacing animals who wanted nothing more than to rape and marry White women. These frightening individuals would not be content until there was a complete "overthrow of civilization in the South." Griffith's film portrayed the Black legislators who had served during Reconstruction as drunken, barefoot oafs working to legalize interracial marriage and limiting the rights of White voters. The film's final act tells the story of the origins of the Ku Klux Klan, a group that brought together people from the North and South, "former enemies ... united in their Aryan birthright,"[11] defenders of justice and protectors of women. "Liberty and union are one and inseparable now and forever!" the film proclaimed. And in case anyone missed the point that White + Klan = Christian Goodness, the film's final scene included an image of a serene Jesus celebrating along with the ebullient crowd of White people who had gathered after the Klan rescued the movie's young star, actress Lillian Gish, from a terrifying Black pursuer.[12]

The film opened in Los Angeles on March 3, 1915, and critics hailed its thrills, historical accuracy, and educational value. Despite the glowing reviews, the movie sparked controversy almost immediately in the Black community, leading to riots in Philadelphia and Boston.[13] The NAACP understood that *Birth of a Nation* came at a particularly fraught time, when many northerners had little personal exposure to African Americans and a massive exodus of Black people from the South was underway. Black leaders did not want this movie to be the majority culture's introduction to people of color, so, hoping to limit the film's reach, the NAACP's national office mailed flyers to local chapters asking the leaders to demand that the movie be banned from their area, a strategy that was successful in places such as Denver.[14]

Local efforts to ban the film in Kansas City, Missouri, were less successful, but not through any lack of effort by residents of Montgall Avenue. Throughout the summer of 1915, H. O. Cook, Chester Franklin, and other members of the NAACP's Grievance Committee met to strategize about how to respond to the film's Kansas City premiere, scheduled for October 1915. The group was savvy enough to appreciate that any publicity would bring added attention to the movie, so they were restrained in their objections and kept their concerns out of the newspapers. The very public protests in Boston, New York, and Philadelphia only brought extended runs of the film.[15]

Cook, Franklin, and others met with city officials in June 1915 and proposed an ordinance stating, in part, that no person or film "shall exhibit in Kansas City, any obscene or immoral film or picture (or any film or picture tending to cause strife or disturbance of the peace between persons of different races, colors nationalities, or sections)."

Although the ordinance passed the lower house, 15–0, it met resistance in the upper house when two aldermen began "a campaign of evasion and delays" that continued throughout the summer.[16]

As the date of the Kansas City premiere approached and members of the Grievance Committee realized that their proposed ordinance had been defeated by stalling tactics, they proposed their plan B at a special meeting with Mayor Henry Jost. They asked him to appoint a committee of six people, three Black and three White, to review the picture and delete the most offensive scenes. The mayor did appoint a committee to preview the film and delete the most objectionable parts, but he selected an all-White panel of men to complete the task.

The Kansas City, Kansas, NAACP proved more successful in keeping *Birth of a Nation* from premiering when Kansas governor Arthur Capper banned the movie altogether. (It did not play in Kansas until 1923.)[17] The Kansas City, Missouri, NAACP's Grievance Committee could take some satisfaction knowing that when the film opened on October 24, fifteen scenes had been eliminated, and their low-key approach had kept unwanted publicity away. The unnamed *Kansas City Star* reviewer called the movie "a monument to filmmaking." And as if Kansas Citians would be immune from the harmful attitudes about Black people that *Birth of a Nation* portrayed, he dismissed the controversy by proclaiming it "largely a matter of locality."[18]

Jackson had strong bonds and professional associations in the community and with her Montgall neighbors. She took an active role in raising money for Wheatley-Provident Hospital, a facility established by her neighbor, John E. Perry (2451, and whose story follows in chapter 6); she and Anna Jones were members of the Social Service League, who delivered public lectures at the old City Hospital; and for a time she served as president of the Book Lovers Club, a group that included many of her neighbors, such as founders Anna Jones and Daisy Cook. Jackson was on the board for the Florence Crittenden Home for Colored Girls and served as matron at the Home for the Aged and Indigent Colored People.

As important as she was to the larger Black population, Jackson should also be remembered for her role in creating the smaller African

American community that developed on Montgall during the first half of the twentieth century. Just as the Cooks had, Charles and Frances Jackson opened their home to a number of people, providing temporary (and in one case permanent) housing for newcomers to Kansas City, including Charles and Willie Mae Greenstreet (2455), who stayed with the Jacksons while their home across the street was built.[19]

In 1906, when the original Lincoln High School moved to its new home at Nineteenth Street and Tracy Avenue, the district hired a number of new faculty members, many of whom came to live on Montgall Avenue, including two women who moved into the Jacksons' home. One of them, Fredericka Sprague, was hired to head up the Domestic Science Department, and the other, Carolyn Brydie, was hired to teach Latin. Sprague, granddaughter of the famed abolitionist Frederick Douglass, eventually married John Edward Perry and moved across the street. Brydie, however, remained in the Jacksons' home for the rest of her life, caring for Charles and Frances until their deaths.[20]

In addition to Fredericka Sprague and Carolyn Brydie, school district records indicate that many educators lived on Montgall during the first two decades of the twentieth century. The Cooks housed Lucile Hunter, a teacher at Lincoln, and Katherine Wright, who taught at Garrison School. Amanda Wheeler taught at Phillips and moved into 2440 Montgall, in the home owned by John Day.[21] By opening their homes, Montgall residents were not simply providing a kindness—they were offering much-needed lodging to "proper" young women looking for housing in a safe neighborhood. For them, Montgall was a refuge.[22]

Carolyn Brydie, known as "Miss Brydie" to the thousands of students she encountered, was born in Athens, Georgia, in 1878, one of seven children born to Eugene and Camilla Brydie. Educated at Atlanta University, she started her teaching career at a school in Augusta, Georgia, but was hired away in 1906 when Lincoln High School expanded its curriculum.[23]

Although Brydie was hired to teach Latin, she did a lot more than that, especially in the early years. She directed plays, including the school's productions of *The Merchant of Venice* and *The Drum Major*,

Carolyn E. Brydie. 1926 Lincoln High School
yearbook, Thatcher Family Collection, Kansas
Collection, RH MS 1250, Kenneth Spencer Research
Library, University of Kansas Libraries.

and she served as the faculty sponsor for the yearbook.[24] It is not
known whether she received extra money for these duties, but evidence indicates that her regular pay may have been about half of
what a male teacher received. In 1913 the average monthly pay for
female teachers was $74.92, while men earned $137.40.[25]

Brydie was well liked by her students, and Lincoln's senior class of
1916 singled her out.

She has been the prop of the Senior Class, has grieved at our grievancs
[sic], smiled when we smiled, and worked for us incessantly. For our
programs, our plays, commencement exercises, and even our conduct

and dignity, we are indebted to this beloved woman. And in a simple manner we wish to publicly thank her. The Class of 1916 also takes this means to leave with her the impression that, regardless of the number of colleges or the professions we might follow in years to come, the name of Miss Carolyne [sic] Brydie will always be dear to us.[26]

Later classes showed their affection by poking fun at her, such as a joke that appeared in the 1926 yearbook: "How old is Miss Brydie? Answer: Quite old—I heard she taught Caesar." And the class of 1928 (the year her neighbor Lucile Bluford graduated) willed to her "a little more patience to go with her already sweet disposition."[27]

Brydie was with the faculty in 1911 when the teachers made it their mission to visit every student at his or her home, "studying particularly the conditions under which the pupil lived and did his work," so the school could "render the very best service possible to the individual pupils."[28] She was also there as the teachers and students battled overcrowded conditions.

Lincoln's Nineteenth Street and Tracy Avenue facility, designed to accommodate 250 students, was by 1919 serving 640 during the day and more than 700 at night. That year, 424 girls shared sixty lockers, each of which measured 12 by 15 by 10 inches. The lockers were stuffed in the school's basement or shoved along the school's stairway landings. Up to five girls shared each one, relying on them for books, gym clothes, lunches, and winter coats. In addition to the locker shortage, Lincoln High girls faced intolerable conditions when it came to bathroom facilities, for the school had only two toilets to serve all the girls, toilets that were known to overflow or have their water supply cut off for no apparent reason. When the girls played basketball, they walked for blocks to find an appropriate space, because Lincoln offered no such accommodations. (Boys walked to the Paseo YMCA.) The Assembly Hall, where Brydie directed her plays, was also inadequate. It seated four hundred, but more than twice that number were known to attend the performances.[29]

Given the White community's overall apathy toward the city's Black population, it is hardly surprising that the school district allowed these conditions to persist. What is surprising, however, is how the faculty, including Brydie, spun the situation, trying to turn this injustice into a gift. As faculty sponsor of the 1922 yearbook, Brydie was responsible for how these overcrowded conditions would be framed and remembered by the students. That year, the yearbook editors acknowledged that classrooms were taxed "to their utmost capacity" and that students never worked with "less than two classes in a room and frequently three." But Brydie remained hopeful as she and the yearbook editors concluded that the students "gained much in self control" and "learned to concentrate better from this inconvenience."[30] One student, Lucile Bluford (2444 Montgall), not only absorbed this optimistic perspective but chose to see the struggle as a source of strength, and she was known throughout her life for her positive disposition (see chapter 8 and later chapters).

Brydie continued her education throughout her career, earning her master's degree at the University of Chicago in 1908, and twenty years later, another degree from Chicago that certified her as a counselor. She was on staff in 1935 when Lincoln moved into its current building. She remained in the new building for thirteen years, teaching the children and grandchildren of her former students until her retirement.

Brydie was also known to go above and beyond when it came to students in need. One evening she returned home late. The Russells, the family that had been persuaded by Principal Cook to come to Kansas City in 1928 and had moved into 2434 Montgall, was already sitting down to eat when Brydie pulled into the driveway accompanied by one of her students, the "most bedraggled creature" Gwendolyn Russell had ever seen.[31] Brydie directed Joshua Russell to fetch the young girl's trunk from the back of her car and informed the family that they had a new houseguest. The girl, Christine MacDonald, had recently lost her parents, and her older brother had started mistreating her. He beat her up so badly that she missed several days of school. When Brydie heard about the abuse, she went to the girl's home, gathered her things, and brought her to her home on Montgall. MacDonald ended up staying at 2434 Montgall for the rest of high

Carolyn Brydie with Gwendolyn Calderon, 1934. Courtesy of
Gwendolyn Calderon.

school. When it was time for college, Brydie supported her through
that as well. During World War II MacDonald became a member of the
Army Nurse Corps and eventually settled in Iowa.

Carolyn Brydie appeared to enjoy being surrounded by people, and
her home was a crowded, lively place, especially after the arrival of
Joshua Russell and his wife, Josie, in the 1920s. The Russells lived
with Brydie for twelve years, and Josie gave birth to three children
while the family resided there. Only when a home across the street
(2461) become available in 1941 did the family decide it was time to
move on, although their oldest daughter, Gwendolyn, remained with
Brydie.[32]

PART 2

THE HUB OF A COMMUNITY
MONTGALL AVENUE FROM
1920 TO 1940

2451 Montgall: John Edward Perry and
    Fredericka Douglass Perry
2453 Montgall: Homer Roberts
2447 Montgall: Chester Franklin and Ada Crogman
2444 Montgall: The Bluford Family
2457 Montgall: Piney Brown
2449 Montgall: The Pittman Family

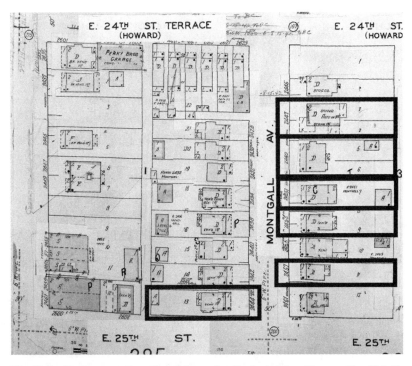

The Hub of a Community—detail from the *Sanborn Map, Kansas City, Vol. 3, 1909–1950*, p. 360. Bold outlines added to indicate the homes of Montgall's business leaders and families. Missouri Valley Special Collections, Kansas City Public Library, Kansas City, Missouri.

*Controversies are settled on merit, not argument. When
a man thinks that a negro cannot perform,
his opinion can be changed by a demonstration of ability.*
John Edward Perry, *Forty Cords of Wood* (1947)

6

The home at 2451 Montgall belonged to one of the most influential couples in Kansas City history, a hard-working pair who understood poverty—he from personal experience and she from her work with homeless youths in the city. John Edward Perry was a self-made man, the son of slaves who came from nothing to became one of the city's leading citizens; Fredericka Douglass Sprague Perry had a middle-class upbringing and was the granddaughter of one of the most famous Americans in US history, Frederick Douglass.[1] Together these two played a role in dozens of civic, charitable, and educational organizations from the Niles Home for Negro Children to Lincoln University, groups that touched and improved thousands of lives. Like several of their neighbors, they dedicated their lives to the service of others. But while Anna Jones, Ollie and Myrtle Cook, and Frances Jackson became active in civil rights organizations that vehemently protested Jim Crow, John Perry had an altogether different outlook. He welcomed segregation and maintained that it was the best way to help members of his race. He was so committed to it that he played an active role in not only establishing a Black municipal hospital in Kansas City but also helping other cities such as Saint Louis and Houston set up their own separate hospitals for Black patients.[2] In supporting segregation, Perry sided with those like Booker T.

John Edward Perry. Black Archives of Mid-America.

Washington who believed that patience and accommodation were the most effective way for Blacks to achieve equality. His view was that if African Americans developed skills in their separate institutions, they would win the respect of the White community—an outlook likely informed by a childhood defined by poverty.

Perry was born April 2, 1870, in Clarksville, Texas, the child of former slaves, Louisa White and Anderson Perry. Perry goes into great depth to describe the sacrifices his parents endured to ensure that their only son would succeed. He also came to believe that this path was open to any Black man willing to sacrifice and work hard. It was a message he preached in his autobiography, *Forty Cords of Wood*.

Fredericka Douglass Sprague Perry. Courtesy of Gwendolyn Calderon.

Perry's paternal grandfather, Ches, was brought to the United States from Madagascar, and his grandmother was a wet nurse who cared for Perry's father, Anderson, in the slave owner's house. Perry's mother Louisa was a field slave who picked cotton alongside her own mother under the scorching Louisiana sun, where malaria and typhoid were as common as the reptiles and rodents in the fields. Perry appreciated the strength and spirit that his mother's family

exhibited, and he summed up these qualities through a story he relayed in his book. When his grandmother, Louisa, was about ten years
old, she lived on a Missouri plantation in the southeastern corner of
the state. One day a trader came looking for a girl who could serve as
a nurse for his family, and he believed that Louisa could serve in this
capacity.

> The overseer directed the trader across the fields to an old Indian
> looking woman [Louisa's mother and Perry's grandmother]. He ad-
> vised that if the old woman would consent, he would sell the girl but
> he could not do so otherwise. The reply was that he would purchase
> both of them if they met the requirements. On approaching the old
> lady he said, "I came down here to buy you nigger; open your mouth
> and let me see your teeth."
>
> The reply was, "What do you think I am—a horse?" Disgusted at
> such impudence he said "I ought to slap you down." Exasperated with
> unrequited toil, brutality, and humiliation, she looked him straight in
> the eye and said, "If you put your hands on me, I will do my best to try
> to kill you with this hoe."
>
> The trader returned to the overseer and remarked, "That is a dan-
> gerous old woman; I would not have her on my place."[3]

This dangerous woman, Perry's grandmother, was sixty-eight years
old when the Civil War ended, and in her later life she survived by
making rag carpets out of scrap material. Eventually she saved enough
($200) to buy a piece of land in town. Five years later, she built a four-
room house—two rooms for herself and two rooms to rent.

Perry's parents married in 1865, and although Perry believed his
father was the source of his intense work ethic, it was his mother
who took to calling him "Doc" when he was still a baby. Both believed
that he would be of "great service" to his race (27). When his father
learned that a new school for the children of former slaves was established in nearby Marshall, Texas, he found work cutting and selling
wood so his son could attend. The title of Perry's book, *Forty Cords
of Wood*, refers to the amount of wood that his father had to cut (a
cord measures eight feet long, four feet wide, and four feet tall) for

the twenty dollars needed for his son's tuition. Before he set out for Marshall, Anderson gave his son a guidebook on manners and friendship. "The book gave wonderful ideas on economy and thrift, my daily companion and was included in my list of belongings to be taken" (53). Not only did this book echo the self-reliance messages preached by leaders like Booker T. Washington, it also reinforced lessons that the young Perry learned from his parents—that the greatest assets in life were "industry, integrity, honesty, courteousness, obedience, helpfulness, patience, and punctuality" (11). Perry lived these lessons and preached them to his readers:

> Be sure to give an honest day's work. Do not shirk, but work and then work some more. The two most essential elements, aside from toil, are love and order.
>
> An idle mind is the devil's workshop.
>
> When you work, it requires all of your time to attend to your own affairs. (11–12)

Like other conservative leaders, Perry acknowledged that prejudice existed but said that the problem was not the attitudes of Whites but the members of the oppressed minority who needed to work harder to prove their worthiness.

After high school, Perry attended Meharry Medical College in Nashville, Tennessee, an all-Black school founded by the Freedmen's Aid Society. He was then accepted into a medical program in Chicago, where, for the first time in his life, he found himself amid large numbers of White students and doctors. In 1901 he described the experience in a piece he wrote for a politically conservative publication: "To think or say that the success of the physicians of our race has been impeded in the least by their White brethren in the professions is erroneous," he wrote. "They [the White physicians] were found to be broad-gauged gentlemen of the purest type; ready to lend at any time a helping professional hand to medical representatives of a long depressed race."[4]

Interestingly, Perry remembered his colleagues a little differently in his autobiography forty-six years later in which he described the moment he arrived in Chicago and discovered that he was an "un-welcome matriculant." The school accepted him without realizing he was Black. He was told: "We can't say that we cannot accept you because it is against the laws of Illinois to refuse a student because of his color. We can say that we would rather not have you and can't do much for you" (193–194). Perry was determined to stay in school even though it meant that he would have to stand outside of the classroom to attend some of the lectures. On the rare occasions when an instructor did welcome him into his class, he faced students who crowded him out and forced him to the back. These experiences convinced him that separate hospitals would be needed if large numbers of Black men and women were going to be adequately trained in medicine. Black surgeon Daniel Hale Williams further reinforced his dream of an all-Black hospital when he heard him speak in Saint Louis. Williams told the crowd that they must build their own medical institutions. "If you sit idly by and wait for Providence and luck, you will be here a thousand years, so leave this amphitheater with determination to have more hospitals, better medical men and more scientific surgeons" (245).

Perry wrote that this was the moment he knew he would start a hospital. Another ten years passed before Perry realized his dream. He moved to Kansas City in 1903, the same year a historic flood brought another Black physician, Thomas Unthank, into prominence. Unthank was called on to treat African Americans who had been displaced by the flood and were temporarily housed in the city's convention center. Perry became friends with Unthank and two other physicians, J. F. Shannon and M. H. Lambright. "It would be difficult to find three men more unselfishly interested in the general welfare of the community as a whole than the late Shannon, Unthank and Lambright," Perry wrote, adding that the doctors also shared his sense of humor. "I doubt if there are four men in this country who have laughed more than Shannon, Unthank, Lambright, and Perry. . . . When the load became heavy, the highway of life rough, and the clouds of despondency were low and threatening disaster, momentarily the burden was laid down and some one of the four would start a laugh, which gave relaxation" (280).

Although the four men did not establish a traditional practice together, they operated as a unit: if a patient's regular doctor was unavailable, a "brother physician" would step in (280). However, the men did establish a business partnership in 1904 with the opening of the People's Drug Store at the northeast corner of Eighteenth Street and Paseo Avenue. This store, the first Black business in the vicinity of Eighteenth Street and Vine, opened December 17 to much fanfare. In addition to providing much-needed medicine for the city's African American community, it became a gathering place, a space where Blacks could purchase a glass of lemonade or other refreshments. According to Perry, before People's Drug, only two places in Kansas City would sell a soda or ice cream to people of color (305).

Perry originally moved into a home at Twelfth Street and Vine and set up his medical practice along Twelfth Street, turning his residence into a four-bed facility, Perry Sanitorium. Perry was content with his small establishment, but Unthank persuaded his new friend to dream bigger. In 1903 Kansas City voters approved $225,000 worth of bonds for a hospital to replace the twenty-five-year-old, 175-bed facility, a place so inadequate for the city's burgeoning population that it was not uncommon that cots were set up in the hallways, and that two patients would be assigned to one bed.[5]

After Colonel Thomas Swope donated land for a new municipal hospital overlooking the city's new Union Station, Unthank saw an opportunity to turn the old hospital into a facility for the Black community, and the doctors began a public campaign for it.[6] He and Perry set up a meeting with the editor of a leading newspaper to make their case. Because the *Kansas City Journal* had run stories about public health, the physicians believed they had an ally in swaying public opinion.[7] Unthank and Perry told him that most of the Black community was treated by Black doctors, and they reminded him about the rates of tuberculosis, diphtheria, and smallpox in the Black community. What captured the editor's attention, though, was the threat to the White community that these diseases posed. Unthank and Perry argued that Black people could bring these diseases into the White community through their work as chauffeurs and maids. A hospital for the Black community was needed to protect White people. According to Perry (355), the newspaper's public health argument swayed readers, and attitudes began to change after he ran an editorial in support of the Black hospital. In 1906 Unthank and Perry stumped for the Republican mayoral candidate, Henry Beardsley, with the slogan "A City Hospital for Negroes." Beardsley won after gaining support from the city's Black population.

On October 8, 1908, 68 of the 126 patients in the old city hospital were moved into the new facility on top of the hill. African Americans, Mexicans, and Whites with contagious diseases were left in the old facility, which became the "Kansas City General Hospital for Colored," fulfilling the dream of not only Perry and the other physicians but also those who supported Jim Crow. "We were off to a new experiment, such as never had been attempted in any municipal institution of which we were aware," Perry wrote.

> The building was unsanitary, the equipment dilapidated, and the entire environment was one of gloom and despair. Light was furnished by old coal lamps and other features were equally discouraging. Several days were given to a process of cleaning, and I am confident that more than a million insects, such as roaches, bed bugs, and flies, were destroyed. The men put on overalls and at times were on their knees, scrubbing floors, and cleaning other equipment in the dejected institution. (363)

Despite the conditions, Perry was hopeful. His optimism, however, was short-lived as he discovered obstacles, especially attitudes carried by White physicians with whom he worked. These attitudes are best articulated by another history of the Old City Hospital, which emphasized the wisdom and generosity of the White doctors.

> To appreciate fully the history of the development of the hospital facilities especially devoted to the health of the colored people of

Kansas City and now under the supervision of Nebro [*sic*] doctors and assistants, one must place himself in a position and at a time when no such opportunities existed for the indigent colored patients or for the doctors of their own race to attend them. Next, one must take into consideration the spirit and the courage of the white men who took up the cause and sponsored the project for a separation of the hospitals and the creation of separate staffs, and the great inspiration that this progressive movement gave to Negro medical men to advance in their profession on their own efforts—a movement that has been of wide influence in other communities in stimulating the establishment of similar institutions.[8]

The history goes on to describe how Unthank with Perry and others "pressed their agitation" and the White community eventually came around:

The problems of adjustment to these newly created opportunities were no light ones. The colored men, realizing their deficiencies and their inexperience in dealing with general health problems, and awed by the mounting mortality rate of their race had much to learn to cope with the new conditions that confronted them. . . . They were obliged to rely upon the support of their white staff associates of the General Hospital, and this support and guidance . . . [was] freely and sympathetically given.

Given the prevailing attitudes within the White community, it is no wonder that conflicts arose at the hospital, conflicts that Perry and Unthank addressed during a meeting with the hospital superintendent Dr. Jabez Jackson. Perry recalled this meeting vividly:

Dr. Jackson said, "What can I do for you gentlemen?" In his usual brusque way, Unthank replied, "By George, we came down here to talk to you about the old city hospital building. We feel that we should have the advantage of the clinical material. How in the h—l do you think we can ever be the kind of doctors we ought to be, unless we have the advantages equal to others?"

While Unthank spoke, Dr. Jackson listened attentively until he had completed his remarks. He then cautiously but forcefully said, "To be frank with you gentlemen, I do not believe that a colored man has the capacity to learn surgery. There are times in surgery when you must call to your finger ends a dozen different things in a flash of a moment and reach a conclusion right now. Damn it, I do not believe a colored man can think that fast."

One of Dr. Unthank's characteristics was his wit and ready answer for any statement made, but this remark "knocked him out." He dropped his head with a surprised expression on his face. For a moment, quietness prevailed as Dr. Jackson looked at him as a rooster in a bard [sic] crows over another. When he was assured by his quietness that no response was in evidence, he turned his eyes toward me, as I sat with a broad smile, as if to say, "Now what have you to say?" The author said, "Doctor, don't you think you might give us a chance?"

He fixed his steel grey eyes on me, looked at the ceiling, at the floor, at Unthank and finally again at me. With a changed countenance, he said, "It may be that you haven't had an opportunity. If that's it, this city, this state and this nation are guilty of a woeful neglect of closing the door of hope in the faces of men that might make good doctors and a contribution to the community's welfare. I don't know, but I shall look into this matter and you will hear from me."

Dr. Jackson was a man of temper, so was Dr. Unthank. It would have been an easy matter for an argument to have upset our plans. I am a great believer in Providence. That was one time that Providence closed the mouth of Dr. Unthank. (362)

It was that simple, as Perry recalled in 1947. On October 1, 1911, four Black doctors were put on the staff of Kansas City's General Hospital for Colored, including John E. Perry. Perry's story, though, illustrates just how complicated Black progress was in twentieth-century Kansas City, and how dependent every Black person was on attitudes of every White person. Perry had his share of personal indignities. Once, when a White surgeon discovered that he would be assisting Perry during surgery, the White doctor stormed out of the operating room just before the procedure was to begin. Eventually, the surgeon returned and berated Perry, "If any one has his feelings on the floor, they had better take them up because I am going to step on them in a minute." Perry described how others stood by silently and awkwardly waiting for him to respond. When the doctor asked Perry what he thought, Perry chided the doctor with his good-natured response. Perry said that, except for the ministry, he believed that the medical profession was the greatest in the world. "To properly represent it requires men of culture, dignity and refinement. Men who are so lofty in their ideals, though armed with authority, at no time would they impose upon others associated with them" (367).

Perry wrote that the surgeon's face turned red with surprise but his demeanor changed in that moment, and the two became friends, so much so that this doctor requested Perry every time he needed assistance in the operating room. We will never know if Perry remained as calm as he claimed with the emotionally charged doctor, but he clearly felt that appealing to the doctor's character helped him. And he believed that this approach would eventually change White attitudes, which would end discrimination and discriminatory policies.

Racial tensions were not limited to the physicians but to the interns as well. When the Black interns felt that White students were given priority in the operating room and in patient care, Perry reported that the Black interns "wanted to raise a 'row.'" Perry remained true to form, and he advised them "to be punctual, observant and attentive to such responsibilities as were delegated to us and wait. Experience had taught me that it is very difficult to continue indefinitely to ignore an individual who possesses unquestionably commendable qualities" (364).

The situation came to a head in August 1912, when all the interns, Black and White, sat for an exam. When the tests were graded, all five of the Black interns failed. The hospital board worked swiftly, and several members voted to remove them. Board president W. P. Motley, however, suspected that something was amiss and had the exams regraded by physicians who were not associated with the hospital.

When the results came back, all five Black interns passed. Those who earned the top four scores, both White and Black, were offered positions at the hospital.[9]

Throughout his life, which spanned more than ninety years, John Edward Perry saw the change as overtly discriminatory remarks and actions became more the exception than the rule, at least among certain segments of the White community. This transformation fueled his sense of optimism. Less visible, however, were unaddressed and unspoken attitudes and new forms of racism that may not have been as personally offensive but were every bit as damaging, perhaps more.

Perry's experiences with the city hospital occurred at the same time that tensions between the White establishment and the Black teachers on Montgall Avenue were mounting, tensions that his future wife, Fredericka Douglass Sprague, saw firsthand as a resident of the street, although there is no record of her response.

Fredericka was born on August 9, 1880, the fifth of seven children born to Nathan Sprague and Rosetta Douglass Sprague, who was the oldest daughter of Anna and Frederick Douglass. Fredericka and her siblings grew up outside of Washington, DC. Fredericka's father was frequently unemployed, and her mother relied on her parents for support. As an adult, Fredericka moved to Missouri and joined the faculty of the Lincoln Institute in Jefferson City, teaching in the school's Home Economics Department. In 1906 she moved into the home of Charles and Frances Jackson on Montgall Avenue so she could accept a position at Lincoln High School, where she headed up the Home Economics Department.[10]

John Edward and Fredericka married on July 3, 1912, and moved into 2451 Montgall, where they remained throughout their thirty-year marriage. "The greatest problem during our married life was not one of eking out an existence, but rather making an effort to brighten some corner in the lives of others environed with gloom, sorrow and despair," Perry wrote (318). One of the misconceptions about John and Fredericka Perry involves whether they had children. Perry did not mention his son in his autobiography, yet he did have one, Eugene Boone (E. B.), who graduated from Lincoln High in 1919. Some scholars have assumed that E. B. was John and Fredericka's biological son,[11] but the facts do not support this conclusion. (He would either have graduated from high school when he was only six years old or been born out of wedlock, conceived before Fredericka and John arrived in Kansas City.) The only real mystery that remains is who E. B.'s biological mother was. Unfortunately, Perry did not offer any clues.

Despite being overlooked in his father's autobiography, E. B. appeared to maintain a close relationship with him. After all, E. B., who lived Houston as an adult, named his son John Edward Perry Jr. During the 1940s Perry's grandson moved to Kansas City and lived with his grandfather on Montgall so he could attend an integrated Jesuit high school in the city.[12]

Social mores of the day put a halt to Fredericka's teaching career after her marriage, but her departure from education allowed her to focus on other ways to help the city's Black community and provide needed services to the underserved, especially young girls. She helped found the Civic Protective Association, a fundraising group for those needing legal services. In 1941 she organized the Black community in opposition to the city's police chief, Lear Reed (see chapter 12). She also raised funds to bring a statue of John Brown to Kansas City, Kansas. Erected in 1911, this statue is still standing.[13]

Perhaps Fredericka Perry's biggest contribution to Kansas City, however, was her support for orphaned girls. Because Missouri provided no foster care for people of color, she organized the Big Sister Association, which sought to place girls in foster homes. Before she became involved, girls in the Niles Home for Orphan Children had to leave after they turned twelve. If no homes were available to take these girls in, the courts sent them to an institution for juvenile offenders until they were seventeen. Fredericka understood not only the inherent injustice of this practice but also the danger of placing such a vulnerable population together with those who have a criminal history. She organized club women to rent a facility, which became known as the Colored Big Sisters Home for Girls, and she convinced a juvenile court judge to place these girls in the home on a trial basis, with her serving as the superintendent. Donations of food,

clothing, and other essentials made it possible for fifteen girls to acquire homemaking skills in the home's first year alone.[14] On April 5,
1934, her grand experiment became a permanent part of Kansas
City's Black community with the opening of the Big Sisters Home at
2326 Brooklyn Avenue.[15] The facility also secured funding from the
Greater Kansas City Community Chest, resources that had traditionally only gone to White children. Fredericka Perry and others were
able to convince officers of the charity that the funds would benefit
the White community in the long run because the girls who graduated from the Big Sisters Home would eventually be hired as maids
and cooks for White people.

Three years after John and Fredericka Perry married, Dr. Perry was
able to fulfill his dream of his own hospital when the sixteen-bed facility that he started, Perry Sanitarium and Nurse Training School,
merged with another institution to become Wheatley-Provident
Hospital. Not long after the merger, the hospital moved into an abandoned Catholic school on Forest Street, where it served Kansas City's
Black community until the 1970s.[16]

While Perry had more control over who practiced at Wheatley-
Provident than he did at the city hospital, he continued to see all the
"attitudes, dispositions and impositions" among the White doctors
associated with it. A story about one White surgeon brought in to
perform abdominal surgery is particularly noteworthy. Perry wrote
that after successfully completing the procedure, but before he had
closed the wound, the surgeon found a tumor. He informed the patient's loved one what he found and told him that it would cost an
additional fifty dollars to remove it. Perry was incensed as he watched
the encounter. "The poor ignorant man was shaking with fear and
no doubt thinking of assuming another responsibility. The operator
said, 'Hurry up or I will close up and let it go!' The poor fellow said,
'Go ahead!'" (341). After the operation, Perry told the surgeon that he
would never again practice at Wheatley-Provident.

This particular doctor aside, Perry found that most of Kansas City's
physicians were extremely helpful, most notably pediatrician Katharine Richardson, who is best known for establishing Children's Mercy

Exterior of Wheatley-Provident Hospital, 1940s. Warner Studios
Collection courtesy of the Kansas City Museum/Union Station Archives,
Kansas City, MO.

Hospital, a facility that continues to serve the region and beyond.
Perry wrote that she enjoyed talking to him because her struggles
as a woman "so nearly parallel[ed]" his as a Black man (352). Richardson was aware of the discrimination faced by Kansas City's African American community, and she worked closely with Perry over
the years, even holding free clinics for African American residents at
Wheatley-Provident.[17]

When Richardson could not persuade others that Mercy Hospital should treat Black children, she approached Perry and asked him
whether she could help establish a children's ward at Wheatley-
Provident. Ten days later, she had secured $5,000 to get it started,
and Perry took full advantage of this ward almost immediately. The
hospital started outreach programs, including nutrition classes for
mothers that Fredericka oversaw. During the 1920s, after scientists
discovered the nutritional causes of rickets, the devastating bone-
softening condition that primarily affected infants and children,
Wheatley-Provident took the lead in educating the public about the

links between vitamin D, calcium (or phosphorous), and rickets. Perry also established a dental clinic in the hospital, and to ensure the widest outreach possible, his staff organized field trips so that every Black student enrolled in the Kansas City school district was seen by a dentist.[18]

To fund the venture, Perry convinced city officials that it was an investment. He educated them about the relationship between dental decay and rheumatism, which, if left untreated, led to other health issues. These conditions could have a negative economic impact if they kept someone from performing a day's labor. Taking a page from T. C. Unthank, Perry wrote that he used his "diplomacy and suavity" (375)—and his contacts with the city—to persuade the welfare department to give Wheatley-Provident an X-ray machine.

Perry's beloved wife, Fredericka, died on October 23, 1943, at Wheatley-Provident Hospital. His autobiography makes no mention of a fall in their home, only that she returned from a downtown trip "seriously ill" (320). But her death certificate indicates that she died from "pericardial effusion," or excess fluid in the sac around the heart, and "general septicemia," or a bloodstream infection that resulted from an abrasion on her limb, a wound she received after falling in her Montgall Avenue home.[19] Her unexpected death devastated both her husband and Kansas City's Black community. "Love and loyalty were among her principal assets," Dr. Perry wrote. "Tenderly, she devoted her life to husband and children who came under her supervision. With kind words and noble deeds she so indelibly stamped her personality upon the minds of those with whom she was most closely associated that she will always be affectionately remembered" (319–320).

Perry had a strong relationship with his Montgall neighbors. He was a shareholder in Ollie and Myrtle Cook's Home Seekers Savings and Loan; he and Ada Crogman Franklin (2447) served together as members of the board for the Niles Home for Negro Children; and he provided medical care for many of them, including performing surgery on Ada and signing the death certificates for George Gamble (2445) and John Bluford (2444). But unlike his neighbors who were vocal about civil rights, specifically segregation,[20] Perry remained

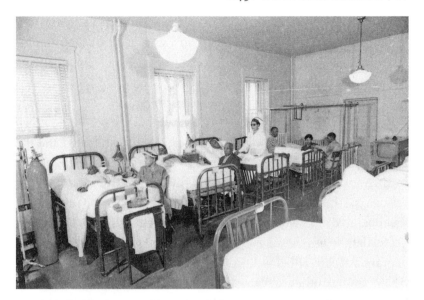

Interior of Wheatley-Provident Hospital, 1940s. Warner Studios
Collection courtesy of the Kansas City Museum/Union Station Archives,
Kansas City, MO.

true to his conservative message by preaching separation and patience. And when it came to one of the most important civil rights issues of the twentieth century—school integration—Perry maintained
a unique and powerful position.

In 1938 Lloyd Gaines, a young man with a promising future, was
denied admission to the University of Missouri Law School because
he was Black. Because Missouri's school for Black students, Lincoln
University, did not have a law school, the state did what it always had
done: offered to pay his tuition at a neighboring state's law school.
Gaines, however, refused the voucher, and with the help of the
NAACP's chief legal counsel, Charles Houston, he sued the university. The case eventually made its way to the Supreme Court, which
ruled that Missouri's voucher system was unconstitutional. It was
a decision with far-reaching implications: if the state had to offer a
separate—and equal—law school, the door was opened to the state's
other separate institutions, its schools and hospitals, which it might
also have to prove were equal.

After the decision, the state had a choice: either allow Lloyd Gaines into the University of Missouri or set up a separate law school at Lincoln University (which had changed its name from Lincoln Institute in 1921). Perry was on Lincoln University's Board of Curators during this critical period, and at a meeting on June 26, 1939, the issue came up when one of the members moved that the school establish a law school for the upcoming fall semester. Perry protested and the board secretary recorded his reaction. "Dr. Perry characterized the setting up of a law school at Lincoln University at this time as a subterfuge, stating that an effective law school could not be established and operated at Lincoln University under such a plan. He vigorously protested the passage of the motion and requested that the minutes contain a record of his protest."[21] On the surface, Perry appeared to be reacting to the state's hasty attempt to establish a law school that would be the equivalent of the University of Missouri's already established program—all within two months. However, according to his autobiography, his position was more nuanced.

> The decision in the Gaines case brought to the board through legislative enactment some serious and difficult problems. The board was mandated to establish schools of journalism and law. Several members of the board did not share the opinion of the Legislature, yet we were under orders and a good soldier or a good citizen always obeys the law. We felt and still feel that as appointees, it is our indispensable duty to do all in our power to direct these departments to the highest degree of efficiency. Our thought was, the number of Missourians desiring to pursue such courses would be limited. The cost would be great and finally regarded as a wanton expenditure of public funds. (452)

Perry protested not because Black law students' education would suffer under such a slapdash plan but because a new law school would be a strain on Missouri's tax base. And although Perry did not specifically predict the role that economics would play in ending segregation, he understood—and saw firsthand as a curator of Lincoln University—how expensive Jim Crow was. Over Perry's protests,

Lincoln University's law school opened September 1, 1939, with a staff of six.

Although the school was specifically established for him, Lloyd Gaines never attended Lincoln; he never attended any law school. He disappeared shortly after the Supreme Court decision and was never heard from again. His disappearance led to much discussion and speculation in the Black community about what happened to him. Some reported that he had gone to Mexico to escape his notoriety; others said that he was bought off by a group of wealthy MU alumni who did not want him to attend the university; and still others believed he had been murdered. Even though Gaines never attended Lincoln, he succeeded in putting economic pressure on Missouri.[22]

Since its beginning after the Civil War, the state's college for Black residents, Lincoln Institute/University, was a liberal arts college, but it added the law school in 1939 and a graduate school of journalism in 1942, after Montgall resident Lucile Bluford filed her own lawsuit (see chapter 8). The academic expansion strained the state's budget, and other Black students who wished to continue their studies out of state found it more difficult to receive reimbursement. "I am writing you again in regard to the tuition aid for Negro students," wrote Adell M. DeBoe in 1943. "As you no doubt know, my tuition claim has not been paid."[23] Sara Slaughter also sought compensation for her work at the University of Illinois. "I represent many Negro students throughout the state who have sat quietly by only hoping to receive their tuition sometimes [sic] in the near future. I have waited a year to be re-enbursed [sic] for the sum of fifty-dollars."[24]

Lincoln president Sherman Scruggs expressed his frustration in a letter to Missouri's attorney general, Roy McKittrick.

The Board of Curators of Lincoln University finds itself in a most embarrassing situation when attempting to answer the requests of residents of Missouri, students in attendance at institutions of higher learning in other states, seeking the reimbursement for fees paid as tuition for courses taken in the institutions of the states in which they were in attendance during the biennium 1941–1942.

These requests and the inability to meet them by the Board of Curators have given the Board and the students as well much unpleasantness and unfavorable status before the admission officers of the various institutions in which these residents of Missouri are in attendance. The general reputation of the State has been in great jeopardy.[25]

Lincoln University's law school remained open until 1944 when the state ended its appropriations, citing the cost.

By 1947, when Perry published his autobiography, "Separate but Equal" was in its final days, but the ever-cautious Perry wasn't rejoicing.

Personally, the author has wondered how many Negroes of the state would vote to close all Negro schools and combine them in one educational system. One of the greatest schools in America was established and developed by a Negro. For the length of time of its existence, it is questionable if any school equals Tuskegee Institute for its service to the nation and its influence upon the lives of individuals. (454)

After Fredericka's death, Perry moved to Houston for a time to live with his son and to advise the city's Black doctors about how to establish their own teaching hospital for Black physicians.[26] While there, he met and married Ora M. Brown. Perry, then in his eighties, returned to Kansas City, where he continued to see patients out of his Montgall Avenue home. He died in Houston in May 1962 at the age of ninety-two.

John Edward Perry and Fredericka Perry were a Kansas City power couple: a brilliant, self-made physician and the granddaughter of the nineteenth century's most famous African American. They were in a unique position to affect change, and they succeeded. But in lobbying for their respective causes, they argued for very practical reasons how the institutions they supported would benefit White people. He argued that a separate hospital would keep the communicable diseases, which were running rampant in the Black community, away from Whites; she promoted the Big Sisters Home so that young Black girls could be properly trained as maids for upper-class White families, approaches that would keep Black people subordinate.[27]

John E. Perry was proof of what a Black man could accomplish in America in the generation after the Civil War. Born in rural Texas into abject poverty, he reached a position where he could influence some of the most powerful White leaders in his adopted city. Having achieved such a level of professional success, he could have helped continue the trajectory of his life and assisted other people of color in their struggle for assimilation and acceptance. As a physician, he could have challenged the status quo and used his understanding of human biology to promote racial equivalence. Instead, he seemed to have absorbed just enough of the day's White supremacist scholarship that rationalized Jim Crow laws. As such, Perry convinced himself that the *only* way for Black people to succeed was through separate institutions, an approach that exacerbated racial divisions for future generations. Perry's approach to civil rights, like that of other Black leaders in the conservative movement, emphasized accommodation and patience, and he was the very symbol of a "good" Negro, a man expected to be humble and thankful for any opportunity that the White establishment offered. In Perry's case, he was grateful for the opportunity to take over one of the city's castoffs, an out-of-date medical facility, to serve the city's Black community. Perry and other conservative leaders believed that the only thing Black people needed to do was work harder. The fallacy, of course, was that the problem was with the oppressed minority. The true problem, however, was with the racial attitudes of the dominant culture, a part of which would never see a person of color as smart, patient, or accommodating enough to be accepted.

Helping draw Kansas City's color line, Perry contributed to making Jim Crow more and more the norm, and the color line increasingly difficult to cross. And although Perry may have been able to rationalize that a line was needed for the health of his community and the education of other Black people, some in Kansas City's White community would continue to push these limits into more areas of American life, areas that had nothing to do with health or education.

As will be explored in the next chapter, this was a phenomenon that neighbor Homer Roberts experienced firsthand.

Homer Roberts, the Negro car salesman heading the Roberts Company at 18th and Paseo is reputed to have sold one or more cars of every make represented in Kansas City in the past two years.
    Kansas City Sun, December 11, 1920

7

Like his neighbor, John Perry, Homer Roberts was bright, hard-working, and highly successful. Unlike the urbane doctor, however, Roberts was an affable man, someone described by the press as "hustling" and "astute."[1] While Perry spent most of his professional career in Kansas City, living on Montgall Avenue for more than five decades, Homer Roberts left Kansas City after twenty-five years, a dozen of which he spent on Montgall. Despite this abbreviated time frame, Roberts made a name for himself with his keen business sense, and he deserves credit for his role in helping transform the Eighteenth Street and Vine area into an economic hub for the city's African American community. While his Montgall neighbors concentrated on strategies to lift up members of their race, Roberts's primary focus was on his own various business interests. But his entrepreneurial endeavors did benefit the Black community by creating jobs. He also engaged with Lincoln High students and promoted other Black-owned businesses.

Roberts's time in Kansas City can be divided into two parts: before World War I, when he worked as a chauffeur and the manager of several clubs and theaters along Twelfth and Fourteenth Streets, and after the war, when he built one of the largest businesses in Kansas City and

Homer Roberts, circa 1947. Black Archives of Mid-America.

the first US car dealership owned by an African American: Roberts Motor Mart.

Roberts was born in the small community of Ash Grove, Missouri, in either 1882 or 1885.[2] When he was young, his family moved to Wellington, Kansas, and he attended Kansas State University and the Tuskegee Institute, where he displayed an aptitude for engineering and for a new invention: the automobile. Roberts migrated to Kansas City in the early 1900s, where he found work as a chauffeur in the Eighteenth and Vine area. By 1914 he had saved enough money to purchase the New Theater at 2411 Vine, a facility that the *Kansas City Sun* was eager to promote as "the finest and most up-to-date motion picture house owned and operated by negroes in the United States." The four-hundred-seat theater had "the most modern" film projector that money could buy and was decorated with oriental rugs, mahogany furniture, and oil paintings "from the world's famous artists."[3] Roberts went on to manage other clubs such as the Autumn Leaf Club, a bar that operated in the Eighteenth and Vine area for decades. In 1941 it was the scene of a widely publicized incident of police brutality (see chapter 12).

Roberts enlisted in World War I because he believed that it was "an honor for individuals of the Negro race to fight for and protect the country."[4] He failed his first physical exam because of an overlapping toe on his right foot, but he eagerly offered to have the "defective member" amputated. This persistence paid off: he was eventually accepted (with or without all ten of his toes). As a soldier he displayed the same enthusiasm that he exhibited in civilian life. Realizing that any modern army would become increasingly reliant on motorized vehicles, Roberts saw a unique opportunity for Black chauffeurs. He approached the War Department with the idea of enlisting chauffeurs as a special class of soldier that would drive ambulances and serve as mechanics. "As a class of workers, none are more thrifty and intelligent than our Colored chauffeurs of this city," wrote the *Kansas City Sun* in its report on Roberts. "No wonder when Homer Roberts introduced the idea of enlisting as a body in the War Department he met with such warm and enthusiastic response."[5]

The newspaper exaggerated the reception the military brass gave to Roberts's idea of a special class of "Colored Chauffeur Mechanics," for nothing ever came of it. What Roberts did accomplish, however, was to persuade a number of his friends to enlist, demonstrating just how engaging and persuasive the businessman was. Roberts was commissioned as a first lieutenant in the 325th Field Signal Battalion, and he oversaw the communication for the all-Black Ninety-Second Division. When the Allies were ready to make their final major assault of the war in September 1918, Roberts was there, setting up communications in the Meuse-Argonne Offensive. It was a critical job, considering that this battle was the longest frontline assault the

Allies put together. The fighting was so intense and Roberts's mission so dangerous that two men under his command were cited for their bravery. When Roberts returned home and discovered that W. E. B. Du Bois was gathering information for a history of Black involvement in the war, the veteran lieutenant reached out to him, writing a letter that has been preserved among Du Bois's papers: "I feel that I am in a position to give the most complete history of [the 325th Field Signal Battalion] available, as I was the first man enlisted there-in and afterward was commissioned First Lt. S.C. from the ranks."[6]

After the war, Roberts started the enterprise for which he is best known in Kansas City: automobile sales. His venture started small, but it grew to become the biggest Black-owned business in the city. According to B. S. Restuccia, Roberts was successful because he was able to put White car dealers in touch with members of the Black community. He knew that White dealerships were not especially welcoming to Black customers because of the personal interaction required to sell an automobile. So Roberts acted as a middleman, arranging the sale, the financing, and the delivery of various vehicles. Roberts earned a commission for every sale he facilitated. Eventually he had enough money to start his own business with his personal collection of used vehicles, and he set up an office at 1509 East Eighteenth Street. In a modest announcement in the May 31, 1919, issue of the *Kansas City Sun*, Homer Roberts announced that he was open for business. Under the heading "Used Car Bargains," Roberts declared that he had eight cars, ranging in price from a $300 Studebaker to a six-cylinder 1919 Nash Touring Car, a "real bargain" at $950 (approximately $14,000 in today's money).[7] As his business began to flourish, he employed more sophisticated advertising techniques, printing the names of his customers, many of whom were his Montgall Avenue neighbors such as Dr. John Perry, Ollie Cook, and Frances Jackson.[8]

As a testament to his business acumen, he encouraged readers to ask his customers whether they were satisfied with their purchases and service. In other ads he showed his level of racial consciousness as he appealed to the "Black soul," saying that he couldn't satisfy people who would be happy with "Caucasians discarded junk," people

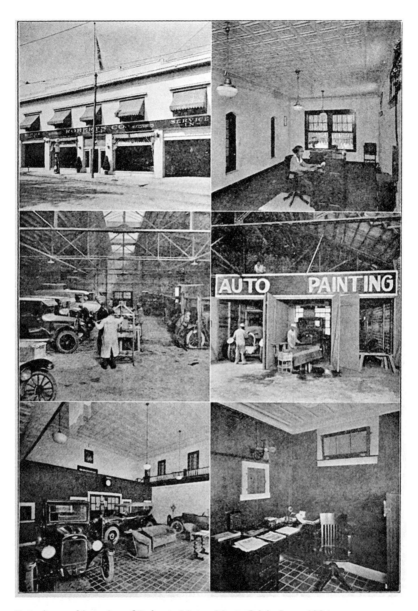

Exterior and interior of Roberts Motor Mart. *Crisis,* June 1924.

whose satisfaction "must be derived from the presence of 'Uncle Tom's blood in their veins.'"[9]

Roberts was a member of Negro Businessmen's Noon Day Club, sort of a Black chamber of commerce. Organized to promote Black businesses, the club adopted the motto "Race Patronage for Race Enterprises." Roberts was proud of his use of Black labor in the design and construction of Roberts Motor Mart, which opened in 1923. He even coordinated with staff at Lincoln High to have students work on the construction of his new facility.[10]

Roberts settled into married life after he wed teacher Floy King in June 1920 and moved to 2453 Montgall. The couple, however, did not engage with their neighbors as others had. For example, neither Roberts nor his wife is mentioned in the numerous letters that his neighbor's father, William Crogman, wrote after his five-month stay on Montgall, and the couple's names are noticeably absent from various club memberships that frequently listed other residents of Montgall. It is possible that the more cultured members of Montgall sniffed at the entrepreneur who got his start in the clubs along Vine. Or perhaps his detachment could be traced to the attitude of Roberts himself, for, at least according to Roy Wilkins, Roberts's friend Joe LaCour "hated the affectations of Kansas City's Black middle class."[11] It is possible that the car dealer felt the same way.

Although he was not fully engaged in neighborhood activities, Roberts was committed to racial equality and helping his community. One of his business partners, Kenneth Campbell, was a graduate of Lincoln High School, and he married Sarah Rector, one of the richest women in America. Rector's wealth came from oil discovered on her family's land in Oklahoma, property she had been allotted as a member of the Creek Nation. Although the acreage had been considered worthless when it was given to the Native population (which is why the federal government parted with it in the first place), the discovery of oil changed its value tremendously. Rector's family leased the land to Standard Oil Company, and by the time Rector was ten years old, she was making the enormous sum of $15,000 a month.

Her family moved to Kansas City in 1920, and she married Campbell in 1922. The couple built one of the most elaborate homes in Kansas City, at Twelfth and Euclid Avenue, and entertained some of the most famous African Americans of the era, including jazz musician Count Basie and boxer Joe Louis. Roberts's other partner, Thomas Jefferson Brown, who was also known as "Big Piney," migrated to Kansas City from Pine Bluff, Arkansas, and had a brother who lived on Montgall (see chapter 9). In Roberts Motor Mart, the trio created a one-stop shop for customers that stretched on Vine from Eighteenth to Twentieth Streets and included a filling station, tire and battery repair, an upholstery and painting department, and a sixty-car garage. Roberts Motor Mart opened July 29, 1923, and from 1923 to 1928 the business flourished, becoming the largest employer of African Americans in the city.[12]

Five years later, in the summer of 1928, Roberts, his business partners Brown and Campbell, and his friend Ulysses Arnold showed up at Swope Park's public golf course, complete in their "golfing outfit[s]" and ready to play. The golf course manager intervened, informing them that he would need special permission from the park board before he could allow the foursome on the course. This permission never came. Instead, the manager explained to Roberts that "Negroes ha[ve] no more right to attempt to play golf on the public courses in Kansas City that were not provided for Negroes exclusively, than they would have to attempt to use the public bath houses, the swimming pool at Swope Park, the public tennis courts and the baseball diamonds, all maintained by the city."[13]

Roberts explained to a *Kansas City Star* reporter what happened next. "Several of us wrote the park board and asked for a conference," he said. When they got no response from the park board, the four men filed a lawsuit. "So far as the law is concerned, we have no question about the standing of our case. As taxpayers we help support Swope Park."

Circuit court judge Brown Harris agreed—to an extent—for rather than integrating Swope Park's course, though that would have been the fastest, fairest, and most economical solution, Harris ordered the city to establish a separate course for Black players. "Negroes have a right to their exclusive golf courses just as they have a right to their exclusive schools, separate from white persons," he ruled. "It is the opinion of the court that the city should, without being driven to it, accede to the modest request. . . . There is no better crime deterrent in Kansas City than its public parks and playgrounds. If it is good for the white race it is just as good for the Negro race." After acknowledging that African Americans had rights as taxpayers, Harris could not help but take a swipe at Roberts—and any other African American who dared to stand up for civil rights. "Any attempt on the part of the Negroes to carry on litigations in this manner just has a tendency to lower the standing of the Negro race by their trying to force themselves where they are not wanted and would lead toward race riots in the future." The city complied and built a course, but its location, right next to the city zoo, shows a level of contempt on the city officials' part. Years later, one Black golfer remembered the stench playing on the segregated course and how, when he stopped to eat a sandwich, he was greeted with a "whiff of the zoo animals."[14]

The establishment of this golf course is significant for several reasons, including how it illustrated, by 1928, that enough of Kansas City's Black population had the leisure time to devote to a game of golf. (Editor Chester Franklin was another avid golfer, and on July 31, 1942, after being turned away from Golf Course #1, he filed his own lawsuit against the city. His case was dismissed.)[15] But, perhaps most importantly, the judge's decision cemented the second-class status Kansas City assigned to Black citizens, highlighting the uncomfortable intersection between racism and classism in twentieth-century America. A golf course is different from a hospital, swimming pool, or a school. At those institutions, separating the races was justified, however falsely, by using a health, decency, or safety argument. But how could White leaders rationalize segregating a space where people (primarily men) choose to spend their leisure time, where players have only the most minimal of contact? One answer: social class.

For decades, Kansas City's elites had been able to physically remove themselves from less desirable elements by means of exclusive neighborhoods, private schools, and country clubs. But in the ruling against Roberts and his friends, Judge Harris appears to have extended this same "courtesy" to middle-class Whites, denying upper-class Black men entry into a middle-class White social space. With this ruling, the judge demonstrated how fully he had absorbed the southern ideal of gentility and class and how far the divide stretched between Black and White America. Swope Park Golf Course #1 was for middle-class Whites, and the much inferior Golf Course #2 was designed for the Black professional class, those who had the time to use it, residents such as Homer Roberts. In Kansas City's caste system, no one was lower than an African American, no matter how educated, enterprising, or loyal to his country. It was one more indignity designed to demoralize Black men who dared to seek entry into White social space.

It is not known whether Roberts ever used the separate course at Swope Park. Just after the decision, he moved to Chicago to specialize in a popular vehicle of the day, the Hupmobile.[16] His timing for a new business venture, right before the bottom fell out of the US economy, could not have been worse. In addition, he was opting to specialize in a vehicle known only by the most fervent automobile connoisseurs, so his ultimate failure as a car dealer is hardly a surprise.[17] But the unflappable Homer Roberts was not down for long, and he managed to reinvent himself yet again. When the United States entered World War II, Roberts reenlisted in the army and was assigned to a training base for the Thirty-Second Division. He was later transferred to Washington, DC, where he served in the press branch of the Negro Interest Section for the US Army. Roberts was responsible for sending out press stories and photos of Black soldiers to Black newspapers, like the *Call* and its counterparts in other cities like Chicago and Pittsburgh. Throughout the war the *Call* featured stories and large photographs of all-Black divisions like the Ninety-Third. While White reporters tended to ignore African American soldiers, with the exception of Black entertainers, Roberts understood that the African American community was desperate to read about Black soldiers in battle, and he is credited with bringing these stories to the Black press, including the newspaper that belonged to his former Montgall neighbor, Chester Franklin.[18] Roberts was discharged from the army with honors, and he died in Chicago in 1952.

Roberts's business partner, Thomas "Piney" Brown, remained in Kansas City to oversee the Vine Street business, but like Roberts's Hupmobile enterprise in Chicago, Roberts Motor Mart could not outlast the Great Depression. It closed shortly after Roberts's departure. In 2017 a fire started by a homeless woman, who had found shelter at a nearby address, consumed the building that had housed Roberts Motor Mart.[19]

I have to get a house in 1924 if I am to have my heart's desire. I want to do what you want, sweet boss, so you will smile and praise me. I want to do what you want because I love you. Anyway you take it I want just what you want.
Chester Franklin to Ada Crogman (undated letter)

8

Chester Franklin was a passionate man: passionate about his work, passionate about justice, and passionate about the love of his life, Ada Crogman. When he promised her a home, he understood that there was only one place he could go: Montgall Avenue, a safe block where they, as descendants of slaves, would be welcomed. And the house that he built for her on Montgall Avenue was grander than any other home on the street. It was a showpiece, with carved oak paneling and leaded glass windows, a breezy sunroom, and a fireplace in the primary bedroom.

Like most of their neighbors, the Franklins' life journey to Montgall began far from Kansas City. Chester Franklin's parents were part of the first great wave of migration of African Americans to the North after the Civil War. George and Clara Bell Franklin were Exodusters, former slaves who believed that Kansas would offer a better future for them and their only son, Chester, born on June 7, 1880, in Dennison, Texas.[1] In 1887 the family set out for Nicodemus, the all-Black community in northwestern Kansas. Somewhere along the way, though, George and Clara changed their minds and decided to go to Omaha, where "Chet" developed a reputation as the smartest kid in the school.[2] When Chester showed no interest in becoming a barber like his father but instead wanted to run a newspaper, George made an unusual move—he

Chester Franklin and Ada Crogman, circa 1945. Black Archives of Mid-America.

changed his profession. George and Clara scraped together enough money start the *Omaha Enterprise*, which they published while he attended school. After high school Chester attended the University of Nebraska, but he was forced to leave when his father became ill. When George's health did not improve, the family moved to Denver, believing that the climate would help. In 1898 they purchased the *Colorado Statesman* and renamed it the *Star*. When George died in 1901, mother and son continued the business for a dozen more years, until Chester Franklin grew restless and sought a new challenge: a larger newspaper with a wider circulation. In 1913 Franklin and his mother moved to Kansas City.

World War I delayed the start of his newspaper, so mother and son operated a printing business to establish themselves in the community. Franklin began playing volleyball at the Paseo YMCA (in a building that H. O. Cook helped get started and on a team that became the first subscribers of his newspaper, the *Kansas City Call*), and he even shared advice to students at Lincoln High, where he spoke about his school experiences. He advised the students to turn "toward the sun." Franklin told them:

> This is what your High School is for. I can give no illustration better than by saying this: An artisan takes a piece of iron, casts it into a mold and when it is removed it is shaped into whatever design he desires it to be. You can come into the High School, pass away your time and be satisfied with yourself in the rough or you can do as the artisan, make yourself what you wish to be. This school can give you the tools and equipment with which to work, but you must do the work yourself.[3]

Franklin continued at his print shop, joined the NAACP, and was a member of the Grievance Committee, which met with city leaders to try to keep D. W. Griffith's *Birth of a Nation* from playing in the area. As a part of that protest, he was introduced to city hall, a place he would become more familiar with in the years to come. "I have seen [him] pound his fist on the desk of former Mayor John B. Gage to make a point about the scarcity of Negroes in jobs at city hall," remembered his *Call* successor, Lucile Bluford. "He was frequently in the office of the Superintendent . . . making an appeal for a new Lincoln high school [a campaign that took years] or to correct some injustice done to Negro children or Negro teachers."[4]

Franklin was fearless when it came to civil rights, and he took the struggle to the public with his newspaper, the *Call,* which began circulation in 1919 as veterans returned home. Setting up shop in the Eighteenth and Vine area, the heart of the city's Black district, Franklin understood that publishing a newspaper for the Black community was more than reporting and editing—it was a crusade. "The serious Negro editor never lacks for issues to charge his batteries; the issues are all around him," he told a *Kansas City Star* reporter years later. "His hardest task is to concentrate his efforts on one reform at a time, to keep from scattering his shots. He learns through the years that the Negro's problem is not the Negro's alone, but is America's problem, affecting all its citizens, interacting among them in the growth of democracy."[5]

As an institution, the Black press did more than serve as a megaphone to address injustices confronting a marginalized population; it offered African Americans the opportunity for recognition—for its readers to feel legitimate. Dowdal Davis, *Call* sales manager, declared in 1951 in a speech in Chicago:

> How many times have you seen an account of a Negro social function ... ? From the attention given it from mass media, one would assume that Negroes never got married—never received promotions, never established businesses or went on vacation trips or bought homes, had babies, went to college, wore smart frocks, or even attended church. One would imagine from the studied indifference of radio and television—with a few notable exceptions—that there were no Negro singers, dancers, musicians, artists, actors, announcers or newsworthy happenings outside of perhaps Jackie Robinson and Dr. Ralph Bunche. What the Negro citizen wants is nothing more nor less than what every other man wants. That it is withheld makes it no less desired nor avidly sought.[6]

Davis's speech was delivered during the Negro Newspapers Publishers luncheon at which his boss was being honored. Davis spoke about not only Franklin's contribution but also the larger role the Black press played in twentieth-century America, and why local newspapers—and their editors—were supported and cherished by their readers. Davis continued:

> And it is because of these facts that there is a Negro press. It is because man must have the comfort and inspiration of knowing that he—the individual—is a vital and important part of some accepted organized society. It is because he does want to know what his fellows are doing—what his friends have accomplished—what is happening in those fields where he has a deep personal concern. He must have the consoling knowledge that his problems are being dealt with and given attention—that the deficiencies under which he labors and lives are being remedied. He wants to take pride in the mention, no matter how brief, of something worthwhile that he has done. He needs the

balance of knowing that his part in the national life is not confined to that meager bit of information he gets from general media. The Negro press gives him those things. It tells him where he is going and how he may get there. It is his bulwark against a not-always-too-appreciative world. It is his means of self-expression. It tells him where he can go without fear of embarrassment or refusal, where he can buy with assurance of equality in service and substance—who his friends are and who wants his trade. It tells him all of the things toward which mass media display no interest. He has no need to wonder if the ad he reads "means me" or if the story he encounters applies to every man. Its appearance in the Negro press is his guarantee that it does "mean me." The Negro press is a companion, a guide, a friend. It is current for 168 hours every week—read again and again—referred to constantly—and passed on to a friend or neighbor when it has been thoroughly exhausted. Compared to the life of the average daily which is usually about as long as it takes to eat breakfast or to ride home on a subway or bus, the Negro newspaper is clearly a mature, constant, and trusted confidant. It has no substitute.

Franklin understood the value and the power that his newspaper wielded for its readers, just as those around him understood his value and power. "C.A. Franklin was a giant of a man, physically, mentally, and spiritually," said Lucile Bluford. "He was a big man of stature. He had a strong voice and when he spoke people listened not only because he could make himself heard, but because he always had something worthwhile to say."[7]

Roy Wilkins, who was Franklin's managing editor in the 1920s, also remembered his intensity. "His silvering hair had retreated from his forehead, leaving him a high, deeply crinkled brow, on which sat his ferociously bushy eyebrows, and he had a square, solid jaw.... He was all business." All business, that is, until he met his future wife, Ada Crogman. According to Wilkins, she "made a new man out of the editor of the *Call*."[8]

Ada was a lady: educated, proper, and refined. "Little Jam," as her father affectionately called her, grew up in a busy, lively home on the

Call pressroom, 1940s. Papers of Dorothy Hodge Johnson, Dowdal Davis Jr., and John Hodge, Kansas Collection, RH MS 549, Kenneth Spencer Research Library, University of Kansas.

Clark University campus where her father, William Crogman, taught in the Classics Department, and her mother, Lavina, created a warm and nurturing environment for her and her seven siblings.[9] Her childhood home was a popular meeting place for the students in Atlanta. Ada remained close to her family throughout her life, especially her "Sweet Papa" from whom she frequently requested advice. In the letters that remain, she asked his opinion on everything from her professional life to her spiritual one.[10]

Born on St. Martin Island in the Caribbean in 1841, William Crogman was a traveler and had sailed around the world several times before his twentieth birthday. These trips were possible because Crogman, who had been orphaned as a young child, was adopted by a sea captain who saw his potential. The captain eventually brought William to his New England home, where the youngster flourished and excelled at Pierce Academy in Middleborough, Massachusetts, completing his coursework in half the time it took his classmates. After graduation, Crogman decided to devote his life to Christian education and the elevation of his race, a mission that brought him to Atlanta's Clark University, where exceptional students from Morehouse College and its sister school, Spelman, went on to earn master's degrees and doctorates.

Ada attended Emerson College in Boston, and after earning a degree in dramatic arts she was hired by the National Playground and Recreation Association. The job took her around the country to work with young people, including the students at Lincoln High School. During the 1922–1923 school year, she organized the Story Tellers Club and led her students in the "art of correct story telling." Armed with their new skills, students ventured into the community, including a visit to the Orphans Home on November 12, 1922, where the Lincoln students told tales of Thanksgivings past and present.[11]

Two men changed the trajectory of Ada Crogman's life once in Kansas City: Chester Franklin, and Lincoln High music teacher and composer N. Clark Smith. Just as other residents of Montgall Avenue had ideas for racial uplift, Crogman did too. While working in Ohio, she wrote a show about the history of the Negro race, from the "golden age of Egypt through savagery to civilization," for which Smith arranged the music.[12] *Milestones* showed pivotal moments in African and African American history and brought Crogman a fair amount of national attention in Black communities across the country. At a moment when gospel and the blues were changing the landscape of American music in places like Kansas City, Crogman—possibly with guidance and influence from N. Clark Smith—asked her audiences to look backward at the Black community's role in the development of American folk music, specifically spirituals, music that she felt many were "ashamed to sing."[13]

Crogman opened *Milestones* with a scene of Moses begging a Pharaoh for his freedom, to illustrate, as she explained, that "darker races were supreme at this time." The show continued with scenes in an African village, showing "idol worship," and a violent scene when European marauders devastated the Africans' way of life. "They [came] in and destroy[ed] all the peace and contentment," Crogman wrote in an early letter to Chester Franklin. Crogman wanted to remind White audiences that people of color "did not leave the shores of Africa of their own accord but were driven away." A slave market scene followed in which children were sold away from a devastated mother, who sang "Sometimes I Feel Like a Motherless Child." Next was a scene from a southern cotton field, in which the actors sang more spirituals, including "Swing Low, Sweet Chariot." An actor playing Abraham Lincoln appeared, and the cast sang "Free at Last." After the show's depiction of emancipation, *Milestones* turned into a lesson on African American achievements. It included some of the most acclaimed individuals in US history, including poet Phillis Wheatley, activist Sojourner Truth, Frederick Douglass, Booker T. Washington, composer and conductor Samuel Coleridge-Taylor, businesswoman Madam C. J. Walker, and Du Bois, among others. For the show's finale, Crogman honored the men who served in the Great War and included the song "Lift Every Voice and Sing," which is known as the African American national anthem.

At the time, racial tensions were high as the Great Migration brought millions of African Americans into northern cities, and Crogman felt the show was a "racial panacea." She explained to Franklin: "It helps the white race. They don't know as much about us as they should know . . . all the good things."[14]

The show toured the country throughout 1923 and 1924, including performances in Dayton and Youngstown, Ohio, Marion, Indiana, and Chicago, with a different cast in each city. When *Milestones* premiered in Cleveland, Crogman used 575 amateur actors, and she told a newspaper reporter that her show "gives a large group of people an opportunity for self expression," in addition to "stimulat[ing] race consciousness and creat[ing] greater race pride."[15] *Milestones* played in Kansas City on December 15 and 16, 1924, at the Grand Theatre as a benefit for the children's ward at Wheatley-Provident Hospital. Despite the budding romance between Crogman and Franklin, he did not have a role in the production. She did persuade Roy Wilkins to play Moses, however.[16]

One member of the audience was so moved by Kansas City's production that she wrote Crogman a letter of thanks. It was Katharine

Milestones, 1924–1925. Black Archives of Mid-America.

Richardson, the pediatrician who had approached Perry about the children's wing at Wheatley-Provident. Richardson wrote that *Milestones* was "one of the most profoundly impressive things I had ever seen. I am sure that feeling was shared by every one of the white people in the audience."[17] Richardson described how one member of the audience, the pastor of one of the largest churches in the city, cried after watching the scene with the slaves on the auction block. She wrote that the preacher felt as she did, and that the show needed to be seen by more people to help with race relations.

Ada Crogman's professional and personal life were riding high during 1923 and 1924, the years that *Milestones* toured, for along with the show's success, her fervent courtship with Chester Franklin blossomed, a relationship that can be traced through letters he wrote. Although most of this correspondence is undated, there is a marked difference in tone in the various letters that survive. "Dear Miss Crogman," began one (presumably early) letter in which he informed her that he would be sending her a box of chocolates. By the fall of 1923 he was starting his letters more affectionately: "Ada, darling!" and filling them with rapturous prose: "Ada I love you, that you know. Ada will you marry me right quick. . . . And then if you say yes, and you will won't you Ada darling—I will carry you off to the preacher man and—and lose what little reason I possess. Who wants to be sensible and sober sided if by loving Ada one loses his wit?"[18]

He told her he wished to memorize a poem for her and asked her to send him one. "Listen I have turned Tennyson over and am disappointed. He did not love enough to talk about it, and since I am moon-struck, I want poetry and love poetry at that." Later in the letter, though, he demonstrated that he didn't need to rely on any other poets to express his feelings: "Ada, I love you. Distractedly definitely infinitely and all the other ways." In another letter dated only "Wednesday evening" he enclosed a watch and told her of his plan to buy her a wedding ring, "with Tiffany setting of platinum."

Franklin's affection extended beyond the letters, and those close to the couple understood the depth of their relationship. "I have never seen a fonder husband," wrote Roy Wilkins. "Franklin became cheerful and generous and, to everyone's surprise, suddenly began prying time away from the sixteen-hour days he put in at the newspaper to be with his new wife."[19]

Franklin wasn't the only one smitten or changed by the relationship. "I fully understand now how it happened, and why, after harpooning your whale, you quietly withdrew to your igloo and let the rest of the world pass by," William Stewart wrote to Crogman after Franklin came on the scene. In a letter he told her of the two Ada Crogmans he had observed, one before she met Franklin and the other after. Stewart reminded her of the determined woman, elbowing her way through a throng of people, "as though there was not a man on earth capable of assisting." The second image was one of a "lady who sat so helplessly to be waited upon" as Franklin knelt before her, assisting her with her boots. "Can you blame me for smiling just a small smile at seeing you not only submit to but apparently enjoying this little courtesy from the big man. How helpless ladies become when they are fortunate enough to have such chivalrous husbands."[20] Ribbing aside, Stewart understood his friend's attraction.

> After meeting him the first thought that ran through my mind was "he sure is a bear," but after spending more time and then seeing and reading his Call, I came to the conclusion that he is too big to be called a bear.... You know this country is so big and contains so many people

who make a pretense of doing, that we must stop and admire the man who is really doing the things the others pretned [*sic*] to do. Hence, I join with you in saying I, too, admire this Lochinvar who came out of the West and believe him to be all you claim for him and more.

There was no pretense when it came to Chester Franklin, only drive, and after he won Ada's heart, he returned to business. In a letter to Ada dated "Tuesday morning, Dec. 11" [1923?], four years after starting the *Call*,[21] Franklin was savoring the troubles that his adversary, Nelson Crews, publisher of the *Kansas City Sun*, was experiencing, and Franklin laid out his plan to undo his competitor. The letter was addressed to his "Sugarkins," and it apparently was a response to an inquiry from her:

No, the Sun has not gone down yet, but it was mighty foggy around it the last two weeks. Thanksgiving week, it was four days late, a fatal error, and last week it was all boiler plate. That is the cheap filler stuff with which we fill space when we have no time to put in worth while reading matter.

Mr. Dabney as head of a proposed band of 25 is actively trying to raise money with which to buy it. . . . Mr. Watkins is his backer and Mr. Street and a few more of the boys who have ambitions.[22] There are others who are the tools. But there are not 25, and it takes 25 at $100 apiece to raise $2500. They figure poorly. When they have that amount and have paid off debts and acquired the property, they will have no reserve. Right then is when we move up the big artillery. March 1 they are sure to be broke, even if they make every move as they now plan. That is one reason I am selling the job department—so I am free to tend the one big interest.

This same letter also offers insight into Franklin's spiritual beliefs:

I once was an orthodox Episcopalian, a lay reader, cross bearer, member of the choir and was offerred [*sic*] an education for the priesthood. University thinking made me not agnostic, but unorthodox. I doubted the efficacy of prayer, etc., etc. After I came to see that after all in our relations with God, FAITH is the big thing, not hope, or sight, but FAITH.

Its possession is the one supremest joy. That is true in our relations. Faith is the rock on which business is built. It takes us every day in safety amid many dangers. Not a trip, do you make, on train or elevator but you have faith in the builder's fidelity to his calling.[23]

Clearly, Franklin thought a lot about faith and Christianity, once writing a pleading editorial in which he asked God to provide ministers who were "men." He complained about preachers who held defeatist attitudes, who only spoke of divine intervention in times of adversity. "Negro preachers do the race an injustice by making such a one-sided presentation of the relations God has with men.... Our men must quit consoling us for losing. They tie our hands with their whimpering sympathy."[24] Later in life, the Franklins became devout Christian Scientists.

Chester and Ada Franklin married on July 3, 1925, at Ada's sister's home in Philadelphia, and as promised, Chester built his beloved a home on Montgall Avenue. The couple moved into a neighborhood that eagerly embraced them, and their home at 2447 became a hub of the street, especially after Ada invited her parents for an extended stay from January to May 1926. The retired Clark University professor William Crogman became a fixture in the neighborhood, charming almost everyone he met, including his son-in-law, "Uncle Chester."[25] He had a tongue-in-cheek message to John Bluford's wife, Addie (2444), telling her to "behave herself" in his absence by "paying all due respect to the head of the house, and remembering that she is only subordinate," and he teased Charles Greenstreet (2455) that the next time he called him a "kid," he would "knock him out in the 5th round."[26]

After his departure, the letters to his "Little Jam" provided a glimpse into the strength of the Montgall community. "It was not without some reluctance that I bade farewell to you and the good-hearted people of Kansas City who lavished so much kindness and consideration on your mother and myself during the five months we were sojourning in their midst," Crogman wrote. "I shall begin to write soon to my friends." Crogman went on to promise that he would send notes to Mrs. Cook, the Gambles, the Perrys, the Jacksons, Miss Brydie, and the Greenstreet household.[27]

Another letter read:

I am sorry, very sorry to learn of the serious illness of Mrs. Perry. Tell her to think of all those who love her, and look up and live. Give my regards to Prof. and Mrs. Cook. Tell Mrs. Cook I received the card she sent me late in the summer, when she was in the extreme northwest corner of the United States, enjoying the beauty and grandure [sic] of the scenery of which I have heard so much.

Give my regards to Miss Bryday [sic] and Mrs. Jackson, and . . . Please extend my regards to [Mr. Greenstreet's] better half and tell her to hold the reins tight on him. Among all these I do not forget Mr. and Mrs. Gamble. As to "honey sweet and sugar pie," tell her I received her letter and will write soon. In conclusion, I give you the liberty to tell every body who knew me in both cities of Kansas, that I send my love &c.[28]

Ada wrote to him, "Mrs. Perry says to tell you that she is just as jealous as she can be because you gave Mrs. Bluford one of your photos and didn't give her one. She said that she was going to write you about it herself."[29]

When William and Lavina Crogman returned to Montgall Avenue in 1931 to celebrate William's ninetieth birthday, his daughter made sure it would be an event to be remembered, and several of her neighbors played a role in the festivities. Fredericka Perry served as the mistress of ceremonies. Both J. E. Perry and Carolyn Brydie spoke at the event, and Addie Bluford, Lucile's stepmother, sang "God Will Take Care of You," one of the professor's favorite songs.[30]

Dr. Crogman died on October 16, 1931. Ten days later, Ada's mother, Lavina, died. Ada accompanied her parents' bodies back to Atlanta, where they were buried.

Not long after her parents' death, Chester and Ada Franklin left Montgall and relocated to an apartment above the *Call*. Although

The Franklins and Crogmans on Montgall Avenue, 1926. Black Archives of Mid-America.

there is no explanation of their move in any of the surviving correspondence, it could be that Ada worried about her husband's long hours and did not like him traveling at night, even the short distance between the *Call* offices and their Montgall Avenue home. Another more likely possibility is that the notoriously tightfisted Franklin felt that their Montgall home was an unnecessary expense, given the economic conditions at the time and the fact that the couple owned an apartment above his offices. Whatever the reason, the couple moved to the *Call* building at Twentieth and Vine, where they remained for the rest of their lives, as Franklin's reputation as a businessman, publisher, and crusader continued to grow.

While Franklin's writing lacked the wit and biting criticism that Roy Wilkins's had, he made up for it with his dogged civil rights activism, from pounding on the mayor's desk about police violence, to appealing to the superintendent for a new school, to initiating a lawsuit against the city for the right to play on Swope Park's Golf Course #1.[31]

He was also a Republican and was always on the lookout for ways to help the party, if not for any specific issue, at least as a way to punish the Democrats, a party he described as "sponsor[ing] peonage, lynching, injustice in the courts and all the other evils of the South." And Franklin was savvy enough to realize the possibilities for the Republican Party. In October 1923 he reached out to Missouri's Republican governor, Arthur Hyde, to strategize about how to make the most of the migrants from the South. Franklin told the governor that the migrants were coming in numbers "greater than persons think. ... The republican party can add to its strength, if it will make an effort to get these new citizens."[32] According to Franklin, it wouldn't take much to win their confidence, just "a kindly approach and a genuine interest in their welfare." But if the governor and other party leaders would make the effort, these voters would put "their feet in the republican path."

Still, Franklin was not such an ideologue that he could not appreciate a powerful Democratic ally, especially one with integrity and a good working relationship with Kansas City's Black community.[33] He maintained a cordial relationship with Democrat Harry Truman as he rose up the ranks from judge to senator to president (although the *Call* didn't endorse him in 1948). Truman, in turn, respected the newspaper editor, and in 1950, when Franklin celebrated his seventieth birthday, the president sent warm greetings. A number of other dignitaries turned out to celebrate with the editor, including his former employee Roy Wilkins, who had become the leader of the NAACP; Alf Landon, the former Kansas governor and US presidential candidate; and William Kemp, Kansas City's mayor.[34]

Franklin celebrated civil rights advances during his life—increased job opportunities for Black Americans, the end of legalized segregation in public schools, and the integration of the armed forces—but other problems were looming, including the decline of neighborhoods like the one in which he lived after he married the love of his life. When Chester Franklin died in 1955, most of White America believed that there would be dire consequences if their children associated with Black people. The last great civil rights victory that Franklin would see was the 1954 *Brown v. Board of Education* decision, but the newspaper man did not take time to celebrate. He understood that the problem was rooted not in segregation but in the attitudes of White supremacy that led to segregation. His last columns for his beloved *Kansas City Call* addressed the firing of Black teachers in the wake of the Supreme Court victory, after White parents became alarmed about their children being taught by African Americans. One of his final wishes was to have his funeral in the press room, and his friends and coworkers complied.[35]

Ada lived another twenty-eight years and continued to contribute to the newspaper and live above its press room. She eventually sold her business interest to Lucile Bluford, who had taken over as managing editor. Ada Crogman Franklin died in 1983, and she is buried next to her husband in Kansas City, Missouri.

The second hour chemistry class was organized in September, under the direction of Mr. John Bluford. This class is composed largely of girls.
    1926 Lincoln High School yearbook

9

In 1919, after Anna Holland Jones retired from the Kansas City school district and moved to California, a young family moved into 2444 Montgall Avenue: John Henry Bluford, his wife, Addie Alston Bluford, and John's two young sons, John Jr. and Guion.[1] Like so many others who landed on the block, the family came to Kansas City so John could take a teaching position at Lincoln High School. The family migrated from North Carolina, where Bluford's oldest daughter, eight-year-old Lucile, remained with her maternal grandmother because of their exceptionally close bond. "Cile,"[2] as her family called her, stayed with her grandmother for two years while her father, stepmother, and brothers forged new connections in Kansas City. When her grandmother died in 1921, Lucile joined her family on Montgall and moved into the house that she would call home for the next seventy-seven years.

John Bluford Sr. moved to Missouri because he believed the state offered better educational opportunities for his children and would be a less hostile environment for his family than North Carolina.[3] He was, perhaps, overly optimistic in his assessment. On April 29, 1921, Ray Hammond, a Black man in Bowling Green, Missouri, was dragged from his prison cell and lynched, one of the sixty-four individuals lynched in the United States that year. Bluford's neighbor, Myrtle Cook, responded with a

John Bluford. 1926 Lincoln High School yearbook,
Thatcher Family Collection, Kansas Collection,
RH MS 1250, Kenneth Spencer Research Library,
University of Kansas Libraries.

letter to Republican governor Arthur Hyde: "We urge that this investigation be vigorously prosecuted, not only for proper respect for law and order and the good name of our State, but also for the sake of justice to all of her citizens."[4] Cook urged the governor to voice his support for a bill working its way through Congress, the Dyer bill, which would have made lynching a federal crime. (It passed the House of Representatives but was defeated in the Senate by those who argued that it was federal overreach.) Had this bill become law in 1922, it may have changed the consequences for those who lynched another Missouri man a year later.

The Second Hour Chemistry Class

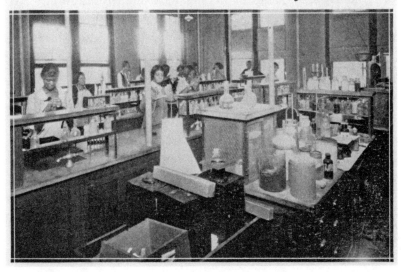

Bluford's chemistry class at Lincoln. 1926 Lincoln High School yearbook, Thatcher Family Collection, Kansas Collection, RH MS 1250, Kenneth Spencer Research Library, University of Kansas Libraries.

On Saturday, April 28, 1923, James Scott, a thirty-five-year-old Black janitor at the University of Missouri sat in a Boone County prison cell wrongly accused of attacking a fourteen-year-old White girl. Sheriff Fred Brown sat with Scott and watched as the crowd that gathered outside the jail morphed into an unruly mob of thirteen hundred, including women, children, "influential citizens," and students from the university. Sheriff Brown could have sworn in more deputies or moved his prisoner to another location to ensure that Scott received due process. Instead, he chose to engage in idle conversation with mob leaders, even as they entered the building and opened Scott's cell with a blowtorch. A concerned citizen alerted Governor Hyde, who ordered the Missouri National Guard to deploy to the county jail, but the Guard never arrived. Too many of its members were already on the scene—as part of the mob. Shortly after midnight, James Scott, having been violently dragged from his cell, was hanged from a nearby bridge.[5]

Montgall residents responded quickly. Chester Franklin urged Governor Hyde to "bring proceedings against Sheriff Brown for misfeasance in office."[6] Myrtle Cook reminded the governor that this was the second lynching in the state in two years and asked him to employ "greater diligence in investigating and in prosecuting this shame of Columbia."[7] Another Montgall resident, Pearl Dabney (2432), as a member of the Kansas City Negro Women's Republican League, asked the governor to do his "best to sustain the constitution of the U.S.A."[8]

Lynchings were just one of the threats to African Americans in 1920s Missouri. In 1922 the two-hundred-plus Black families in Caruthersville, Missouri, awoke to find signs posted on their doors, warning them not to go to the polls on election day. "There is going to be an election Tuesday Nov. 7th for White voters only. Nigger—you are not wanted. Signed K-K-K."[9]

At a plantation in Dunklin County, Missouri, African Americans were being held captive. When a foreman discovered they were trying to leave the plantation just east of the city of Kennett, he told them he would "kill all of them before they should move their [belongings]."[10] Terrorizing Black citizens was so commonplace in rural Missouri that on February 28, 1923, Governor Hyde warned the sheriffs of Pemiscot, Dunklin, Mississippi, and Scott Counties that he had heard reports of the intimidation and that they had best maintain order and protect their peaceful citizens.[11]

Although Montgall Avenue's residents kept abreast of the threats and attacks swirling about their state, they were personally removed from the worst of the violence. The intimidation and dynamite that had rocked the street in 1911 was all but forgotten by the time Lucile Bluford arrived in 1921, and her oral history suggests that she had no knowledge of the terror that Anna Jones and her neighbors endured a decade before. Rather, the young Bluford enjoyed a pleasant childhood, one in which her stay-at-home stepmother baked for the neighbors and prepared the meals that the family enjoyed every night. Bluford recalled that Addie was an excellent homemaker and a warm and wonderful woman who attended club meetings, sang in the church choir, and played the piano.[12] Lucile's father joined the local

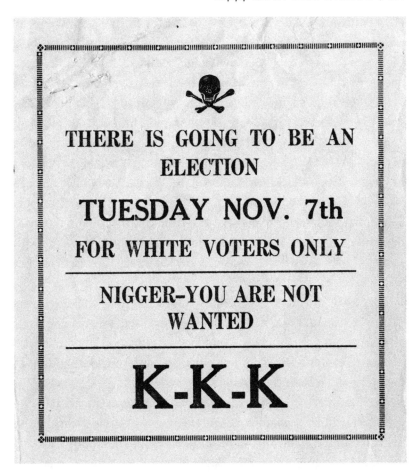

KKK poster. Arthur Mastick Hyde Gubernatorial Papers (C0007), State
Historical Society of Missouri Research Center–Columbia.

NAACP and the Research Club, where he met with fellow neighbors
and teachers, including Principal Cook. For two years, Bluford served
as the secretary of the Home Seekers Savings and Loan Association.[13]
These associations suggested that Lucile Bluford's parents were not
so naive as to believe that racism was limited to the most overt forms,
such as the lynchings and intimidation in rural Missouri. As a member of the Research Club, John Bluford discussed topics ranging from
religion to poetry, and although the meeting's agendas did not always
specifically mention racial equality, civil rights were never far from

the members' minds. "Our philosophy was to outthink and outfox the white man," recalled a fellow club member, Roy Wilkins. "We believed that if we thought deeply enough and talked long enough about the hostile world around us, we would find a way to overcome it."[14]

Situated amid a larger White neighborhood, Lucile and her brothers were protected from some of the indignities confronting other Black Kansas Citians, such as those who lived in the vicinity of a newly relocated city waste transfer site. Garbage was a big news story in Kansas City's Black community in 1923, and that fall the *Call*'s Roy Wilkins followed it closely after the city passed a zoning ordinance that relocated the garbage site from downtown and moved it into the middle of a Black residential neighborhood. "Garbage with Their Meals! Odors from Transfer Yard Penetrate Homes, Churches and Schools Every Hour of the Day and Night" began Wilkins's November 2 piece. The article went on to describe the "trickling rivers of filth" that had brought rats and other vermin to an area one block away from a Black church and an elementary school. "If garbage is a nuisance along the Inter City viaduct it is nothing less than that in the midst of a residential section."[15]

The Blufords were especially attuned to Wilkins's column. "Roy was always talking about some interesting thing that happened in the community, some kind of discrimination or something interesting. And I'd always pick up the *Call* and say, 'Well, let's see what Roy is talking about this week,'" Lucile recalled.[16]

The young Bluford resisted her parents,' especially Addie's, efforts that she conform to a traditional gender role. She never learned to cook, and she told her father he was wasting his money on the piano lessons forced on her. She knew from a young age that she would have a career, and not one in education—dreams that were possible growing up in the Montgall environment of the time. Lucile also remembered her father taking her to hear national civil rights leaders, such as NAACP executive secretary Walter White and civil rights litigator Charles Houston, whenever they came to town.[17] And no gathering was larger or more important than the NAACP's annual conference in the summer of 1923, which Kansas City hosted. Wilkins was there for the meeting's tumultuous opening session, the first story he ever wrote for the *Call*.[18] "Thousands and thousands of Kansas Citians, delegates and visitors, were stirred to white hot enthusiasm by the drama that was enacted on the platform."[19]

Governor Hyde had been asked to speak at the opening meeting, but he was unable to attend. In his stead he sent an aide, W. B. Brown, who probably wished he was anywhere else. Less than a minute into his speech, after Brown referred to African Americans as "darkys," the audience erupted in jeers, yells, and boos. For more than five minutes the crowd "seemed determined to clap the speaker down," Wilkins reported. Only after pleadings from NAACP leaders Arthur Spingarn and James Weldon Johnson was Brown allowed to continue. Then it got ugly.

Brown proceeded to read a letter from Governor Hyde, who urged "devotion to fundamental institutions—industry, thrift, individual achievement, rather than the pursuit of so-called equality." After Brown finished, James Weldon Johnson rose to respond, and, as Wilkins wrote, "launched [into] an attack upon Gov[ernor] Hyde's letter." Wilkins transcribed Johnson's speech:

> His Excellency advises patience, thrift, industry and intelligence. Patience? We know that patience is a foundation upon which we have to build. But who has been more patient than we? *(Applause)* Who has endured more hardships, suffered more insults, bent to more humiliation than we? Thrift and industry? Look around you, sir, at these thousands who by thrift and industry, by study and by devotion to the church have made themselves worthy to enjoy the rights of American citizens, but sir, do they enjoy them? *(Wild applause)*

Johnson turned to Brown and pounded his hand on the table. "We are here to serve notice that this is a fight to a finish for the rights guaranteed [to us] as American citizens by the Constitution." At this point, the crowd rose to its feet and thundered its applause.

But Johnson was not quite finished:

The *Star*, a great, powerful paper, which ought to know better, advises us to stop talking about lynching, stop harping on hardships and talk about the great achievements of colored Americans. We would like the *Star* and Governor Hyde to tell the white people about our achievements. We know all about theirs. We have neither the time nor the money to meet together and congratulate ourselves upon our achievements. We are concerned with justice. In this fight we are struggling not for distinction from America, but for oneness with America.

The convention included a silent parade in which Kansas City's African American community, all dressed in white, walked wordlessly through Kansas City's streets in both Kansas and Missouri.

* A year after the convention, in 1924, Lucile Bluford entered Lincoln High and embraced all that the school had to offer. She took an interest in civics and in 1926 was elected chair of the school's first civics club. She was editor of the yearbook, was elected class vice president, was active in the school's NAACP club, and became a part of Lincoln's debate team.[20] When she wasn't in school, she spent time giggling with her two best friends, Gwendolyn Butler (later Gwendolyn Jones) and Thelma Arnold, as they walked home from school. She recalled her trips to the Central High School library where she checked out books for debate and other projects.[21]

What Bluford does not mention in her 1989 oral history are the reasons for her frequent trips to the Central High School library. One of them was the fact that Lincoln High did not have a librarian—or even a real library, for that matter—and that its reference library consisted of "a few dilapidated sets of encyclopedias and ramshackle bookcases." Despite its stellar reputation, Lincoln High School had never received the same resources as its counterparts. Instead, Bluford and the other students had to settle for castoffs, receiving materials only after one of the other schools received new ones. Overcrowding was so serious during her years at Lincoln that many of her classes were held in stairwells. Students were so packed into some classrooms that

Lucile Bluford
School Editor

Lucile's yearbook photo. 1926 Lincoln High School
yearbook, Thatcher Family Collection, Kansas
Collection, RH MS 1250, Kenneth Spencer Research
Library, University of Kansas Libraries.

if a visitor wanted to enter, they had to stand and fold their chairs so
that the door could be opened.[22]

But years later, when Bluford sat for the oral history, she did not
talk about the physical inadequacies at her alma mater. Instead, she
only shared the positive experiences: being a part of the debate team,
writing for the school newspaper, and attending various club meetings. She enjoyed high school, where she first became interested in
journalism, and she was sad when it was over.[23]

Bluford's recollections about high school speak to her positive disposition and affable nature. She had a hopeful outlook throughout her life, a quality her fellow classmates picked up on as early as 1928, when they wondered whether she would ever "express gloom."[24] Lucile Bluford was valedictorian of Lincoln's class of 1928 and enrolled at the University of Kansas in Lawrence. Four years later, she graduated from KU with honors, journalism degree in hand.

Just as she had been able to escape more brutal forms of racism on Montgall, she also avoided some of the most vile discrimination in Lawrence. But no Black student was fully protected at KU. Five years before her arrival, when the university opened Corbin Hall, its first residence hall for women, Chancellor Ernest Lindley had to assure the Kansas legislature that no Black women would ever live there, so as not to offend the university's southern students. Historian William Tuttle observed that the University of Kansas operated on two levels during the 1920s and 1930s: it opened its doors to Black students, but it did not allow them to live on campus, and although swimming was a requirement for most students, the policy was waived for African Americans.[25] Loren Miller, a Black man who attended KU several years before Bluford, observed that he was excluded from literary and dramatic societies and glee clubs, he was unable to use the school gymnasium, and he was not allowed to attend school-sponsored dances. This discrimination also extended into the classroom. Miller reported on the dean of the Engineering School who "regularly call[ed] in all colored engineering students and advis[ed] them to get out of his school" because there were no engineering firms that would hire them."[26]

The buoyant Lucile Bluford did not recall any specific trouble with her college professors, but that was not the case for her friend and fellow journalism student Marie Ross, who appeared to be far less deferential. Ross, who was a few years ahead of Bluford at KU, had a run-in with Leon Flint, dean of journalism. "Dean Flint told her in so many words ... 'There's no point in your studying journalism because there's nowhere for you to work and you're just wasting your time. You shouldn't be here,' and all that. Tried to get her to withdraw,"

Bluford recalled.[27] Eager to prove the pompous professor wrong, Ross sought help from Roy Wilkins and amassed a collection of nearly two hundred different newspapers, which she confidently flung on his desk.

That the dean of the journalism school at a major university was unaware of one of the most powerful institutions in Black America hints at the depth of division between the two Americas in 1928 and at how successful earlier scholars had been in propagating racial inferiority. Bluford's recollection of Ross's experience also suggests something about Bluford herself. She respected her friend's courage in standing up to her professor, just as she respected Roy Wilkins's fiery editorials in the *Call*, but her easygoing nature made confrontation difficult. At this early stage in her life, she was more concerned with protecting others' feelings than in calling out an injustice.

In 1983, while testifying in the Kansas City school district's desegregation case, she told a story about a conversation she had with her White friend and neighbor, "Abee," who was several years younger than she was. Abee lived nearby, on Twenty-Fifth Street, and when Lucile was preparing to go to college, Abee wanted to know where she was going, and she told him KU. He asked her why she wasn't going to attend the University of Missouri, and Lucile didn't want to share the truth that MU didn't admit Blacks. "I guess I was trying to make America seem a little better and I said, 'Oh, I just would like to go to KU,' and I never did tell him why I didn't go to MU because I didn't want him to know how bad this country was, I guess."[28]

Although she did not recall any specific slights at KU, she experienced the sting of discrimination outside of class. One night she and a friend decided to see a movie at a segregated theater in downtown Lawrence. Instead of retreating to the balcony, the space reserved for its Black patrons, Bluford and her friend sat down in the main section, where the White people sat. Bluford remembered the ushers trying to get her attention and force her to leave, but she and her friend ignored them. Ushers even stopped the film and turned on the lights, but the two continued to feign ignorance. Only when others started to complain did the attendants give up and let the film continue.[29]

Lucile at KU, circa 1930. Papers of Dorothy Hodge Johnson, Dowdal Davis Jr., and John Hodge, Kansas Collection, RH MS 549, Kenneth Spencer Research Library, University of Kansas.

Although Bluford was part of a successful campaign to integrate a dining hall in the Kansas Union as part of a student group that met with Chancellor Lindley, her preferred strategy for securing equal rights was less direct. Bluford turned civil rights into a moral crusade, and she took advantage of her position at KU's daily newspaper, the *University Daily Kansan* (UDK), to write and publish lessons on righteousness and decency. As telegraph editor, monitoring and transcribing stories as they came across the wire from the United Press Syndicate, she kept students up to date on international and national news: Gandhi's quest for Indian independence, Hitler's rise to the German chancellorship, Al Capone's legal troubles, and the Lindbergh kidnapping. Among those major news events, she sprinkled in less publicized stories that focused on the plight of Black America: a lynching in Maryville, Missouri, and an editorial about Black Gold Star mothers whose sons had died in the Great War.[30] When the group purchased tickets to sail across the Atlantic to visit their sons' graves, they were forced into substandard, segregated accommodations. And even though no bylines were provided in the newspaper, as the only Black member of the staff, she likely had a hand in articulating the newspaper's position in January 1932, when an African American was given nonvoting status on its student council. "The incident illustrates another truth—that by calm deliberate, constructive action, the Negro can finally demand his rights and come into his own."[31]

The newspaper covered George Washington Carver's lecture in Lawrence (titled "What God Put in the Peanut")[32] and the death of Julius Rosenwald, part owner and head of Sears, Roebuck and Company, who had given tens of thousands of dollars to build Black schools in the South and establish Black YMCAs throughout the country, including Kansas City's Paseo Y. And in March 1932, when Bluford's sorority, Alpha Kappa Alpha, sponsored a visit from Langston Hughes, the newspaper covered it too. Hughes, who spent much of his young life in Lawrence, did not hold back his frustrations about the monotony of work that was open to Black people, or his anger about a people who emerged from the "whip of the slave-master" in the nineteenth century only to face the lash of prejudice in the twentieth. Bluford summed up the evening and wrote: "To hear a poet interpret his own works is always an interesting pastime. . . . When the poems express the thoughts and sentiments of a particular group, it is doubly worth while to hear the author read them."[33]

Lacking the edifying wrath of Du Bois or the mocking cynicism of Wilkins, Bluford's reporting and writing was subtler and less confrontational. But then again, she could hardly afford to be too outspoken as the only Black woman working on an all-White and majority male editorial board. In a column titled "Seeing Race through Colored Glasses," which focused on the isolation that the school's international students experienced, Bluford could have been talking about her own experiences:

He finds himself, in a great many instances, an involuntary member of the "out" group. . . . Students do not avoid his company, nor do they seek it. His presence at social gatherings is not frowned upon, but at

the same time it is not invited. He is subject to no stringent ostra-
cism by his American fellow students and on the other hand he is not
fully accepted. Such is the perplexing social problem that confronts
the foreign student when he attempts to orient himself in university
life and surroundings upon his arrival.

Bluford felt that the only solution to the isolation was personal contact. "Until there is aroused a feeling of mutual respect and admi-
ration, founded upon a knowledge of the persons involved, we, who
pride ourselves on our world outlook and wide tolerance, will continue to turn thumbs down on the foreign student."[34]

If the goal of a university education is to secure employment, Bluford attended college at perhaps the worst time in American history,
entering in 1928 as the economy roared and the stock market neared
the peak of its frenzied growth, and graduating in 1932, before any
of the New Deal job programs were able to provide any relief. As a
student, Bluford watched as her professors and other KU staff took a
10 percent salary cut, and her classmates were anxious. Bluford again
sought to educate her mostly White, mostly upper-middle-class
readers about the plight of African Americans. "If 1932 presents a
dismal outlook in employment to the white men and women who will
be graduated in June, what must the outlook be to Negro seniors?"[35]
Ironically, Bluford's prospects were better than most of her White
classmates in the School of Journalism, and certainly better than
other women in her class. The *Kansas City Star*, for example, had yet
to hire a woman in 1932.[36] Bluford, though, had no trouble securing a
job. After graduation, she moved to Atlanta to work for a daily Black
newspaper, but she found the heat and the segregated buses intolerable. After several months she returned to Kansas City and eventually found her way back to her former neighbor at the *Call*.[37]

By 1939 Lucile Bluford's professional career had taken off. In her
seven years at the newspaper, she had worked her way from city reporter, to managing editor, to editor of one of the country's most
prestigious Black publications. But in 1939 she made an important
decision, one that would have taken her out of the workplace and back

into the classroom. She decided to sue the University of Missouri for admission into its Graduate School of Journalism. Although returning to school was not especially appealing to her, she understood that success in her case would open the door for future generations. This battle would make national headlines and would make Lucile Bluford a hero not only in Kansas City but across the country.

It is likely that Bluford would have never engaged in this struggle without encouragement from the NAACP.[38] As managing editor of the *Call*, she had achieved professional success at an influential publication that was still growing in circulation. And up to that point, she had avoided confrontation, preferring to appeal to an individual's conscience. But in 1939 the struggle for integration was at a crossroads, and it needed good soldiers willing to take up the swords. Lloyd Gaines had won his battle against the University of Missouri, and although the state responded by setting up a separate law school for Black students, the NAACP understood that establishing and maintaining these separate professional and graduate schools, which were supposedly on par with the White schools, would be cost-prohibitive. Civil rights leaders wanted to keep up the pressure. All they needed were qualified students willing to engage.

Lucile Bluford stepped up.

She applied and was accepted to MU's Graduate School of Journalism, and in September 1939, when she appeared at MU to enroll, it looked at first as if she might succeed. "There were other people of color there from all parts of the world," she said. "Not American Negroes, but Indians and Chinese, all kinds of folks ... And nobody paid any more attention to me than they did to them or anybody else." But after about twenty minutes of standing in line with people from all over the globe, Bluford was reminded of the unique space that the descendants of slaves occupied in US society—and the lengths to which the state was prepared to go to maintain African Americans' second-class status. Someone tapped her on the shoulder and told her that the registrar, S. W. Canada, wanted to see her in his office. When Canada informed her that she could not enroll at MU, she protested and claimed that the Gaines decision made it possible. The registrar replied that the decision wasn't final because it "had not come down from the Supreme Court to the Missouri Supreme Court, to the District Court, and then to the university."[39]

Bluford's legal team, which included civil rights giants Charles Houston and Thurgood Marshall, filed a petition for a writ of mandamus, and in February 1940 she entered a packed courthouse in Boone County, Missouri, to plead her case. She answered questions from the prosecution about her work at the *Call* and her correspondence with her attorneys. Her position as managing editor at the newspaper worked against her as prosecutors argued that she had nothing to gain from a graduate degree in journalism because she was already gainfully employed. "It was true," Bluford said in 1989, "but we couldn't admit it back then."[40] Students from nearby Stephens College, an all-girls' school, came to show their support for Bluford and interrupted the proceedings several times with spirited applause. The judge was not as supportive, and in the end he determined that the case was more about "litigation" than "education."[41]

Despite the loss, Bluford and her attorneys fought on. They filed a lawsuit in the federal court against Canada for his refusal to admit her and another suit against the university, arguing that the journalism courses that the state had scrambled to put together at Lincoln University were not comparable to the graduate courses at MU. Every semester from 1939 to 1941, Bluford showed up to enroll at the University of Missouri, and every time, she was rebuffed.[42]

The years-long struggle and rejections took their toll on Bluford. "Is there nothing that can be done at this moment to force Missouri U. to admit me in view of the fact that Lincoln's school is not ready on schedule?" she wrote to Charles Houston in February 1941. "I am losing patience with the orderly but slow procedure of the courts and my mounting ire at Missouri's continued evasion of justice at a time when my brothers are being drafted to fight for 'democracy' may drive me to return to Columbia Friday and attend classes—a permit to enroll be damned. They can't do more than eject me."[43]

Through it all, the university and its registrar remained steadfast—even though conditions were changing all around them. The country

Lucile with students from Stephen's College, 1941. Papers of Dorothy
Hodge Johnson, Dowdal Davis Jr., and John Hodge, Kansas Collection, RH
MS 549, Kenneth Spencer Research Library, University of Kansas.

marched closer to war, and Bluford's boss, Chester Franklin, worked
to ensure that jobs in the defense industry would be open to African
Americans, a mission that took him out of the office and the city regularly. With Franklin's absences, Bluford was left to assume more and
more responsibilities at the newspaper, managing staff and covering

the news, and during the summer of 1941 there was a lot of it, including a growing crisis involving police brutality in the city's Black community (see chapter 12). Bluford's role within her family was also changing as she became the caregiver for her parents, both of whom were in declining health, and her brother, John, who was struggling with his mental health. By the fall of 1941 she was exhausted. "I hadn't planned to go through the attempt-at-enrollment procedure again and I'm not at all keen on it," she wrote to Houston on September 10, 1941. "I certainly hope it will be the last time."[44]

Sensing her diminished interest, Houston responded with an upbeat letter dated September 15, 1941:[45]

> Dear Lucille: [sic]
>
> Last Saturday Thurgood was in town, and we had a conference: Hastie, Marshall, Nabrit, Ming, Ransom and I. Your case was one of the main topics of discussion.
>
> All the boys hope you will see the thing through. They feel that we are right down to where the going is tough, and that the State does not intend to either put a school of journalism at Lincoln or allow a Negro to go to the University of Missouri unless the pressure is kept up on it to the very end.
>
> No one knows what may take place in the world and the country between now and February 1942, so it is barely possible that if we are in a shooting war this may be the face-saver which will permit Missouri to enrol [sic] you under the guise of being patriotic....
>
> It is too bad that there are not more students applying to the University of Missouri, but it simply shows that we are paving the way for those who will come in the next decade. After all look where the Mississippi River rises. So it goes.

Six days later, Bluford gave Houston her report about her most recent rejection by Canada and the reason for her delayed response. "Please pardon me for being so late making this report to you, but my brother was taken to the hospital Wednesday, my mother is not well and I am tired and busy as the dickens."[46]

Bluford's case ended in a decidedly undramatic fashion. Although

Lucile at the *Call*, 1940s. Papers of Dorothy Hodge Johnson,
Dowdal Davis Jr., and John Hodge, Kansas Collection, RH MS
549, Kenneth Spencer Research Library, University of Kansas.

Houston had hoped that MU would surrender under the flag of patriotism and admit a thirty-year-old Black woman into its graduate
school, the university did something altogether different: it closed
its entire graduate program in journalism, declaring that it could no
longer justify offering this degree because of the number of students
and faculty that had been called up for service.

In the years after her lawsuit, Bluford remained a civil rights
leader, and she used the pages of the *Call* to make her views known.
Her work and the stories she covered are documented in the chapters
that follow.

... I dreamed last night
I was standing on 18th and Vine
I shook hands with Piney Brown
And I could hardly keep from crying
    Big Joe Turner, "Piney Brown Blues"

10

The teachers and professionals who lived on Montgall Avenue sought to negate stereotypes about racial immorality and inferiority through their lives and work, and they railed against institutions that they believed spread decay. And for many of Montgall's residents, there were no more dangerous or vile places than the clubs along Twelfth and Fourteenth Streets, which they believed "carr[ied] hundreds of negroes into the vortex of hell's running stream."[1]

Not everyone on the block fit this mold. One Montgall Avenue resident not only frequented the clubs and bars north of Twenty-Fifth Street, he also made his living there: Walter "Piney" Brown (2457).

There were actually two Piney Browns: "Big Piney" and "Little Piney."[2] The brothers, Thomas Jefferson and Walter, migrated to Kansas City from Pine Bluff, Arkansas, which explains their woodsy nickname. Thomas was known as "Big Piney," most likely because he was older and, perhaps, taller, although Walter stood well over six feet.[3] The brothers were drawn to the pulsing energy along Twelfth and Fourteenth Streets, and they were soon acquainted with some of Kansas City's biggest power brokers of the day. One was Homer Roberts (2453), the entrepreneurial dynamo who managed clubs before World War I and built Roberts Motor Mart. Another was

Felix Payne, a gambler, politician, night club owner, newspaper editor, and close business associate of Kansas City's Democratic boss, Tom Pendergast. While Thomas (Big Piney) partnered with Roberts, Walter (Little Piney), who lived on Montgall Avenue, became associated with Payne.

The Brown brothers represented a different kind of migrant to Montgall Avenue, compared to the street's first Black homeowners, such as Anna Jones and Hugh Oliver Cook, who came from middle-class origins and were educated in the North and East. The Browns were also different from the more polished John Perry and Chester Franklin, who had also reached a level of professionalism and respect in both the Black and White communities. Despite Perry's and Franklin's humble beginnings in the hard Texas soil, they had been raised by parents who had poured all their dreams into their only sons. As adults, the physician and newspaper publisher were dutifully living out the weight of these expectations. Thomas and Walter Brown were more like the migrants who started arriving in the urban areas in the North and Midwest a decade later as part of the Great Migration. And like those five hundred thousand migrants who sought to escape the oppressive conditions in the South, the Browns had to appreciate that their economic and political opportunities would be greater in Kansas City than in the more rural Pine Bluff, Arkansas.

Although Kansas City never saw Great Migrant numbers like New York, Detroit, and Chicago, more than seven thousand African Americans came to Kansas City during the first two decades of the twentieth century, and eight thousand more arrived in the 1920s. By 1930 Kansas City had 38,574 Black residents, which represented 9.7 percent of its total population.[4]

The new migrants brought new sounds to the clubs in the city's Black district, and the Brown brothers were fans. Although not musicians themselves, they supported the jazz music fermenting there, a genre that benefited from generous patrons. And no one was more supportive than Walter "Piney" Brown of Montgall Avenue.

"He knew everybody, and everybody knew Piney," said Kansas City jazz giant Count Basie. "Piney was like the patron saint to all musicians," recalled saxophonist Eddie Barefield. "He used to take care of them. In fact, he was like a father to me. . . . Most all the playing and jamming happened at Piney's place. Piney was a man, he didn't care how much it cost. . . . If you needed money to pay your rent, he would give it to you and take you out and buy booze. He was a man you could always depend on for something if you needed it, as a musician."[5] In 1928 Walter's older brother Thomas was with Homer Roberts the day he was turned away from Kansas City's municipal golf course, and he was one of the plaintiffs in the ensuing lawsuit, which resulted in the city creating a separate golf course for Blacks.[6] A year later, when Roberts moved to Chicago, Brown remained in Kansas City and took over the daily operations of Roberts Motor Mart.[7] After the economy collapsed and the business folded, Thomas Brown also moved to Chicago. He died soon after.[8]

Walter Brown remained in Kansas City, where his relationship with Felix Payne deepened. Among Payne's nightclubs was the very successful Sunset, a club managed by Walter Brown. It was the place where blues giant Big Joe Turner got his start.

Long before his "Shake, Rattle, and Roll" shook up the music scene in 1954, the Kansas City–born Turner tended bar at the Sunset, where he became known as "the singing bartender" because of his tendency to sing when business was slow. Piney appreciated his young employee's talent so much that he hung a speaker over the outside door to attract customers.[9] Years later, Turner expressed his gratitude with the popular "Piney Brown Blues," in which he dreamed of standing at Eighteenth and Vine so he could shake hands with Piney Brown.

All of the big names played at the Sunset, including bandleader Benny Goodman, drummer Gene Krupa, trumpeter Harry James, and brothers Jimmy and Tommy Dorsey. And while patrons remembered the Sunset for the undeniable talent, the musicians remembered it for its manager. "We used to go to Piney Brown's place on Twelfth Street with Count Basie," recalled composer Mary Lou Williams. "He used to play, and there was a little bench. Everybody used to sit on the bench, and whoever was next, they'd go and play, and they just loved it. . . . He'd give us money; he was very kind to the musicians."[10]

Piney Brown was not the first resident of Montgall who had an ear for music or a heart for musicians. Ada Crogman sought to draw attention to gospels and spirituals in her *Milestones* show, and H. O. Cook had close family members who were musicians, including both his brother and his son. There is also some evidence that Cook himself dabbled in the art when he welcomed the "Unbleached Minstrels" into his home in 1906.[11] Where Brown differed from his neighbors was in the kind of music he supported. Crogman was clear in her appreciation for spirituals, and Cook's tastes appeared to lean toward the vaudeville sound. But the jazz musicians that Brown supported were in a different category, partly because of where the music was played—in the city's clubs, where drinking and gambling were rampant. These were the very places that many Montgall residents had railed against for decades.

But no amount of preaching could keep people, Black and White, away. "Kansas City was a good time," recalled bandleader Sam Price. "We had some supporting fellows like Felix Payne and Piney Brown . . . and those were the kind of fellows that really helped to sponsor jazz in America."[12]

As supportive as Piney Brown was, though, another Kansas City figure also deserves some credit for cultivating Kansas City's jazz sound: Democratic boss Tom Pendergast, who ensured that the police stayed out of the clubs throughout Prohibition (1920–1933) as long as they carried liquor from his distributorship.[13] The clubs were open all day, every day, which provided time for musicians to hone their skills and experiment with new sounds. Kansas City was a haven, supported by the "Pendergast Prosperity" in the early 1930s, when the lean years of the Great Depression shut out opportunities for musicians in other cities as clubs closed and bands split up.[14] Because the clubs were open 24/7, Kansas City was an attractive destination for some of the most talented musicians in the country.

If Walter Brown's salary came from managing the clubs, his real money came from gambling. Even so, one longtime resident of Montgall Avenue recalled him fondly. "Piney was what you would call a 'Gentle Giant,'" said Gwendolyn Russell Calderon (2432). "We all knew that he made his money gambling, but he was just so nice! And he was so good to all of those musicians."[15]

But Brown's high-rolling life and illegal activity did not last, and in 1939 Pendergast was indicted for income tax evasion. On November 6 of that year, Walter "Piney" Brown was arrested for gambling at the Autumn Leaf Club. Brown posted $1,500 bond and moved to California, where he died not long after.[16]

While Anna Jones had brought the urbane W. E. B. Du Bois to Montgall Avenue, and Ada Crogman and Carolyn Brydie hosted an evening with General Benjamin Davis,[17] the first Black man to rise to the rank of brigadier general, Piney Brown invited struggling musicians to sleep on his couch and brought boxing great Joe Louis to Montgall. His neighbors remembered Louis sitting on Piney's front porch reading "the funny papers."[18]

This change on Montgall reflects a larger reality for the Black experience in America's northern and midwestern cities, for Thomas and Walter Brown's arrived in Kansas City at the same time thousands of European immigrants did. Scholars who have compared these groups tend to conclude that although both groups faced bigotry and racism, the Europeans eventually assimilated into the dominant culture while African Americans became increasingly isolated. Academics discuss the phenomena in the abstract, but there was nothing abstract about what happened to the residents of Montgall. Thomas "Big Piney" Brown discovered the two Americas at the golf course, and Walter discovered it on Montgall. Montgall Avenue's early White residents, Boris and Anna Kittis (2428), Adam Hildebrand (2430), and Richard Mayberry (2432), all left the street in the early twentieth century. While the particulars of their departures are not known, taken together and viewed through the larger prism of the assimilation of European immigrants across the country, it is likely that these families exited the street after having come to a "fuller sense of their own Whiteness and a more secure footing as Whites," as historian David Roediger aptly described.[19]

This sense of inclusion—and exclusion—was something that builder Jesse Clyde Nichols played up and played upon in the years to come, a history that is explored in the next chapter through the experiences of the Pittman family from 2449 Montgall Avenue.

[The] linking of place, race, and behavior worked to racialize urban space thereby focusing public attention on the behaviors of blacks as the cause of urban problems and, in effect, justifying their segregation from the white population. Over time, this connection between race and place, in Kansas City and elsewhere, became an important impetus and justification for maintaining the color line in housing, for disinvesting in racially mixed and nonwhite areas, and for directing investment resources into racially homogenous, all-white neighborhoods.

    Kevin Fox Gotham, *Race, Real Estate, and Uneven Development: The Kansas City Experience, 1900–2000*

11

The home at 2449 Montgall Avenue was occupied by one family—the Pittmans—for more than a hundred years. Arthur Pittman, like his neighbors Chester Franklin and John Perry, was born in Texas, but like his other neighbors H. O. Cook, John Bluford, and Joshua Russell, Pittman came to Kansas City to teach at Lincoln High School. Arthur and Marguerite stayed with Ollie and Daisy Cook for some time after arriving in Kansas City, but in 1914, when their home was completed, the couple moved across the street to 2449 Montgall, where they raised four children— Arthur Jr., Keith, Marguerite, and the baby, Paul, who, when he was born in 1928, "came in time for Thanksgiving dinner!"[1]

Montgall Avenue was a bustling, active place in the 1920s. Teachers Arthur Pittman, John Bluford, and Carolyn Brydie attended to the needs of their students, while their principal wrote his master's thesis. John Perry raised money for the children's wing at Wheatley-Provident Hospital, while Homer Roberts and Chester Franklin expanded their thriving businesses. When not supporting various Republican Party candidates, Myrtle Cook established the Home Seekers Savings and Loan with her husband in 1926. Fredericka Perry and her best friend and neighbor Pearl Dabney (2432) started the Big Sisters Home to improve the lives of girls in foster care. And after

Arthur Pittman. 1926 Lincoln High yearbook,
Thatcher Family Collection, Kansas Collection,
RH MS 1250, Kenneth Spencer Research Library,
University of Kansas Libraries.

Milestones finished touring, Ada Crogman Franklin joined the board
of directors for the Niles Home for Negro Children, hosted her parents for an extended stay, and threw lavish dinner parties at her tony
Montgall home.

The 2400 block of Montgall was the kind of street that Walt Disney would have felt comfortable in at the start of the twentieth century. It was, after all, just four blocks west of Disney's childhood home

and only two blocks from where he had a paper route in the early 1900s.[2] And like the idyllic neighborhoods for which the Walt Disney Corporation is known, the street was brimming with children. These youngsters included the Pittmans' four children, Lucile and her two brothers at 2444, the Russell family at 2434 and later 2461, and five children in the Anderson household at 2428, the home formerly occupied by Boris Kittis. These were the halcyon days of Montgall Avenue, a time when the youngsters, who were well served by their teachers during the day, spent their off-school hours riding bicycles, building snowmen, and playing hide-and-seek, hopscotch, and baseball. And when the children weren't running to Callison and Swartz, the corner grocery store at Twenty-Fourth and Prospect, for a neighbor, they were climbing trees and playing jokes on their parents, such as when the young Paul Pittman distracted his mother while others picked pears from her backyard trees.[3] Gwendolyn Russell Calderon, who has lived at 2434 Montgall her entire life, recalled how "Aunty Pearl" (Dabney at 2432—the Mayberrys' former home) would give her orange slices, while the gruff Mrs. Patterson (at 2430—once owned by the Hildebrands) only passed out stale peanuts. Calderon's favorite treats, however, were the red-and-white mints from Marguerite Day (at 2442), because she usually distributed them after giving an impromptu concert on her baby grand piano.[4]

Arthur and Marguerite Pittman were integral members of the neighborhood. The family belonged to Saint Augustine's Episcopalian Church and introduced several of their neighbors to their place of worship, including the Blufords and Carolyn Brydie.[5] Arthur Pittman was a member of Montgall's whist club, a group that met every Friday and included Joshua Russell, John Bluford, and Ollie Cook. Every Valentine's Day the men hosted a "Sweetheart Dinner" for their wives, and each woman received a five-pound box of chocolates from local candy manufacturer Russell Stover.[6]

Marguerite Pittman was a stay-at-home wife, mother, and caregiver who used to joke with her youngest, Paul, that he could never play hooky from school by feigning illness, not with a doctor on one side of them and a pharmacist on the other. (John and Fredericka

Children on Montgall Avenue, circa 1937: Collins Anderson, Sue Anderson, Rozelia Russell, and Gwendolyn Russell. Courtesy of Gwendolyn Calderon.

Perry lived to the south, and a pharmacist, Sydney Johnson, moved into the house just north of them after Chester and Ada Franklin relocated to an office above the *Call*.) In addition to raising her young children, Marguerite cared for her father, Charles, who suffered from a type of dementia. Charles died of pneumonia on May 1, 1926, in his daughter's home.

Arthur Pittman taught science at Lincoln High School for over twenty-five years, and he experienced the school's evolution under Principal Cook's leadership from a more traditional curriculum to one that offered more practical skills such as carpentry and masonry. In 1911, his second year of teaching, Lincoln had an enrollment of 311; eight years later, enrollment had more than doubled, with an additional seven hundred attending night school. Pittman tolerated the overcrowded conditions until 1936, when the new facility opened at Twenty-Second Street and Woodland Avenue. Pittman, however, chose to remain in the old building at Nineteenth and Tracy, which became R. T. Coles Junior High. He stayed until his retirement in 1953.

Although Lincoln High's faculty was known for its caring attitude, teachers were also committed to academics. For his part, Pittman encouraged his students to trace scientific terms back to their Latin roots.[7] Although traditional with regard to curriculum, he appeared to exhibit progressive attitudes regarding gender, and he encouraged female students to pursue the sciences. During the 1925–1926 school year, Pittman taught an all-female physics class. He asked the seventeen girls in his third hour to observe science in everyday life and keep up with scientific advancements by following and reporting on stories carried by the *Saturday Evening Post* and *Popular Science*. His students also conducted experiments in electricity, light, magnetism, and heat. (That year, John Bluford's second-hour chemistry class was primarily composed of females.)[8] Although the number of females pursuing math and science paints an image of a very forward-thinking culture at Lincoln High School, it may have had more to do with the economic reality facing many Black males at this time. In his master's thesis, Principal Cook addressed the falling attendance rates for his male students, many of whom were forced into the world of work.

For those who remained in school, they could have participated in one of Pittman's extracurricular activities, including the Thrift Club, whose members declared that thrift was patriotic and the foundation of character. This club encouraged students to deposit money in a school bank, where it would remain for the academic year, barring any extenuating circumstances. He also led several fundraising campaigns for various charitable organizations. For example, in 1917 Lincoln students raised $48.25 for the hospital and children's home.[9] And in the fall of 1919, when Kansas City launched a $2.5 million capital campaign to build a memorial for the veterans of the Great War, one of Kansas City's most prominent businessmen, lumberman R. A. Long, came to Lincoln High to encourage faculty and students to contribute to the cause. Soon after, Arthur Pittman and John Bluford, as sponsors for the school's war memorial campaign, raised $2,809.20 (nearly $42,000 in today's money) toward what would become Liberty Memorial.[10]

As Pittman and other members of Lincoln's faculty encouraged values such as thrift and community involvement, not far away, Jesse

Pittman's class. 1926 Lincoln High School yearbook, Thatcher Family Collection, Kansas Collection, RH MS 1250, Kenneth Spencer Research Library, University of Kansas Libraries.

Clyde Nichols, known as J. C., embarked on an endeavor that would reshape Kansas City and change the lives of those at Lincoln High School in fundamental ways. Nichols was acquiring land around Brush Creek to create a shopping center—coincidentally, the same area that Rufus Montgall had cleared and tilled fifty years before. But Nichols was not a farmer; he was a real estate magnate, and his signature masterpiece, the Country Club Plaza, became the first (and some would say the most beautiful) suburban shopping district in the nation. Nichols went on to build the neighborhoods that surrounded the Plaza district, including Westwood, Fairway, and Mission Hills. These attractive areas were known for their aesthetic qualities and featured curved streets, fountains, statuary, and other outdoor ornamentation, all designed to create an image of wealth and class—and all designed to last for the long term. Nichols wasn't just selling homes—he was selling a lifestyle, a place where the country's growing middle class could go to escape the grit of the city and "where your children will get the benefit of an exclusive environment and the most desirable associations," associations that did not include Blacks.[11]

Nichols went further than banning specific groups from his property, though, because his homeowners automatically became members of neighborhood associations, which automatically re-newed these restrictions after twenty-five years.

Twenty years after the Tenth Ward Neighborhood Association gathered to discuss ways to remove the teachers on Montgall for "economic reasons," as the city prosecutor argued in 1911 prior to the dynamite attacks on Montgall Avenue, Nichols was able to spare his tenants from the possibility of ever needing to discuss people of color moving into a neighborhood. Like Judge Harris's ruling against Homer Roberts that allowed middle-class Whites to avoid African Americans on the golf course, J. C. Nichols allowed middle-class homeowners to avoid facing the possibility of ever living near Black people. These individual actions of shutting out the Black commu-nity from the dominant culture had a cumulative effect.

Nichols's influence extended beyond his own subdivisions, and as a member of the Kansas City Real Estate Board, a position he held for a number of years (1912, 1913, 1915, 1920, 1921, 1936, and 1938), he had ample opportunity to put this ideology into practice, locally and beyond. "In Kansas City, the origin of racially segregated neighbor-hoods was not the foreordained consequences of decades of an un-changing racial prejudice or overt discrimination by ordinary White residents," according to scholar Kevin Fox Gotham, who studied the role of race in Kansas City's real estate market. "Early-twentieth-century racial prejudices, negative stereotypes of Black neighbor-hoods, and subsequent discriminatory acts were cultivated and dis-seminated through the organized efforts of housing reformers and elite real estate interests, community builders, and homeowner as-sociations."[12] But the devastating ideas about race and neighborhood that Nichols peddled were about to extend to an entirely new level.

In 1929 the stock market crashed, which caused millions of real and imagined dollars to suddenly disappear. Hundreds of banks closed as economic activity ground to a halt. Arthur and Marguerite Pittman's children were in elementary school when the United States suffered through the worst economic crisis of the twentieth century. When President Herbert Hoover's policies failed to kickstart the economy, voters elected a new president, Franklin D. Roosevelt, who was eager to try anything to get Americans back to work. This included efforts to extend the federal government's hand into the nation's floundering housing industry. Enter J. C. Nichols and his close associates at the National Association of Home Builders and the National Association of Real Estate Boards.

Although business leaders traditionally loathe government regulation, real estate developers understand that government involvement can be vital for their enterprises. Zoning laws, for example, play a role in stabilizing property values in certain areas by protecting neighborhoods from industries and other structures.[13] Also, savvy real estate professionals, like Nichols, saw the benefit of a more regulated financial system, one that could streamline home mortgages. Before the 1930s, home sales often required enormous down payments, with mortgage interest payments often tied to inflation, meaning that payments could vary widely from month to month. For years, Nichols and other real estate magnates had lobbied Congress for federal regulations that would lower down payments and make longer and more stable terms for loans. Now, in the midst of the economic calamity, government officials were all ears. And when the feds responded to the crisis by changing housing market policies, they rescued one segment of society—at the expense of another.

J. C. Nichols was a chief architect of the Federal Housing Administration (FHA), an agency set up during the Great Depression that set the standards for home construction and insured the loans made by banks. Its underwriting manuals, according to Gotham, could have been written by Nichols himself. They warned land developers and realtors that if a neighborhood is to retain stability, it needed to be racially homogenous. Further, living in an all-White neighborhood was "an indicator of upward mobility and financial success, and an outcome of hard work, thrift, and resourcefulness."[14] In creating the FHA, the federal government turned the belief that Black people had a negative effect on real estate values into federal policy. Now, according to the federal government, any integrated neighborhood, like the one surrounding Montgall Avenue, was seen as "in transition"— and seen as transitioning the wrong way.

In addition to the FHA, the federal government created the Home Owner's Loan Corporation (HOLC), which was charged with refinancing home mortgages that were at risk of foreclosure. To get a better understanding of the properties it was dealing with, the HOLC began a nationwide study to assess property values and the "credit-worthiness" of the owners. The survey included every street in every major American city, including Kansas City. The first criterion that the HOLC looked at was race. Homes located on all-White streets were seen as the most desirable properties and were awarded the corporation's highest score, a 4. Integrated streets, primarily home to working-class families, were given 2s and 3s. All-Black streets were given a 1, the lowest score.

In 1939, when HOLC surveyed Kansas City, the 2400 block of Montgall Avenue was colored red on the map, indicating that its residents were at the highest risk for foreclosure and their properties were the least valuable. As far as the federal government and the rest of White America were concerned, the men and women of Montgall were some of the least creditworthy people in the country. With J. C. Nichols's blessing, the federal government, through the HOLC, pulled the rug out from under these hardworking Americans.

After these maps were released, banks and other private lending institutions refused to make loans to any redlined area. Because banks wouldn't lend to anyone who wanted to buy a home on Montgall, the block's residents could only sell to those who were able to pay cash. This caused steep declines in the price of their homes, the residents' most valuable asset, and it robbed the parents on Montgall Avenue of their ability to transfer the wealth accumulated through homeownership to the next generation.

Although H. O. Cook and Anna Jones were forced to contend with racist individuals and discriminatory neighborhood associations back in their day, they were able to purchase a new home in a desirable area because they had enough money to do so. A generation later, racism was so woven into the housing and lending industries that a relocation to an area like what Montgall Avenue was in 1904 would have been all but impossible by 1940. This policy was like a virus that

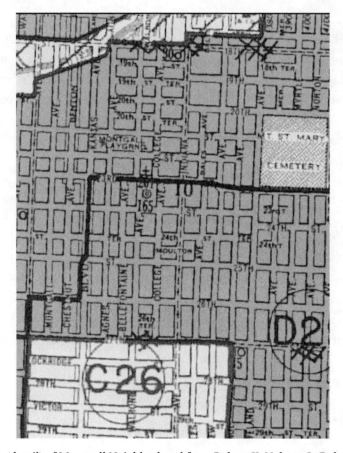

Map (detail) of Montgall Neighborhood from Robert K. Nelson, LaDale Winling, Richard Marciano, N. D. B. Connolly, et al., "Mapping Inequality: Redlining in New Deal America" *American Panorama*, ed. Robert K. Nelson and Edward L. Ayers, accessed January 8, 2023, https://dsl.richmond.edu /panorama/redlining/#loc=15/39.081/-94.556&city=greater-kansas-city-mo.

spread deterioration to the area. Montgall's residents, like most of Black America, became trapped on one side of the increasingly impermeable color line. And just as a virus attacks the most vulnerable patients first, those who were the first to feel the effects of these new policies were Montgall's most vulnerable—its children.

For thirty-five years, the Black children on Montgall had to walk past the all-White Irving Elementary School to attend Wendell

Phillips Elementary. Irving Elementary, at Twenty-Fourth and Prospect, was only one block away from their homes. But Irving was reserved for White children. Gwendolyn Russell, born in 1933, recalled
the year that it all changed, and she no longer had to walk a mile to
school. In 1942, when she was nine years old, she finally got to attend the formerly all-White Irving because enough Black families had
moved into the surrounding area—and enough White families had
moved out. As a way to signal to the larger community that the building was now educating Black students, the Kansas City school district
changed the school's name from Irving to Booker T. Washington Elementary. Russell noticed other changes in the neighborhood as well,
such as the installation of iron bars on the windows of her next-door
neighbors, the Dabneys (2432). "I thought their house looked like a
prison!" she said.[15]

Not long after, she said, Miss Brydie installed bars on her house at
2434.

In 1940, when one of J. C. Nichols's new subdivisions opened in
Fairway, Kansas, many of the all-White buyers were able to qualify
for the federal government's FHA loans, which required less money
down and more time to pay off the balance. Later, loans through the
Veterans Administration became a major source of support for returning veterans, many of whom purchased homes in Nichols's subdivisions. Racial covenants, however, continued to keep those homes
off-limits to Black families.[16]

The federal government's Servicemen's Readjustment Act of 1944,
or the GI Bill, which included guaranteed loans for housing and education for returning veterans, had a limited impact for Black veterans
in Missouri and elsewhere because state institutions like the University of Missouri continued to deny access to Black students.

Arthur and Marguerite Pittman's four children graduated from
Lincoln High School.

Although Arthur Jr. would have preferred to remain in Missouri,
he moved to Iowa, where he earned his degree, eventually fulfilling
his dream of becoming a veterinarian. He married Elizabeth "Betty"

Davis in Omaha and spent his professional career treating the horses at the Ak-Sar-Ben race track. The Pittmans' second son, Keith, also studied veterinary science at Iowa State University. After graduation, he moved to Los Angeles and started his own practice. He married and had a son. The Pittmans' only daughter, Marguerite, attended Fisk University in Nashville, Tennessee, and then transferred to Ohio State, where she met and eventually married Arthur Diggs, a physician who interned at Kansas City's General Hospital #2. Diggs served in the Ninety-Third Division during World War II and returned to Ohio after the war. The couple raised their two children, Arthur Odell and Marguerite Catherine.

Paul Pittman secured a job at the post office and remained on Montgall Avenue and watched as housing and other federal policies began to choke off his neighborhood. He did not put bars on the windows of his home, and he experienced break-ins on several occasions, including an incident in which thieves stole brass sconces and a chandelier from his dining room.

Some scholars have minimized the impact that Nichols's racial bans had on Kansas City's Black community. Using average-income data for Black families, in 1990 historian William Worley concluded that it wasn't any written regulation that kept Blacks away from Nichols's subdivisions but rather the real estate developer's minimum cost requirements, which meant ownership was "out of the question."[17]

Such an assertion only reinforces a narrow view about Kansas City's Black community in the early twentieth century, that is, to be Black meant to be poor. But a closer look at the 2400 block of Montgall Avenue highlights, in particular, how these racial policies disproportionately impacted the Black professional class—the very people who devoted their lives to lifting other members of their race out of poverty.

There is a direct line between the ignorance about the Black community and individual experiences of the residents of Montgall Avenue in the early twentieth century. In 1963 scholar Clifford Naysmith commented about how the Black community was treated by the White press in nineteenth- and twentieth-century Kansas City.

> The newspapers [from the nineteenth century] published more news of all kinds concerning the Negro community than their counterparts of the 1960s. In both periods the social visibility of the Negro population is considerably lower than that of the dominant white community. Negros tend to make news when they make trouble. But the press of the [1870s] did a better job of reporting the constructive and cultural activities of the Negro population than does the contemporary press.[18]

The division between Kansas City's Black and White communities—as well as those throughout the country—continued through the twentieth century with devastating consequences for the people of Montgall Avenue.

PART 3

THE TRANSFORMATION
OF A COMMUNITY
MONTGALL AVENUE
FROM 1941 TO 1998

Residents Reach Pinnacle of Power, 1941
Wartime Abroad, Changes at Home, 1942–1954
The Civil Rights Two-Step, 1955–1967
Surviving Riot, Attacks, and Decline, 1968–1998

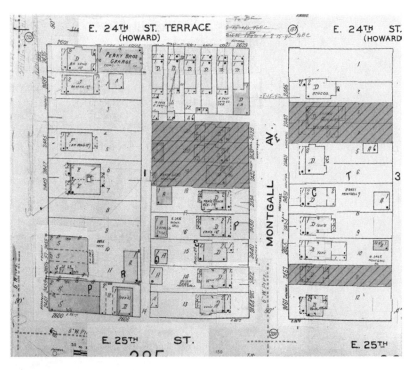

The Transformation of a Community—detail from the *Sanborn Map, Kansas City, Vol. 3, 1909–1950,* p. 360. Shaded areas added to indicate Montgall's homes that are no longer standing. Missouri Valley Special Collections, Kansas City Public Library, Kansas City, Missouri.

The Call *believes that America can best lead the world away from racial and national antagonism when it accords to every man, regardless of race, color, or creed his human and legal rights, hating no man, fearing no man, the* Call *strives to help every man in the firm belief that all are hurt as long as anyone is held back.*

Kansas City Call motto

RESIDENTS REACH PINNACLE OF POWER, 1941

12

At its beginning the 2400 block of Montgall Avenue represented Kansas City's Black power elite, home to intellectual leaders such as Anna Jones, Hugh Oliver, and Myrtle Cook. It was also home to some of the city's most important Black businessmen, such as Chester Franklin and Homer Roberts. In 1941 these powerful individuals, already well known in the city's Black community, were making their voices heard outside of African American circles, and their influence was felt in Kansas City's larger White culture and at every level of government—federal, state, and local.

Montgall residents took up various different causes that year. Chester Franklin was engaged in the battle that he took the most pride in and considered his legacy: opening up defense industry jobs for African Americans. Lucile Bluford was in the third year of her battle against the University of Missouri for a seat in its Graduate School of Journalism. And John Bluford and Fredericka Perry were engaged with Missouri governor Forrest Donnell to oust Kansas City's new chief of police after one of the city's most notorious cases of police brutality, the murder of Harrison Ware.

A Fight for Fairness in Employment

In 1940, as the shadow of war swept over Europe, the United States stepped up production of war goods for its allies overseas. That year the federal government awarded the California-based North American Aviation a contract for a bomber plant in Kansas City. As construction neared completion, *Kansas City Star* readers learned that "Negroes [would] be considered only as janitors and in other similar capacities." North American's president, James Kindelberger, declared that "under no circumstances would Negroes be employed as aircraft workers or mechanics in the plant."[1]

Chester Franklin was eating dinner when he read Kindelberger's words. He became so enraged that he could not finish, and he stormed out.[2] This was a pivotal moment, and Franklin understood that. Over the years he watched African Americans lose ground to Whites when it came to high-paying union jobs. Although some unions accepted Black workers, such as the Musicians' Union and the Organization of Hotel and Restaurant Employees, others, especially those in the American Federation of Labor, forbade Blacks through gentlemen's agreements, traditions, or outright bans.[3] Once Franklin realized that African Americans were not going to receive any of the higher-paying jobs at the bomber plant, he went to work. He contacted members of the NAACP, church pastors, and various club leaders, and in a remarkably short amount of time, he had created a movement. On December 8, 1940, Franklin presided over thirty-five hundred people who had gathered at Municipal Auditorium to discuss African American employment in national defense work. He told the crowd that the "Kindelberger attitude [was] at cross purposes with the democracy [the country was] seeking to defend" and that they should stand together and fight until this injustice was resolved.[4]

In New York City another Black leader, A. Philip Randolph, had the same concerns. Years before, Randolph had organized the Pullman porters into a powerful union, and as the war began to draw the United States in, he, like Chester Franklin, was determined to confront the federal government about defense industry contracts.

Randolph called for a demonstration in Washington to draw attention to unfair labor practices, and he set the date for July 1, 1941. He anticipated ten thousand demonstrators, but once Franklin and others became part of the protest, Randolph's estimate was increased to a hundred thousand. When President Franklin D. Roosevelt heard about the planned march, he agreed to meet with the Black leaders. Randolph, Franklin, and others traveled to DC and told the president that the only way they would call off the march was if concrete action was taken.

On June 25, 1941, Roosevelt issued Executive Order 8802, which declared that there would be no discrimination in the defense industries "because of race, creed, color, or national origin." Only companies that agreed to follow these federal antidiscrimination policies would be awarded government contracts. In addition, the president set up the Fair Employment Practices Committee to investigate discrimination complaints.[5]

Roosevelt's response to Black leaders was a bold move for the executive branch. By choosing to reach past Congress, which had an abysmal record on civil rights, he provided future presidents a path toward racial justice. It was an approach that other chief executives would return to in the decades to come. Roosevelt's order was a triumph for Black America not only because it provided opportunities but also because the minority community had been heard. For a seasoned newspaper editor like Chester Franklin, whose primary audience was Black readers, the victory was empowering.

But the sixty-one-year-old could not rest on his laurels for long. Not long after Roosevelt signed his historic order, another controversy ignited Kansas City's Black community.

Speaking Out against Police Brutality

Police brutality was nothing new in Kansas City. Reports of such treatment date back to at least 1882, when a police officer shot and killed an innocent Black man. That year, when officers refused to investigate and the grand jury refused to indict the shooter, Black leaders created the Negro Protective League, which offered a forum for victims to air their grievances before city officials. (This reform was led by W. W. Yates, husband of Anna Jones's friend Josephine Silone Yates.)[6]

Black victims of police brutality learned that they could find a sympathetic ear at the *Call*, and Lucile Bluford remembered listening to many of these battered victims when they stopped by the newsroom to share their stories while nursing their bruised limbs. Staff at the *Call* noticed a spike in the number of complaints in 1939 after the city hired a new chief of police, Georgia native Lear Reed.[7] (Reed was the chief when Piney Brown was arrested in November 1939 after police raided the Autumn Leaf Club.)

Reed arrived in Kansas City determined to bring order to the region in the post-Pendergast years, and he started by focusing on the clubs that had been allowed to flourish under the Democratic boss. But the police department's assault did not stop there, and Kansas City's Black professional class also endured the change in policing. Carl Johnson, Kansas City's NAACP chapter president, tracked the deteriorating relations between Reed's department and the Black community months before the situation reached its peak. "Police brutality and disrespect for the rights of Negroes in particular is at its worst in the history of Kansas City," he wrote to the *Kansas City Star*'s editorial board. In the letter he told of Black teachers who were stopped and ticketed for no reason. He went on to describe "Negro professional men and others whose wives have been fairer in color than others have been stopped on the streets within the Negro districts and questioned as to the identity of their wives or company and grossly insulted if they resented it."[8]

When Kansas City hosted physicians from Michigan, the Black community reached out to Reed and requested the police department's cooperation and support to make the doctors' stay "a pleasant one." Despite the request, "Two Negro physicians from Michigan and their fair skinned wives were insulted at 18th and the Paseo and the officers threatened to knock their teeth down their throats because they resented the approach made by the officers in an effort to assistain [sic] whether their wives are white or colored."⁹ In addition, officers began initiating raids on the clubs, sometimes two or three in the same evening. And any Black man who encountered an officer, whether he was a suspect or a witness, should expect trouble. The problems between the police and the Black community came to a head on a moonless night in July 1941.¹⁰

On Saturday, July 26, Harrison Ware, forty-nine, was with his friends at the Autumn Leaf Club, a place with ties to two former Montgall residents: Piney Brown and Homer Roberts.¹¹ The club had been targeted by Reed's officers so often that its owner, Felix Payne, got a restraining order to stop the police from the ongoing harassment. The order was in place for several months until it was lifted by another, less sympathetic judge. Shortly before midnight, Officers Charles LeBaugh and Dewey Ellis stormed the club, brandishing their pistols and shouting, "Get back to the wall! All of you, get back to the wall!" The men, Ware included, obeyed and took seats along the walls. LeBaugh went from one man to another shouting, "Who feels lucky tonight? Who thinks he can win?" When he got to Ware, for whatever reason, he announced that he had found "the gamekeeper." LeBaugh grabbed Ware by his shirt collar, pulled him to his feet, and struck him, knocking him across the room. The officer walked over, picked him up again, and struck him a second time. Ware landed against the hall's pool table and picked up a pool ball, which he used to hit LeBaugh. The two became entangled in a fight, and LeBaugh shouted to his partner, "Kill the Black son of a . . ." When LeBaugh freed himself, Officer Ellis shot Ware in the groin. Ware staggered, found another pool ball, and threw it toward Ellis as LeBaugh shot him. After Ware fell, LeBaugh walked over to him, leveled his pistol, and shouted more expletives. Ellis told his partner to cool down, that he had done enough. But LeBaugh was not done: he kicked the dying man and then asked whether anyone else in the room "wanted some of it."

Clifford Warren (who would move to 2457 Montgall) arrived at the Autumn Leaf to calm the distraught crowd. Warren and his partner, Leon Jordan, were two of the Black officers who remained on the Kansas City police force during Reed's tenure, and they not only helped maintain order but also gathered witnesses to take to headquarters. Once the witnesses arrived at the station, however, they learned that the White officers had no intention of accurately recording their accounts. One witness was told he was lying, and others were ignored altogether. Instead, LeBaugh's and Ellis's colleagues fabricated their own version of events and wrote affidavits suggesting that Ware had behaved violently and resisted arrest. If the witnesses didn't sign the fabricated statements, they were threatened with death.[12]

After the incident, Chief Reed reported to the board of police that the Autumn Leaf Club had been a constant source of trouble. He reported that he had looked into the shooting and concluded that his officers were not to blame for the incident and that they were forced into action "by a man viciously resisting arrest."[13]

Kansas City's larger Black community—including many residents from Montgall Avenue—responded quickly and forcefully. Harrison Ware's murder was the *Call*'s lead story on August 1, 1941, under the headline "Policemen Shoot, Then Kick a Dying Man." A huge, graphic photograph showed Ware's body, lying face down so that readers could see the bullet holes in his back.

The *Call* conducted its own investigation and interviewed nearly a dozen men at the club that night. All told a remarkably similar story, one in which Ware was attacked and acted in self-defense.[14] A few days later, more than a thousand men and women attended Ware's funeral. The hearse, which passed police headquarters on its way to Lincoln Cemetery, had a huge red-lettered sign that read "Victim of Un-Americanism of Dewey Ellis and Charles LeBaugh."[15]

Carl Johnson, president of the local NAACP chapter, asked for a special prosecutor and a grand jury investigation. He wrote to the police board and asked that Officers Ellis and LeBaugh be dismissed immediately, and he organized a mass meeting for August 4 at Jamison Temple at 1815 Paseo. More than two thousand people showed up to hear him and Montgall Avenue resident Fredericka Perry speak.[16] Under Johnson and Perry's leadership, the crowd developed a list of

Harrison Ware. *Kansas City Call*, August 1, 1941, Miscellaneous Series, 7433, Forrest C. Donnell Gubernatorial Papers (C0194), State Historical Society of Missouri Research Center–Columbia.

demands, which included the firing and prosecution of Officers Ellis and LeBaugh. They also requested that a special committee on police brutality be formed within the chapter's NAACP organization.

Chester Franklin wrote to Governor Forrest Donnell to inform him of the situation brewing in Kansas City's Black community—not only Harrison Ware's death but also the "Gestapo"-like police practices that Reed had brought to Kansas City. On receiving the letter, the governor invited Franklin for a meeting to discuss the situation.[17]

John Bluford and Fredericka Perry were part of a delegation that traveled to Jefferson City to meet with the governor, and they relayed stories about the brutality that Kansas City's African American community had to endure.[18] The leaders told the governor about James Williams, who was beaten so badly while in custody that he committed suicide rather than endure more torture. Williams's undertaker, T. B. Watkins, reported that bruises covered his entire body.

The delegates told Donnell about James Partee, who was at home with his wife when police officers forced their way into his residence and struck him across the face, knocked him to the floor, and kicked

Montgall residents meeting with Governor Donnell. *Kansas City Call*, August 8, 1941, Miscellaneous Series, 7433, Forrest C. Donnell Papers (C0194), State Historical Society of Missouri Research Center–Columbia.

him in the ribs before dragging him outside while yelling racial epithets at him.

They told him about Walter Davis who, on May 8, 1940, was assaulted by police at Eighteenth and Woodland and was left lying in an alley south of Eighteenth Street. Twelve days later, on May 20, Marcellus Ford, who had no criminal record, was kicked in the back and pushed down the steps after police showed up at his home in response to a reported domestic dispute.

The group piled story on top of story: police who forced a landlady and some of the male residents of a boardinghouse to disrobe and be photographed either nude or semi-nude as a way to build "evidence" in a supposed disorderly house case; Black teenagers who were driven from their own neighborhood at Twenty-Second and Prospect (one block east of Montgall) because it was in an area where White youths liked to socialize; an incident in which police pushed and hurled racial epithets at women and children at the annual Halloween parade at Eighteenth and Vine.

In addition to the brutal attacks, the harassment, and the illegal searches, Franklin, Bluford, and Perry told the governor about Black officers who had been let go from the department. When Reed took over as chief, there were thirty-two Black men on the force; when Ware was murdered, there were fewer than ten. After the meeting, Governor Donnell demanded answers, from both Reed and the Board of Police Commissioners, and he asked for an investigation.[19]

Although the Montgall delegates found the governor sympathetic, others were less compassionate: "The negroes of this community have not been mistreated in any way," wrote Richard Righter, partner from the prominent law firm of Lathrop, Crane, Reynolds, Sawyer, and Mersereau.[20] Another Kansas Citian, Eldridge King, believed that the governor had been persuaded by a "few negro thugs."[21] Chief Reed responded to the governor and assured him that there had been no abuse of power. "One of the first instructions I gave as Chief of Police was that the law in Kansas City would be applied equally and impartially to all." As the investigation continued, Reed remained steadfast and defended his officers. "Police get rough only with roughnecks," he declared.[22]

The police commissioners echoed Chief Reed's beliefs. "The evidence so far does not justify suspension of the men," concluded board president and prominent local attorney Edgar Shook.[23] In its lengthy (forty-four pages), unfocused, and often dismissive report, the commissioners criticized the *Call* for what it called one-sided reporting. They then addressed the governor's concerns, case by case, beginning with the apparent suicide of James Williams, who suffered a skull fracture while in police custody. The board acknowledged that the police had him in custody on June 9, 1941, where he was questioned by officers about the death of another man. While conceding that Williams had "received a sharp blow," the commissioners maintained that officers struck him only after he reached for a gun, an allegation they believed even though Williams was handcuffed at the time. If the officers got a little rough with Williams, the commissioners said, it was justified, as the evidence against him in the murder case "was very strong."

When it came to the Halloween parade, the board repeatedly described the crowd of mothers and children as "unruly" and "hard to handle." They concluded that the officers' reactions were appropriate.

As for unlawful searches of Black men around Eighteenth and Vine, the commissioners contended that police officers' actions were actually preventing homicides. They told the governor that

> a certain type of Negro ha[d] gotten into the habit of drinking a cheap grade of wine, which sometimes causes the drinker to lose all self-control when so intoxicated.... Since the best way to reduce crime is to prevent its commission, and, since statistics have shown that the majority of assaults and killings have been done by drunken Negroes in possession of knives, we have come to the conclusion that this policy of disarming Negroes is the only possible solution.

The Board of Police Commissioners contended that it was acceptable (and perhaps commendable) for Kansas City police officers to treat African Americans differently from White Americans because it was not the consumption of alcohol by itself that led to unlawful behavior; rather, alcohol combined with Blackness made them dangerous.

When the board finally got to the case that initiated the investigation, the death of Harrison Ware, they started with a long description of the Autumn Leaf Club, calling it the "most notorious gambling place in Kansas City." They even referenced the restraining order against police harassment, not as evidence of any harassment but rather as proof of the police claim that it was an unruly place. The board conceded that the officers may have exhibited overly aggressive behaviors, but they said it was understandable, given the population:

> It would be surprising if in the routine assignment of officers, some officer or officers assigned to duty in the colored districts may not have been temperamentally suited to administer the law amongst negro people. As the Board has become apprised of isolated instances of unsuitability of an officer for service amongst negroes, it has endeavored to adjust the assignments so as to relieve any such possible source of friction.

The board's report also reflected a new fear about people of color, an attitude that festered during World War II and found fertile ground after the war ended: that communist ideals had infiltrated Kansas

City's African American community. The only proof that the board offered to support this claim was a May 20, 1941, speech before the Shawnee Mission Cooperative Club in which Thomas Kearney, superintendent of "our Technical and Record Division," informed his audience that there were "10,000 communists in Jackson County, 6,000 of whom were Negroes." In a strategy that US senator Joe McCarthy would adopt ten years later, Kearney provided no evidence for his assertion, only his word.

The beliefs about inherent differences between White and Black Americans, that Black people were not as bright or capable and that they were more criminally inclined by nature, were not limited to the police board. Governor Donnell also heard from others who shared the commissioners' attitudes and conclusions. "The percentage of crimes committed by negroes is out of proportion to the percentage of negroes in our population," wrote a citizen named John Fristoe. "Negroes contribute little relatively in taxes yet are a heavy burden in the benefits they receive from taxation."[24] The fact that Reed had let a number of Black officers go since he took charge did not bother Fristoe in the least. "They certainly deserve no more places on the police force, and I can't believe that on the whole [they] will make as good officers as white men since the mentality and standards of their race as a whole is undoubtedly lower." Calling himself a friend of the "Negro" and a "neutral observer of human nature and conduct," James B. Robinson, another concerned citizen, declared that "there is an element of negroes in K.C. which must be kept under some controll [sic]."[25]

While White Kansas Citians sent these kinds of messages, Black groups such as the Missouri State Association of Negro Teachers and the national NAACP organization applauded the governor for taking the complaints seriously and investigating the allegations.[26] Predictably, the newspaper coverage reflected the division between Kansas City's Black and White communities. As the story continued on the front pages of the *Call*, a publication that the police commissioners in their report called "irrelevant and inaccurate," most of the White press sided with Chief Reed. On August 29, 1941, the *Kansas City*

Journal ran a story titled "Chief Gives Ultimatum to Negro Belt" in which it quoted Reed, who had told his subordinates that he would resign if he could not enforce the law. Donnell kept up the pressure, and Reed, unable to withstand the ongoing scrutiny, ultimately resigned from the force. On his departure, Reed told his troops to stay strong.

> I know you are men of guts to have stayed in the department as long as you did prior to July 11, 1939 [the date he came to the department]. You must have been waiting for the light to come. It came.... No class is criticized as frequently, as unjustly and as unfairly as policemen. There always is an element against you. Jesus didn't please everybody, so I know a policeman can't.[27]

Predictably, the chief's resignation was applauded in one community and denounced in the other.

On September 4, 1941, S. B. Gregg of the Morrison Gregg Mitchell Grain Company wrote to Governor Donnell:

> I just want you to know that the members of this firm and the employees are mighty sorry to lose Chief Reed. He has been the best Chief of Police we have had in this town since I can remember, and I have been here about 50 years. Of course, the crooks in town, and there are a lot of them, don't want a good man that they can't handle, and Chief Reed was that type of man.[28]

Kansas Citian George B. Tracey echoed Gregg's sentiments: "Reed has taken the knife and razor away from the Negro. He has taken the Gun and dope away from the north end Italian or Dago as he is commonly known.... If Chief Reed does no more, he should have earned the gratitude of the entire city."[29]

Harrison Ware's killing was a turning point in Kansas City history—an event that brought police brutality to the attention of the White community, at least for a while. The year 1941 can be seen as a pinnacle for Montgall Avenue. Its past and current residents helped accomplish two remarkable feats: the resignation of Chief Lear Reed and the passage of Executive Order 8802. As for Lucile Bluford, the other Montgall resident who was trying to break down barriers in 1941, her efforts were not as fruitful. After losing yet another battle to enter the University of Missouri, she wrote a piece for the *Call* that highlighted the strategy utilized by the university. Bluford described the attorney hired by MU, Kansas Citian William Hogsett, as saying, "'We speak Anglo-Saxon,' he bellowed in his closing argument. 'We understand each other. If this colored girl wants to study journalism let her go to Kansas.'"[30]

The University of Missouri had continually argued—and the judge and jury agreed—that Bluford was not a serious student. Instead, she was merely a tool being used by the NAACP, a conclusion they reached because the NAACP was paying her defense. Bluford's response, as she articulated in the *Call*, was that

> Hogsett took the only course open to him—a direct plea to the jury to act as white men and put in her place a Negro who dared sue the state for her rights as a Missouri citizen. Of course the NAACP supported my case and provided me with counsel. How else could I have carried it forward? A case like mine costs no less than $3000. Where in the world would I on my small salary get $3000 or even $1000 to carry a case to court.

Rather than calling the jury to treat Bluford as a full-fledged American, Hogsett asked the jurors to identify with their Whiteness and their Anglo-Saxon origins. In doing this he reinforced the notion that to be American was to be White. And Lucile Bluford, because she was inferior to the White students who attended MU, should not have access to the professors and the materials provided there. In making his case, MU's attorney managed to short-circuit the judge and the jurors' rational thought processes by denying a tax-paying citizen her right to attend a tax-funded institution. And once again, justice was denied to Lucile Bluford.

Montgall Avenue had always been home to powerful leaders, but before 1941 their power was primarily limited to the Black community through Lincoln High School and the other institutions they built and maintained. In 1941 that influence extended into White

America, the White police chief in Kansas City and the White industrialists who sought federal defense contracts. But Montgall leaders' strength would not last. At the same time that these leaders achieved the peak of their political influence, the Home Owners Loan Corporation released its ranking of Kansas City's streets. The map's red designation on the 2400 block of Montgall Avenue sealed the fate of every resident who chose to stay on the block, including Paul Pittman, Gwendolyn Calderon, and Lucile Bluford. In 1941 Montgall's residents witnessed significant victories against racism, but new forms of discrimination, particularly those in the real estate, banking, and financial sectors, were laying the foundation of what came next for this Kansas City street.

To a great majority of white Americans, the Negro
problem has distinctly negative connotations. It suggests
something difficult to settle and equally difficult to leave
alone. It is embarrassing. It makes for moral uneasiness.
The very presence of the Negro in America, his fate in this
country through slavery, Civil War and Reconstruction; his
recent career and his present status; his accommodation;
his protest and his aspiration; in fact, his entire biological,
historical and social existence as a participant American
represent to the ordinary white man in the North as
well as in the South an anomaly in the very structure of
American society. To many, this takes on the proportion of
a menace—biological, economic, social, cultural, and, at
times, political. This anxiety may be mingled with a feeling
of individual and collective guilt. A few see the problem as
a challenge to statesmanship. To all it is trouble.

Swedish sociologist Gunnar Myrdal, *An American*
Dilemma: The Negro Problem and Modern
Democracy, 1944

13

In 1942 Lucile Bluford covered two stories for the *Call*. One
was of local interest, the other of national importance,
and both were of historical significance. The first story
involved one of the most famous Americans of the time,
singer Paul Robeson, and it sparked a conversation about
Black Americans' struggle for access to public spaces.
The second story centered on a marginalized Black man,
Cleo Wright, the first man lynched in the United States
after the attack on Pearl Harbor. Wright's killing ignited
a debate about the very meaning of America at a time
the country was fighting tyrannical governments abroad
while denying very basic rights to a significant portion of
its citizens.

On February 17, 1942, Robeson performed at Kansas
City's Municipal Auditorium under the assumption that
the facility would not be segregated. Halfway through
his performance, he glanced up at the balcony, where, it
looked to him, as "if the tickets had been divided in half
with those on the east side of the auditorium being sold
to Negroes and those on the west side to whites."[1] He left
the stage and refused to return, and it was only after a lot
of persuasion that he agreed to continue. When he did,
he began by saying that he had not intended, nor did he
even like, making speeches. He told the crowd that he had
made it a lifelong practice to refuse to sing in segregated

arenas and that he had come to Kansas City with the guarantee that there would be no segregation in the seating. He wanted the audience to know that he was performing under protest.

Lucile Bluford, or rather, "Louis Blue," an alternate identity she adopted when she was unhappy with her prose or when an article was especially political,[2] reported that most people in the stunned crowd greeted his remarks enthusiastically. However, some spectators close to the stage were so offended that they walked out. The singer responded with a song, "Jim Crow." Bluford printed its lyrics alongside the story as they "played significantly upon the situation in the concert hall."[3]

> If we believe in liberty
> Put an end to slavery
> Put an end to slavery—
> Of Jim Crow.

Robeson's protest occurred just after the first lynching the state had seen in ten years, a crime that focused the nation's attention on the Show-Me State.

Early Sunday morning, January 25, 1942, in Sikeston, Missouri, a small town in the southeastern corner of the state, a Black man named Cleo Wright broke into the home of Grace Sturgeon. He spat on her and cut her abdomen before running off. The wounds were not life-threatening, and Sturgeon survived. Shortly after the attack, the town marshal encountered the blood-stained Wright walking down the road. Wright pulled a knife, and after stabbing the officer he was shot four times.[4]

Wright was taken to a hospital where a doctor patched him up as best he could, but because the facility was for Whites only, police were told that he could not stay. He was transported to Sikeston's jail, where a crowd had begun to form. As Wright lay bleeding in his cell, the mob outside grew until it developed into a united force, determined to take action. Someone in the crowd brought a rope and a truck, while others broke into the jail, grabbed Wright, and tied him to the truck's bumper. They dragged him to a Black church, doused him with gasoline, and set him on fire as a shocked congregation stood by and watched. His charred corpse was then dragged through the Black neighborhoods of Sikeston.

Lucile Bluford traveled to the small town to cover the story. Although a segment of Sikeston's Black community believed that Wright and Sturgeon were lovers and her wounds were, in part, self-inflicted,[5] Bluford focused on an aspect that was not in dispute: that the lynching of Cleo Wright, like every other lynching in American history, represented a breakdown of law and order. Bluford wrote that law enforcement officers had known what was being planned and did nothing to stop it. (Her coverage focused on a Missouri Highway Patrol officer who had gone through Sikeston cautioning people to stay home, warning them that something was going to happen.)[6] Bluford was part of an effort that brought attention to this story, and as it turned out, a significant part of the country's population was ready to hear it.

Wright's lynching struck a chord with America's majority population, because it called into question what kind of country the United States was: the nation had just declared war against totalitarian regimes abroad but was denying fundamental democratic rights to a portion of its population at home. And unlike earlier cases of lynching, the US Justice Department responded. On February 10, 1942, US attorney general Francis Biddle wrote to Governor Donnell to announce that the FBI would cooperate with state investigators.[7] It was the first time the federal government prioritized the lynching of a Black man, a practice that continued throughout the Civil Rights era.

Cleo Wright's murder, which was the last recorded lynching in Missouri history, occurred as Black Americans volunteered to fight against totalitarianism. These enlistees included many of those who lived on Montgall Avenue: Manuel Calderon (2434) was a member of the 758th Tank Battalion, the first all–African American tank unit in the war, and fought in North Africa and Italy; Christine MacDonald, the young woman taken in by Carolyn Brydie after her parents died, worked as a nurse in the Army Corps; Arthur and Marguerite Pittman's son-in-law, Arthur Diggs, served in the all-Black Ninety-Third

Division; and former Montgall resident Chester Franklin organized the Brown Bomber campaign, which raised over $285,000 in war bonds. As the war ground on, White leaders began to awaken to some of the injustices confronting African Americans.

In 1944 the Rev. Claude Herman Heithaus, a Jesuit priest at St. Louis University, began his morning worship service: "It is a surprising and rather bewildering fact that in what concerns justice for the Negro, the Mohammedans and the atheists are more Christ-like than many Christians," he said in his quiet, penetrating voice. "The followers of Mohammed and of Lenin make no distinction of color. But to some followers of Christ, the color of a man's skin makes all the difference in the world."[8]

The five hundred young people, most of whom were students, quietly absorbed his message. "St. Louis University admits Protestants and Jews, Mormons and Mohammedans, Buddhists and Brahmins, pagans and atheists, without even looking at the color of their complexions," the priest continued. "Do you want us to slam the doors in the faces of Catholics, because their complexion happens to be brown or Black?" By the end of Heithaus's sermon, the congregation was praying for all the wrongs the White community had perpetrated on Black America. "We are firmly resolved never again to have any part in them, and to do everything in our power to prevent them. Amen." That summer, St. Louis University, the first university in any of the fourteen former slaveholding states to admit Black students to its state universities, enrolled five African American students.

Around this time, the Swedish economist Gunnar Myrdal published his seminal book *An American Dilemma: The Negro Problem and Modern Democracy*, which focused on the lives of former slaves who lived in a country that prided itself on the principle that all men are created equal yet were forced to attend different schools and live in different neighborhoods. Myrdal wrote that it wasn't a "Negro Problem" but rather a "White Problem," namely, prejudice, that kept Black people in a vicious cycle of poverty.[9] Whites oppressed Blacks, which led to poor performance, and this performance was the justification Whites used to continue the different treatment between the two races.

When the *Kansas City Star* addressed the "Negro problem" in Missouri's university system in 1944, it did not appeal to its readers' consciences or to American ideals. Rather, it argued that the state's flagship educational institution, the University of Missouri, "must take down the bars and make the best of what it considers a bad situation" for, as the newspaper predicted, "there will be little or no opposition from the student body or from the general public, and no more attention will be paid to a Negro on the campus than is now paid to a Negro in a bus or railroad coach."[10]

The pragmatic approach to integration reflected the newspaper's more conservative audience. *Star* readers were not the idealistic students that the Reverend Heithaus spoke to, nor were they the left-leaning academic types for whom Myrdal was writing. Rather, they represented a broad spectrum of the population: businessmen, factory workers, and housewives, some of whom, in a time of war, may have been asking themselves very basic questions about the source of America's strength and what the country stood for.

Throughout the war, the *Call* highlighted what the heroic Black soldiers on the front lines contributed. It also pointed out hypocrisy. While earlier atrocities in the Pacific, such as the Bataan Death March, fit the era's zeitgeist of seeing evil motives in the Japanese oppressors, the discovery of the Third Reich's cruelties proved more difficult to absorb. Chester Franklin wrote that when news of death marches emerged from the Pacific, "American opinion ascribed their cruelty to their race, saying no better was to be expected," but stories of atrocities committed by Germany, "leaders in culture, business, and science," brought out a different response, one in which race was never mentioned.[11]

Of all the changes wrought by World War II, one of the more significant was the dismantling of overtly racist language and images in academia and popular literature. While early twentieth-century scholarship was dominated by those who saw moral inferiority and intellectual limitations in the supposed "coarse" Negro brain, postwar social scientists saw the reality of Black life in America through a different and more nuanced lens. This evolution in attitude went hand in hand with other changes in the portrayal of African Americans.

In 1942 a group of Black and White teachers and librarians wrote a series of letters to *Publishers Weekly* about the representation of African Americans in various children's books, which had used gross caricatures and illiterate dialogue for Black characters. Their discussion began a sea change in the world of publishing. By 1945 the editors of *Roget's Thesaurus* agreed to omit the most offensive terms for people of color, including "Blackamoor," "n—," "darky," and "sloe," after receiving a complaint from the NAACP. Editors responded that they were "determined not to be a party to the spread of prejudice and racist doctrine by means of the printed word."[12]

In 1946 President Harry Truman formed his Committee on Civil Rights, a group charged with highlighting injustice, especially as it targeted African Americans. Truman understood that preserving individual liberties was a function of every level of government, and when local authorities failed in that duty, the federal government needed to act. Truman's timing could have been intentional, a preemptive measure to send a message about the federal government's commitment to Black veterans, given the treatment that returning Black soldiers received after World War I.[13]

Lucile Bluford was hopeful about the changes, especially the attention that the White press was giving to civil rights. She believed that the reporting on the Truman Commission was the first time that major (White) newspapers had placed the civil rights issue on their front pages. The country was changing, and African Americans started to feel as if they could—and should—expect to be treated in ways that White people took for granted.[14]

But this progress for Black America masked another, more substantive transformation in society, a change that would propel millions of White Americans into middle-class status and provide tools for them to accumulate wealth for future generations, while leaving Black Americans behind. And nowhere would this be more apparent than for the men and women on Montgall, where the difference between White and Black grew starker in the postwar years.

In Kansas City, African Americans could still not attend the University of Missouri, nor could they move into many of the new housing developments built by J. C. Nichols, where the homes would only increase in value in the decades to come. Instead, Black Kansas Citians were locked into areas of the city that had been redlined by the federal government and shut out by banks. African Americans were limited to streets like the 2400 block of Montgall, which was just beginning to experience the longer-term effects of government housing policies.

In 1945 this block of Montgall still represented the pinnacle of Black achievement, and the children who grew up there were expected to succeed—and they did. A closer look at the street, however, shows some disturbing trends. First, while all sixteen homes were still standing and occupied, more than half of them were owned by people over sixty. Also, among the young people who had grown up on the block and who internalized the ethos of hard work, many ultimately found their success in other cities. A snapshot of the street in 1945 still shows a vital, albeit aging, community. On the street's northeastern corner, one would have found George and Maude Gamble. They had lived at 2445 Montgall for more than two decades, since 1923, when they built their house. In 1946 George retired from his fifty-year career as a brakeman for the Rock Island Railroad. Unlike neighbors who were active in civic and social affairs, the Gambles maintained a relatively low profile, for neither of them appeared on any of the lists as donors or participants in social functions. George and Maude Gamble, however, were impressive in their own way.

"Throughout his 51 years of railroading, Mr. Gamble had a record that few workers in any field can equal. Not only did he earn recognition through long service, but he gave outstanding performance on the job," reported the *Call*.[15] "He was never once reprimanded or 'called on the carpet.'" What the newspaper did not say explicitly, but what made Gamble's career particularly noteworthy, is that he maintained the same position—as a railroad brakeman—even as this position gained in status.

Like every industry, the railroad was segmented racially. Conductor and engineer positions—those with the most prestige—were held by Whites, and more dangerous positions, such as firemen and brakemen, were filled by Blacks.[16] When Gamble joined the railroad, his job as brakeman was one of the most dangerous positions because he had to jump from car to car to manually apply the brakes. As a brakeman he was also responsible for coupling and uncoupling cars, a task that could have easily crushed him if he did not get out of the way before the railroad cars came together. Two innovations improved Gamble's safety on the job significantly: air brakes and automatic couplings. Once the federal government began to require these safety features, Gamble's position became more desirable—and more difficult for him to retain. Although we do not know the specifics about Gamble's life, the *Call* observed that he was one of the few Black brakemen left working for the railroad. The newspaper also noted that when he retired, his job went to a White man because the union, which controlled the job, did not admit Black people.[17]

Just south of the Gambles, at Chester and Ada Franklin's former house (2447), lived Sydney Johnson and his wife, Mayme. Sydney owned Highland Pharmacy at Twelfth and Highland, and Mayme was a nurse. Like the Gambles, the Johnsons never had children.[18] Arthur and Marguerite Pittman were next, at 2449, and by 1945 only one of the couple's four children remained in Kansas City, and on Montgall Avenue—the youngest, Paul, who was just starting his career at the post office. The Pittmans' next-door neighbor, physician John Edward Perry (2451), had spent some time with his son in Houston after Fredericka's untimely death in 1943, but he returned to Montgall with a new wife and his grandson, John Edward Perry II. The young Perry came to Kansas City to attend a Catholic high school, Rockhurst, where he and another student were the Jesuit school's first Black graduates in 1953.[19]

Mary Greer, a teacher, lived in Homer Roberts's former home at 2453, and longtime Montgall residents Charles and Willie Mae Greenstreet were next to her at 2455. Like many of their neighbors, the Greenstreets originally lived with Charles and Frances Jackson (2432) while their home was under construction, and they moved across the street on the house's completion in 1908. Charles worked on the Santa Fe Railroad until his retirement in 1940. In addition, he

Clifford Warren. Kansas City Police Historical Society.

and his wife were partners in Flynn and Greenstreet, one of the few funeral homes in Kansas City that catered to African Americans.[20]

Next to the Greenstreets, in Piney Brown's former home, was the Warren family (2457). Clifford Warren was a Kansas City native. After graduating from Lincoln High School, he went to work at a drugstore, but he joined the police department in 1939 after his store experienced several break-ins. Warren understood that as a Black police officer, he was in a difficult position, especially the role he had in his early days in the department when he had to patrol the Country Club district. When he retired in 1969, he remembered the racial epithets he received while issuing speeding tickets to White Kansas Citians.[21]

Warren, one of the few African Americans to serve under Chief Lear Reed, was on the scene in July 1941 at the Autumn Leaf Club when his White colleagues shot Harrison Ware, and he helped calm the witnesses after the murder. Warren had a stellar record with the KCPD, including a citation he received for the rescue of two children from a burning house. He was promoted to detective, and he and his partner, Leon Jordan, became an effective team, receiving commendations for feats such as the capture of someone suspected of murdering an estate caretaker and who had become the subject of a statewide search.[22]

Warren, like most of his neighbors, was active in his community. He started a club for youths in a run-down dance hall at Twenty-Second and Vine Streets. In addition, he served as a trustee of Second Baptist Church, a member of the advisory board for the Urban League, a board member of the Paseo YMCA, and board member for the Niles Home for Orphaned Children. Of particular note was Warren's interest in mental health, and he served on the board of directors for the Kansas City Association of Mental Health.[23] As a patrolman for the city's Black neighborhoods, Warren had ample opportunity to witness those who struggled on the lowest rung of the economic ladder, a population whose struggle with mental health has been well documented. Seeing the stressors felt by the poor, such as unemployment and the lack of affordable housing, it could be that Warren understood the correlation between poverty and mental health decades before the country's White medical community would see the connection.[24]

Warren's longtime partner, Leon Jordan, left Kansas City for several years to lead a police unit in Liberia, but Warren remained at the Kansas City Police Department. In October 1954 he was named commander of an all-Black unit assembled to combat a crime wave in the African American community and offered a way for Black officers to work their way up the ranks of the department.[25] The unit dissolved in 1957, when Warren became special assistant to Kansas City police chief Bernard Brannon. In this role he served as the public face for the chief with the greater community as well as the liaison between the chief and other department heads.

Warren lived on Montgall Avenue with his wife, Zelda, and the couple's son, Errol. Warren wanted to protect his son from the seamier side of life, so he rarely allowed him to accompany him on calls, but when Errol was fifteen, he begged his father to accompany him one night. Errol had heard about trouble in a nearby neighborhood, where a Black captain on the Kansas City Fire Department purchased a home in the previously all-White area of Vineyard Gardens. Before heading out, Warren cautioned his son that what he would see was not typical human behavior because the "the Devil was at work."[26]

"Those images are seared into my brain.... You would have thought we lived in Selma," Errol said, referring to the Alabama city known for racial violence. "We pulled up to the area and were escorted through the crowd by other police officers. It was all lit up—every house except the fire captain's, which was totally dark, and the neighbors were lining the streets yelling vulgarities at the highest level. There were signs with 'Monkey Face' on them," he said, shaking his head. "It was terrible."

Errol Warren never experienced that kind of discomfort growing up on Montgall, a street where he spent hours riding his tricycle up and down the sidewalks and playing with the Russells, who lived next door. The Russell family lived in the home on the southeastern corner of the block, at 2461, and although they were longtime residents of the street, they were relatively new homeowners. Principal Cook had hired Joshua Russell to teach auto mechanics in 1928, and for twelve years he and his growing family lived with Carolyn Brydie, where four of the couple's five children were born. When the home at the northeastern corner of Montgall, 2461, became available in 1941, Russell and his family moved across the street, except for their oldest daughter, Gwendolyn, who remained with her godmother, "Miss Brydie."[27]

Joshua and Josie (Todd) Russell were another one of the street's power couples, two hardworking individuals who nurtured their children and were integral members of the Montgall community for five decades. Josie Russell grew up in Winfield, Kansas, and traveled extensively as a child. She was educated at Wilberforce in Ohio and Southwestern College in Winfield. After earning her degree from

Southwestern, she accepted a position at Kansas Vocational School in Topeka, where she taught typing and shorthand. It was also where she met her future husband, Joshua, and they married on June 22, 1927.[28] Their youngest child, Frank Edward Russell, was born on October 31, 1944, after the family's move to the east side of the street.

George Gamble, Charles Greenstreet, and Russell were all known for their exceptional gardening skills. Gamble tended the empty lot on the north side of his home and turned it into the "showplace of the neighborhood." Russell had more than a hundred rose bushes in his backyard, and between these two anchors was Charles Greenstreet, who, according to the *Call*, "actively took care of his lawn and garden."[29]

The street had an ethereal quality as giant elms towered over the homes, providing a cathedral-like canopy that created lacy shadows when the sun was out. That aura was enhanced by Russell, who whitewashed the tree trunks every summer to keep pests away (a trick he learned as a youngster growing up in Alabama). In the mid-1940s the 2400 block of Montgall Avenue remained a majestic place, worthy of the remarkable men and women who called it home. It was still, as a resident called it, "the Black Mission Hills," a reference to the high-class neighborhood that real estate developer J. C. Nichols had built just a few miles southwest of the street.[30] Although aging, the 2400 block of Montgall was still vital.

Perhaps the best-known resident of the street was Lucile Bluford, whose battle against the University of Missouri had ended. She worked as managing editor of the *Call*. She lived at 2444 with her aging parents, directly across from the Russells.[31] To the north of her was James Wyatt. He had three young children who had lost their mother to cancer shortly after the youngest, Olive, was born. James later remarried a woman named Nona who, according to Gwendolyn Calderon, was embraced by both the family and the neighborhood.[32]

The Herndons were next at 2440. Morris and Willa Herndon had one son, Danny, who was born in 1935. Danny was an athlete, from a long line of athletes. From 1909 to 1915, his maternal grandfather, Arthur "Chick" Pullam, was the catcher for the Royal Giants, one of

Kansas City's all-Black baseball teams.[33] Danny also played ball, and he played in the city's segregated Jackie Robinson League just as its namesake was making history by integrating major league baseball. His father, Morris, a railroad worker, had to petition the city so that Danny's team could practice and play in the city's parks. Because no White team would play against teams in the Jackie Robinson League, Danny was forced to travel outside of the metropolitan area to find competition. The young Herndon continued playing sports at Lincoln High School and played wing for the football team. Once again, he was forced to travel to find competition, and the team went as far away as Tulsa, Oklahoma; Little Rock, Arkansas; and Columbia, Missouri.[34] Despite the civil rights advances after World War II, such as the integration of the armed services and major league baseball, Kansas City's ruling majority clung to the idea that it was "natural" for the races to be kept apart—especially for its children. Fairyland Park, the popular amusement center at Seventy-Fifth and Prospect, was off-limits to Blacks except for one day a year. (Many Montgall Avenue families, such as the Russells and the Herndons, found Fairyland's policy repugnant and refused to allow their children to go there on the designated day.) The city also used this "natural separation" argument when it maintained separate swimming pools for Black and White residents. In 1939 the city built Parade Park pool for Black residents, and three years later it opened the Swope Park pool for Whites.[35]

Even as municipal pools across the country began to integrate (Saint Louis's did in 1949), Kansas City officials were determined to maintain the "separate but equal" status quo. The problem was that the separate facilities it maintained for Black and White residents were not equal. The Swope Park swimming pool cost $525,000 to build, while Parade Park had cost a mere $60,000 when it was constructed only three years before. Nevertheless, the city held fast to the argument that the facilities were equal. The NAACP disagreed, and in 1952 they sued the city and won. City officials appealed and lost again.[36] Rather than comply, however, officials stubbornly chose to close the Swope Park pool rather than allow Blacks in. For two summers, 1952 and 1953, the pool sat dry as officials awaited court decisions. Only when the US Supreme Court declined to hear the case did the Swope Park pool reopen, and when it did, in June 1954, Montgall Avenue resident Danny Herndon was there, the pool's only Black lifeguard.[37]

Herndon attended the University of Kansas, where he became friends with the basketball star Wilt Chamberlain. In his brief time as a Kansas Jayhawk, the 7'1" athlete spent many evenings and weekends on Montgall, sleeping in a bed that Herndon's mother elongated with a pillow-covered cedar chest placed at the foot of it. Chamberlain met many Montgall residents, including Gwendolyn Calderon, who recalled that he was the only person tall enough to look down on the chandelier that still hangs in her living room.

Next to the Herndons' house was 2436, the home that Ollie and Myrtle Cook vacated in 1943, and where Hughey and Edna Fletcher lived. Hughey was part owner of Consolidated Cab, which got its name when three cab companies—Royal, Blue Line, and Palace—merged. Edna Fletcher worked at the converted Ford plant during the war as a "Rosie the Riveter," cranking out aircraft engines in the reengineered facility, a job made possible because of the efforts of Chester Franklin and others. It was said that Edna Fletcher was so fast and efficient that it took three people to replace her whenever she had a day off. After the war, when Ford encouraged women to return home to make room for returning soldiers, Fletcher was the only woman that the company kept on its payroll, because she was too valuable to be let go. One of her duties was being a "sodder wiper," wiping the seams from car bumpers so smoothly that the fender looked like one piece.[38]

Carolyn Brydie was still living next door, at 2434, with her goddaughter Gwendolyn Russell. Brydie was the counselor at Lincoln High and close to retirement. In 1945 Russell was transitioning to high school, and several years later she was one of the first African Americans to attend the Kansas City Art Institute, where she earned a fashion degree in 1954. Russell won several design competitions, and she even began designing clothes for actress Penny Singleton, best known for portraying Blondie in the 1940s movie series based on the famous comic strip and as the voice of Jane Jetson in the animated series *The Jetsons*. Russell and Singleton developed such a close working relationship that the actress occasionally invited Russell to spend weekends with her in Kansas City's segregated hotels.

Gwendolyn Russell gave up her dream of becoming a professional fashion designer when she accepted a position at Southwestern Bell in 1959, one of two Black women hired at that time. They were the first African Americans to work for the company outside of the custodial department. She had contact with everyone in the building when she delivered mail to each department. Soon after, she was promoted to teller and had a public-facing position waiting on business customers who came into the downtown building to pay their bills. Russell remained at Southwestern Bell for more than forty years, until her retirement in 1989.[39]

Next door to Gwendolyn Russell and Carolyn Brydie, at 2432, lived Fred and Pearl Dabney. Fred was a businessman, a Mason, and a Republican. He was also, apparently, quite the talker, once delivering a four-hour speech—seventy-one single-spaced pages—to his fellow Masons in which he lamented the state of national affairs and the amount of time spent on "the economic side of social and political affairs" at the expense of the "intellectual and spiritual." When Alf Landon ran for president in 1936, Dabney made at least one trip to Topeka with Chester Franklin to help with his campaign.[40] Fred's wife, Pearl Dabney—"Aunty Pearl" to many in the neighborhood—was Fredericka Perry's closest friend, and she had a long résumé when it came to serving the city's Black community. In June 1919, when the city turned over a new bathhouse to the Black community that had previously been used by White residents at Seventeenth and Paseo, she delivered a speech, "A Word for the Children."[41] And in 1934 she worked closely with Fredericka Perry to open the Big Sisters Home for girls over twelve who had lost their parents.

After Fred died in 1949, Pearl stayed on Montgall, and her neighbors watched as she replaced the heavy velvet drapes with venetian blinds and threw out the old, dark furniture in favor of floral chintz-covered pieces. Although Pearl did not have her own children, she enjoyed her nieces and nephews who traveled from Philadelphia to spend summers with her, bringing new games and trends to the Midwest. After her Philadelphia family introduced her to canasta and Chinese checkers, Dabney introduced them to the neighborhood, often hosting tournaments in her fur stole and fishnet stockings. And even though Chubby Checker is credited with bringing the twist dance craze to the country, it was Pearl Dabney who brought it to Montgall Avenue.[42]

Next to the Dabneys lived the Pattersons, at 2430. Ernest Patterson worked as the head custodian at the Katz drugstore at Thirtieth and Prospect. Next to the Pattersons, at the northwestern corner of the block (2428), was a family with deep roots in the area's Black community, Collins and Ophelia Anderson and their five children. Ophelia's grandfather, Ellis Smith, had been a slave in Boonville, Missouri, and gained his freedom when he enlisted in the Sixty-Fifth Regiment of the US Colored Infantry, a group that donated significant funds to the establishment of Lincoln Institute, which later became Lincoln University. Ellis Smith signed his 1864 enlistment papers with an X because he could neither read nor write. By the time he died in 1925 (in his granddaughter's home on Montgall),[43] he had learned to read, and he left an estate of $3,178.98, plus a Studebaker.[44]

Smith's great-grandchildren were still living and excelling in Kansas City eighty years after the Civil War, able to thrive in the safe and stable community that was the Montgall Avenue of their youth. As young children, the Andersons rode their tricycles, operated lemonade stands, and picked fruit from their neighbors' trees. One of Collins and Ophelia's sons, Collins "Buzzy" Anderson, born in 1932, graduated from Howard University's dental school. Buzzy Anderson remained in Kansas City, opening a dental practice at Twenty-Seventh and Prospect, even though many of his friends, such as Danny Herndon and Perry's grandson, John, left the city after college.[45]

Danny Herndon, Collins Anderson, and Gwendolyn Calderon, like all of the other young people on Montgall, entered a new America, one that offered more opportunities for African Americans than ever before, and these three individuals thrived. Their success was grounded in hard work, parents' and teachers' high expectations, and the fact that Montgall itself was a safe environment, free from violence and poverty. Theirs was the last generation who found the neighborhood around the 2400 block of Montgall conducive to this sort of achievement.

Kansas City's Black population increased by 33.9 percent from 1940 to 1950, but housing did not keep up with the numbers. According to the US Census, by 1950 more than half the homes occupied by African Americans were substandard. In 1946 Thomas Webster, executive director of the Greater Kansas City Urban League, complained to city councilman Paul G. Koontz that housing for African Americans was increasingly congested and dilapidated.[46] For the people on Montgall, the grip was tightening as the once-integrated neighborhoods north of Twenty-Seventh Street became filled with poor Black families.

Twenty-Seventh Street became the boundary for the city's Black community, an invisible Berlin Wall maintained by neighborhood associations and local "improvement" groups, and there were violent consequences for any Black Kansas Citian who dared to cross it. On May 21, 1952, when a Black family purchased a home south of Twenty-Seventh Street, White neighbors responded with the same violent tactics used forty years earlier on Montgall. Another bomb exploded on September 7 of that year.[47]

Lucile Bluford had her own encounter with violence after she learned of a neighborhood association meeting being held in a church not far from her home. The curious journalist decided to investigate, and while on a drive with her father (one of John Bluford's favorite activities after he suffered a stroke in September 1942),[48] she stopped at the church located just south of Twenty-Seventh Street. She parked her car and got out to peek in the church's windows to "see what [she] could see."[49] She stayed as long as she thought would be safe, with her ailing father waiting behind in the car. When she returned, she found a "hoodlum" had pulled him from the vehicle and held him by the scruff of his neck, "kind of choking him," shaking him, asking what he was doing. "I got there just in the nick of time," she recalled.

In the decades to come, Kansas City's Black divide pushed farther south as the 2400 block of Montgall became more cut off from the economic opportunities that emerged in postwar America, and its residents increasingly felt the effects of poverty and violence.

The Negro of the South is no longer a docile soul willing to sit by and accept the weekly insults of discriminations heaped upon him. No longer is he content to receive whatever morsels of democracy white Americans feel inclined to dole out to him.

Lucile Bluford, *Call* editorial, March 4, 1960

14

Throughout her life, Lucile Bluford witnessed the great dance for social justice between Black and White America: significant steps forward for the Black community and the subsequent sidestepping response from the White establishment. In 1938 Lloyd Gaines won his court case against the University of Missouri, but rather than allow him to attend the university, the state scraped together a law school at the all-Black Lincoln University. A year later, Lucile Bluford found herself in a similar sidestepping shuffle as she pursued a graduate degree in journalism. In 1952 and 1953, after losing their battle to continue keeping Blacks away from Swope Park swimming pool, city officials stubbornly chose to close the facility rather than comply with the ruling. And in 1954, after the Supreme Court's decision in *Brown v. Board of Education of Topeka*, which declared that separate institutions were unconstitutional, the Kansas City school board responded by redrawing attendance lines as Black families moved into new neighborhoods.

Every step forward and every major court decision was met with joy in Kansas City's Black community: "Mine eyes have seen the glory," Chester Franklin said on hearing the *Brown* decision.[1] Franklin died in 1955 and did not live to see the aftermath of the groundbreaking decision, but his *Call* successor did, and in addition to reporting on how the school district eschewed the court ruling, Lucile Bluford watched the next great dance for justice in America's history, the one involving housing.

Most students of history are familiar with the "White flight" explanation of this postwar phenomenon—that of pent-up demand for homes, which led to millions of White families, all acting independently of one another, to suddenly behave as one and move into new housing developments farther away from city centers. Although this explanation is tidy, it does not tell the complete story of the evacuation of Whites from US cities, and of the racial attitudes White Americans held that persisted after World War II. Specifically, the perception was that when Black families moved into an area, property values plummeted.

Researching the role that race played in Kansas City's growth and development, Kevin Fox Gotham concluded that "block-busting" and panic selling were much more important causes of Kansas City's White outmigration than the "White flight" narrative. Gotham asserts that real estate agents were able to tap into White peoples' latent racial attitudes with talk of rising crime rates and falling property values if a person of color moved into an area.[2]

Lucile Bluford's neighborhood was one of the first to experience this postwar phenomenon, changing from about 60 percent Black in 1950 to more than 90 percent Black by 1960. She had suspected that the exodus of White families had been "inspired by real estate agents with their eyes on commissions," and when she saw the following ad in a local newspaper, she called for an investigation by the real estate board:[3]

Colored in your Block? Want to Sell and Get
All Cash? For Prompt
Appraisal Estimate Call . . .

As Kansas City streets changed from all White to all Black, the process tended to follow a pattern. After the first Black family moved—or was lured—into an area, a profiteering real estate agent would call or go door to door offering his or her services to homeowners, encouraging them to sell "while their home still had value." The agents warned that if the homeowner waited too long, their house would be worth nothing. This scenario played out over and over again, block by block and neighborhood by neighborhood.[4]

Even though the 2400 block of Montgall had been redlined before the war, its homes remained desirable within the Black community long after the HOLC map was released. Most of its residents were not going anywhere, and those who did were able to sell their homes to people who knew the street and understood that it was a safe place to live and raise a family—to people like Joshua Russell, who knew a bargain when he saw one. In fact, people said he could "squeeze a nickel so tight the buffalo would squeak,"[5] so, when 2461 Montgall went on the market for $2,500 in 1941, Russell purchased it.[6] Because of people like Joshua and Josie Russell and Officer Clifford Warren, who bought the house next door about the same time, the street remained a stable and tight-knit community long after the streets around it had started to unravel. But as secure as it was, it could not remain a safe place forever. By the 1950s many of the children who had grown up on the street opted to leave the fragile community surrounding their childhood homes.

In 1959 Clifford's son Errol Warren (2457) married Vesta Duncan, and the couple lived in several residences before settling back on Montgall Avenue, but in a house that was thirty-five blocks south of Errol's childhood home. The couple had a son, Clifford Jr., and for a time the Warrens were the only African Americans on the street. Although the family did not experience bombings or the hateful demonstrations that Errol Warren had witnessed as a teen, they were subjected to a more subtle kind of torment and other micro-aggressions. Warren recalled that his neighbors were kind, all except the man next door who bent over and pointed to his rear end every time he saw them.[7]

The harassment reached a peak when Vesta, pregnant with their second child, was outside playing ball with Clifford Jr. The neighbor yelled at the toddler that if the ball came into his yard, the child had better not try to retrieve it. Vesta snapped, and she tearfully went inside where her husband was napping. "I didn't even take the time to put on pants," Errol recalled. With bat in hand, he went outside and told the man that if he ever spoke to his family in such a way again, he would have to deal with him. Not long after, the young family moved to a more hospitable neighborhood.

Other youngsters who had grown up on Montgall and pushed south beyond the traditional Black neighborhoods also felt the sting. When Josie and Joshua Russell's daughter, Rozelia (2461), purchased a home on East Sixty-Ninth Street, she was told that they were leaving the neighborhood to be closer to their children. "The very fact that they felt the need to tell me why they were leaving told me that they weren't being totally honest," she said.[8] In 1960, when Retha Lindsey, who grew up on the block north of the Russells, tried to rent an apartment on Thirty-Second Street, she was told that it had already been rented. Even so, the "For Rent" sign remained in the window for several more months—until a White occupant moved in.[9]

As neighborhoods began to transition, the school district had multiple opportunities to integrate its schools, and every time the district chose to keep its buildings segregated. Testifying in the Kansas City school district's desegregation case in 1983, Lucile Bluford told the story of two elementary schools that were only three blocks apart, one built for Black students, the other for Whites. When the neighborhood could no longer support the two facilities, Superintendent James Hazlett proposed closing the older facility and sending the White students to the Black building. The school board rejected the plan and voted to keep both schools open, at an increased cost to taxpayers.[10] Bluford saw the fear in the White community—that if White and Black children were in school together, there would be trouble.

After the 1954 *Brown* decision, Kansas City's Central High School was the first formerly all-White high school to undergo the racial turnover. During the 1954–1955 school year, the school's student population was all White. Six years later, at the start of the 1960–1961 school year it was more than 90 percent Black.[11] Central High School English teacher Virginia Oldham remembered the metamorphosis, and she recalled that the first Black students at Central were good students from middle-class families. "But within a summer, the whole make-up of the school neighborhood changed. Most of the children enrolled the next fall were from poor Black families where both parents had to work. Some of these children did exceedingly well in school, but most did not."[12]

Oldham was not a typical teacher. As a member of Fellowship House, a multiracial, nondenominational association of men and women interested in social justice, she was aware of and involved in what was happening in her community. Oldham was part of Fellowship House's Committee on the Practice of Democracy (COPOD), a group that worked to integrate Kansas City's restaurants and theaters in the late 1950s and early 1960s. The group's strategy was fairly simple: pair Black and White members together to spend time out in public. Oldham's partner was none other than Lucile Bluford, who knew the shock value of the Fellowship House's strategy. "People would have you think that a wall was going to cave in or something," she said.[13]

One restaurant that the duo liked to frequent was the Forum Cafeteria on Main Street. "They [the cafeteria line workers] were willing to serve her [Oldham], but they weren't going—they couldn't serve me," Bluford recalled in her 1989 oral history.

> But you couldn't get out, you had to stay in this line. And nobody [the other people in line] was caring, you know. So she [Virginia] got enough food for me. I mean, she got enough so both—and we went on out of the line and went on upstairs and found a place. Well, the people were all upset, you know, the employees got all upset. But they didn't know what to do, so we just sat down and ate.

Modeled after the Congress for Racial Equality (CORE), members of the Committee on the Practice of Democracy understood that it could never call itself CORE because pairing the word "racial" with "equality" made the name too inflammatory, given the city's "Southern orientation."[14] If Rufus Montgall is the symbol of the spread of southern attitudes and Jim Crow to the frontier town, Lucile Bluford, a woman who lived on a block named for the slave owner, is a symbol of Jim Crow's repeal. And Lucile Bluford stood on the front lines as legal segregation in her city began to dissolve.

Bluford carried on the activism of the earlier generation of her neighbors. She picketed Municipal Auditorium, became a member of the Urban League, and was active in the NAACP. She joined the Rev. Dr. Martin Luther King Jr.'s 1963 March on Washington and was appointed to the Missouri State Commission on Human Rights, which investigated complaints and allegations of discrimination in the workplace. "We didn't have any power to punish anybody, other than we could just rule or say that the (for example) Ford Company was wrong and try to work out some kind of plan for them to make up to the man, whatever it was."[15]

Although Bluford also served as the voice for the disenfranchised as editor of the *Call*, she was by no means the only soldier in the fight. In 1958 a young schoolteacher, Gladys Graham, was turned away from a downtown department store when she wanted a drink. Her rejection led to a boycott of some of Kansas City's largest department stores, including local retail giants such as the Jones Store and Emery, Bird, Thayer dry goods store, and Macy's, the national department store. The boycott lasted through the economically important Christmas season, and by April 1959 all five of Kansas City's major department stores had changed their policies to allow African Americans to eat at their lunch counters.[16] Bluford met with the women early on and provided guidance and support.[17]

Bluford also reminded *Call* readers that every voice mattered, and she encouraged them to vote in every election. She understood that her readers' participation in elections became more potent as the city's population changed. In 1950 Blacks represented 12.2 percent of the total population; in 1960, 17.5 percent; and 1970, 22.1 percent. In 1960 Kansas City elected its first Black representative on the city council, Bruce R. Watkins. And it was Watkins who sponsored the public accommodations ordinance that ended segregation in all of the city's stores and restaurants. Bluford remembered the weekly city council discussions: conservatives arguing that it was an example of government overreach threatening individual rights, and more

Protesting downtown Kansas City department stores. Papers of Dorothy Hodge Johnson, Dowdal Davis Jr., and John Hodge, Kansas Collection, RH MS 549, Kenneth Spencer Research Library, University of Kansas.

liberal-minded members seeing the issue from a civil rights perspective. During this period, Bluford started attending the weekly city council meetings. "Week after week they would try to bring it [the public accommodations proposal] up. The opponents would fight it down," she said.[18] The council debated the issue for more than a year before finally voting on September 13, 1964. It passed, and an elated Bluford published an editorial that reflected not only her positive attitude but also the optimism felt within Kansas City's Black community: "We are entering a new era in civil rights and human relations in Kansas City . . . for 18% of the city's population for years has been plagued with discrimination and segregation based upon race. The new ordinance opens new doors. Kansas City is well along its way to really becoming the heart of America when honor, truth, and justice reign supreme."[19]

This modest step forward—the city finally acting to ensure that members of Kansas City's Black community would no longer be forced to stand at lunch counters, purchase clothes without being able to try them on first, or eat in restaurants' kitchens—was undoubtedly positive. But it did not address the declining neighborhoods like the 2400 block of Montgall. Their deterioration was an injustice that not only marred the look of the city but was also beginning to leave a mark on those who lived in these expanding low-income communities, including Lucile Bluford.

These areas have more substandard houses than the rest of the city, high crime rates, and less trash collection and, thus, more rats and fires. More of the residents are unemployed, have less education, receive more public assistance, constitute the bulk of admissions to the general acute and mental hospitals for the indigent, and have less voice in public decision-making. Retail shopping is scarce and tends to be exploitative.

Description of the neighborhood from the federal government's Model City Program, 1973

SURVIVING RIOT, ATTACKS, AND DECLINE, 1968–1998

15

In 1919 John Bluford moved his young family to Kansas City, Missouri, because he believed that his children would have a better future and receive a better education there than they would in North Carolina. His children—Lucile, John Jr., and Guion—grew up in a secure, nurturing environment, in a place that buffered them from the most heinous and dangerous forms of racism. Living on Montgall Avenue did not blind them to the injustices facing Black America—the Blufords' neighbors provided a thorough education about that—but it did give them a secure start in life. It was on Montgall Avenue that Lucile Bluford met her mentor, Chester Franklin, and discovered one of the most significant and potent vehicles for fighting discrimination: the Black press.[1] During that era the Montgall community provided stability and support for the Bluford children and the other youngsters raised there, and Lucile and Guion Bluford were extraordinarily successful. Guion moved to Philadelphia after college and worked as an engineer. His son, also named Guion, became an astronaut for NASA. In 1983, aboard the space shuttle Challenger, he was the first African American to reach outer space.

As for Lucile Bluford, she engaged in the community like very few Kansas Citians, Black or White, ever have, and the list of honors she received illustrates her commitment to her city. She received the Distinguished Service Award from the NAACP, the Martin Luther King Award from the Southern Christian Leadership Conference, and a Matrix Table honor from Women in Communication. She earned honorary doctorates from Lincoln University and the University of Missouri and an award from the Omega Psi Phi Fraternity. She was also honored by the AME Church, the Black Economic Union, the Fellowship House, and the Greater Kansas City Urban League, and she was in the class of 1983 in Missouri's Academy of Squires, an organization established to honor Missourians for their service at all levels of government.[2] But Lucile Bluford also experienced more than her share of personal trauma, events that, sadly, can also be directly attributed to the neighborhood in which she lived, a neighborhood that evolved into a place that brought more than its share of stress and damage, the kind that would create barriers for later residents.

Kansas City's 1968 Race Riot

In April 1968 Kansas City experienced one of the most violent incidents in its history, violence that came dangerously close to Montgall Avenue. While the street escaped the worst of the destruction, it was close enough that its residents were terrorized as they watched the neighborhood around them erupt into chaos. Ironically, the riot that could have meant the destruction of the street started at Lincoln High School, an institution that had played such a central role in the history of Montgall Avenue's residents.[3]

By 1968 an entire generation of students had passed through Lincoln's halls since Principal Cook's retirement in 1943. The teachers Cook hired emphasized thrift and patriotism, but by 1968 they were gone. Teenagers in the late 1960s seemed more cynical than previous generations—and more savvy. Their parents and grandparents had fought in wars that had saved the world from tyranny, but their generation inherited an unpopular war in Vietnam, where the enemy wasn't always easy to determine. Lincoln's students were also not blind to the new America that surrounded them in the suburbs, one from which they had been largely cut off. It had taken trillions of public and private dollars to build suburbia, and billions more to create the Interstate Highway System, which carved up the neighborhoods where they and other people of color lived.[4] So, despite the court victories and changing laws that dismantled Jim Crow, the distance between the two Americas was undeniable by 1968.

An immediate cause of the riots was a decision by the Kansas City school board to hold classes on April 9, 1968, the day that the Rev. Dr. Martin Luther King Jr.'s body was laid to rest. Lincoln High School students were expected to attend school despite the fact that schools in Kansas City, Kansas, were closed. The students were upset and walked out. They organized a march down Woodlawn Avenue and over to Manual High School, where they encountered more students.[5] Others joined the crowd as it headed to more schools and collected more students. Before long, the relatively small group of students had grown into a formidable alliance of demonstrators who planned to walk to city hall to make their case to Mayor Ilus Davis.

As the protest began to take shape, youth leaders were alerted to the situation. These leaders, who regularly held dances at a Catholic high school, formulated a plan to bus the students to Holy Name Catholic Church at Twenty-Third and Benton. They hoped that by providing an atmosphere where the students could decompress with music, burgers, and soda, they could snuff out any potential for violence. Unfortunately, no one informed the police of the plan, and after someone from the crowd threw a brick at a passing vehicle, law enforcement assembled in riot gear, and an officer threw tear gas into one of the crowded buses. The tenuous hold that the community leaders had was gone, and the situation spiraled out of control, particularly among the nonstudents who had joined the protest, a number of whom had thrown rocks at cars driven by Whites. Three days of rioting followed, leaving six people dead and nearly $4 million in damage.[6]

Lucile Bluford first heard about the violence as she returned home from Atlanta after accompanying Ada Franklin to King's funeral. The next day she and other Black leaders, including Leon Jordan, the police officer turned activist, organized a meeting at the YMCA at Thirty-First and Benton to discuss how to prevent the violence from returning. When the meeting adjourned, Bluford and Jordan encountered flames from the Crown Drugstore at the corner of Thirty-First Street.[7]

Other Montgall residents also had stories of terror. Gwendolyn Russell Calderon was more than a little concerned when her future husband, Manuel, did not return home before 10 o'clock, the curfew the mayor imposed the second night of the riot. Manuel Calderon was the manager of an H&R Block office at Thirty-Fifth and Prospect and had been there working on his clients' taxes when someone set fire to an adjoining building. Calderon and his colleagues collected as many records as possible and loaded them into his station wagon. Because public transit had been suspended, Manuel drove each of his employees home, which caused him to miss the curfew. Gwendolyn worried that the National Guard unit, stationed at Twenty-Fifth and Montgall, would shoot first and ask questions later. Fortunately, the guards let him pass, and he made it home safely.[8]

Even though the rioting stopped after three days, the damage wrought by the violence persisted. First was the physical hollowing-out of the already sparse area, with the destruction of businesses like Crown Drugstore, Klein's Grocery Store, and others. Then came the psychological damage, not only to neighborhood residents who witnessed the destruction but also in the larger community. Newspaper coverage of the violence—looting at Thirtieth and Prospect, a bus driver hit by a brick at Twenty-Second and Indiana, and gunfire at Thirty-Third and Cleveland—only fed the narrative that the area was toxic and inhabited by dangerous people who thought nothing of throwing a rock at a police officer or robbing and burning a liquor store.[9] Men and women from the neighborhoods around Montgall picked up on the larger community's reaction. "A net was thrown around the community and the attitude was: 'Whatever happens within it, so what?'" said Herman Johnson, president of the Kansas City chapter of the NAACP, in the *Kansas City Star* immediately after the unrest.[10] The riots also exposed a division within Kansas City's

Black community, a divide that could be seen in the residents of Montgall.

On one side were those like Collins "Buzzy" Anderson, who had grown up at 2428 Montgall and established his dental office in the area. "While I did not participate in the riots, I have nothing but praise for those who did," he told the *Star*. Anderson explained that he did not condone violence, but he understood the limitations of peaceful protests. "Namely, when people speak out and ask for equal rights, those in power can turn a deaf ear. They don't have to do anything because there won't be any reprisals. But when people bring pressure to bear through riots and destruction, those in power are ready to sit and listen and try to work out a solution," he told the reporter. Lucile Bluford, on the other hand, opposed any act of violence, and her editorials expressed not only her dismay but what she believed would have been Martin Luther King's response.[11]

That is not to say that Bluford sat idly by as her neighborhood and those around her crumbled. Newspapers like the *Kansas City Star* portrayed the riots more generally and focused their reporting on the destruction itself, but Bluford zeroed in on the particulars. Her readers were, after all, its victims. And she wanted answers, particularly about the death of an unarmed man, Julius Hamilton, who had not participated in the riots but was killed by a police sniper while he stood in a doorway.[12]

Bluford vs. the Black Panthers

Over the years Bluford continued to believe in the strategy supported by the NAACP, which was to work within the system, particularly the courts, to affect change. But in 1968 this position was out of step with a young population that was tired of waiting. Bluford's steadfast belief that justice would eventually prevail led her into a conflict with another civil rights group, the Black Panthers, after they took offense at her newspaper's coverage of one of their rallies. When the *Call* declared that the crowd was smaller than the group anticipated, Panther leader Pete O'Neal went to various merchants to get them to stop selling the newspaper. This conflict between the *Call* and the Panthers was relatively short-lived, and Bluford reported that a couple of weeks later she met with O'Neal, and they agreed that the Panthers would "watch their tongues" while she was around.[13]

Bluford realized that she was less confrontational than the young leaders who were emerging during the late 1960s, for she also disagreed with the strategy of another activist, Bernard Powell, who had begun attending city hall meetings with his social action committee. "They wouldn't sit down," Bluford recalled. And whenever they disagreed with something being said, they became vocal. Only later, after Powell "became calmer" and "started working through organizations," did Bluford seem to appreciate his efforts to get individuals to take care of their surroundings.[14]

The situation in and around Montgall became more dire in the years after the riot, and its residents experienced more and more trauma, including Lucile Bluford. In 1970 she lost one of her best friends when Leon Jordan, one of Kansas City's most well-known civil rights leaders, was gunned down just a block away from the journalist's home.[15]

Jordan, who had many ties to Montgall, spent a lot of time there, both with Bluford and with his former partner on the police force, Clifford Warren (2457). In 1947 Jordan left the KCPD and moved to Liberia, where he trained police officers. When he returned to Kansas City in the mid-1950s, he began his new career as a political activist within the Democratic Party. Known for his larger-than-life personality and his ability to tell a story, Jordan cofounded Freedom Inc., a political action group that advocated for political awareness within the African American community. Jordan and his friend Bruce R. Watkins organized voter registration drives and endorsed candidates who were sympathetic to civil rights, specifically those affecting the urban core. In 1964 seven of the eight candidates that Freedom endorsed won, including Jordan, who was elected to the Missouri House of Representatives.[16]

When the legislature was out of session, Jordan could be found at his bar, the Green Duck Tavern, at Twenty-Sixth and Prospect, one block west of Montgall Avenue. That was where, in the early hours of July 15, 1970, Jordan was assassinated as he locked up the bar. A man in a stolen brown Pontiac, which had pulled up beside him, fired a shot that caused Jordan to fall. The shooter got out of the car, fired two more shots into Jordan's chest, returned to his vehicle, and sped away. The case has still not been solved. "That was a tragedy," Bluford said. "A great loss to the community and to a lot of people, because Leon had a lot of friends. A lot of people felt that they lost a family member when Leon died."[17] Jordan's slaying was a calculated crime, which was not typical of most of the murders taking place in the once-safe neighborhood.

After Bluford realized that most inner-city violence was unplanned, carried out by people acting impulsively, in 1991 she teamed up with city councilwoman Carol Coe to initiate the "Step Back and Think" program, designed to increase awareness and reduce violence in her neighborhood. "We're asking everybody, if you start arguing with someone, step back and think and don't pull the trigger," she said.[18]

Assault on Montgall Avenue

The details are somewhat hazy—no longtime resident of Montgall wants to remember them—but no one can forget the traumatizing effects of the crimes. Gwendolyn Russell Calderon believes that the rapist who assaulted Willa Herndon was introduced to the street when the Fletchers (2436) hired him to paint their house.[19]

Danny Herndon, who was visiting his parents that Christmas, remembered how inadequate he felt when he discovered that his mother had been raped.[20] Willa Herndon carried this sense of vulnerability until her death in 1992. There is also some indication that Lucile Bluford felt vulnerable after the rape, for she stopped parking her car in the detached garage. Instead, she began leaving it on the street, in front of her house. Her neighbor, Joshua Russell, took comfort in Bluford's new habit. Because he lived right across the street from her, he kept an eye out for her. For the remainder of his life, Russell would

Russell family at parents' fortieth anniversary in 1967. *From left to right*: Rozelia Russell, Gwendolyn Russell, Josie Russell, Joshua "J. K." Russell, Joshua Jr., Josie Mae Russell Cason, and Frank Russell. Courtesy of Gwendolyn Calderon.

wait up for her and not go to sleep until he saw that Lucile was safe at home, even on those very late Thursday nights when she stayed at the office to get the paper ready for print.[21]

After the rape, there was an increased police presence on the street, especially after vandals smashed the headlights of Bluford's car. Gwendolyn Calderon recalled the journalist's surprise that the police prioritized the street by stationing a patrol car there for a time. Although crime remained high in the area surrounding Montgall, the block remained a community. All the neighbors showed up when Joshua and Josie Russell celebrated their fortieth wedding anniversary in 1967, a celebration the children continued every ten years.

John Bluford Jr.'s Encounter with Police

Sometimes the very people hired to protect and serve the area's residents were the ones behaving the most impetuously. This is what

Joshua and Josie Russell's sixtieth anniversary—with
Lucile Bluford. Courtesy of Gwendolyn Calderon.

happened on February 24, 1981, when sixty-seven-year-old John H.
Bluford Jr., Lucile's brother, was approached by Kansas City police officer Bob Thomas not far from 2444 Montgall. After failing to comply
with Thomas's request to drive through a traffic light that was stuck
on red, Bluford was arrested. At some point during the encounter, he
fell and broke his hip. Rather than seek medical assistance for Bluford, Thomas took him to a jail cell, where, Bluford later told his sister, he had to crawl across the floor to get a glass of water.[22]

Bluford was not given the opportunity to make a phone call, nor
was he allowed to post bond, even though he had enough money in
his wallet to cover the $34.25 bail. Lucile found him two days later at
Truman Medical Center, where he remained for four months before

he was transferred to a rehabilitation center for an additional six-month stay.

During those ten months John Bluford underwent five surgeries. "I am sure that you can see how such an incident as I have described to you perpetuates certain stereotypes of the police and brings out unfavorable attitudes toward the Police Department," the seventy-year-old Lucile Bluford wrote to police chief Norman Caron. She could not understand how a police officer could treat her brother, a man who suffered from mental illness, this way. "My concern is not just for my brother and his health and welfare, but for other persons who might find themselves in similar situations because of the 'don't care' attitude of some police officers," she wrote.[23]

The tone of this letter is much like the editorials she wrote fifty years earlier for the student newspaper at the University of Kansas. She wasn't asking the chief to investigate police conduct, something that many civil rights activists most certainly would have done. Nor did she go public with the story. Rather, this was a letter from someone who seemed resigned to the reality in which she and her brother lived, in which people of color were often under attack by those who had been hired to protect them.

John Bluford remained in a wheelchair for the rest of his life, and his sister converted the downstairs den at 2444 into a bedroom because he could no longer climb stairs. Rather than face a long and potentially damaging public lawsuit, Bluford asked the police department to settle with her brother for $50,000. There is no record of whether Bluford ever received the settlement.

Lucile Bluford survived numerous personal tragedies such as the attack on her brother and the murder of one of her best friends. She also lived long enough to see the physical decline of the homes on her street.

Houses on Montgall Start to Fall

The home at 2447 Montgall, which Chester Franklin had built for his beloved Ada in 1925, was the first to be destroyed. Its decline started innocently enough. After Sydney and Mayme Johnson died, the house became rental property, inhabited by people who had no interest in keeping it up and owned by a landlord who had little incentive to maintain it. Eventually the tenants moved out and a hole in the roof went untreated. Before long a family of raccoons took up residence, along with the occasional homeless person who found temporary shelter in the once-glorious home. One morning in the 1980s, neighbors smelled smoke from a fire that most likely was started by one of the transients, and 2447 Montgall, with its leaded glass windows and fashionable sunroom, the home where Ada Franklin hosted elegant dinner parties for W. E. B. Du Bois and army general Benjamin Davis, was reduced to a pile of ash.[24]

The home at 2432 Montgall went next. It was first owned by Irish-born Richard Mayberry when integrated streets were still possible in Kansas City, but it was another forgotten residence by the 1970s. Fred and Pearl Dabney were longtime residents, but after Pearl's death the home went to one of the Dabneys' nephews, who rented it out as a church for a time. Mostly, though, it sat vacant. Later, prostitutes and transients took up residence there. In the 1990s the structure, along with the two homes north of it, 2428 and 2430, was razed after another fire destroyed much of those properties.[25] The Cooks' home at 2436 Montgall, which was purchased by the Fletchers in 1943, was given to Edna Fletcher's niece, Joy Lou. Lou was known for her eccentricities, her six marriages, and her love of dogs. This fondness for dogs, specifically her inability to say no when an acquaintance dropped off a stray, got her into trouble with animal control officials. Eventually Lou found that she could no longer care for the dozen or so canines to which she had given free rein in her house. One morning Lou's next-door neighbor, Gwendolyn Calderon, found that she had abandoned the dogs—and the home. It sat vacant for several years before an investor purchased it for renovations.[26]

For many years, 2457 Montgall was owned by Josie Mae Russell, who had grown up with her family next door, at 2461. This house fell into disrepair, accelerated by Russell's struggle with schizophrenia. For example, whenever her brother showed up to mow the lawn or maintain or repair something in the home, Josie called the police. In 2012 her electricity was shut off, and Josie moved in with her sister,

Gwendolyn Calderon. She stayed for two years before she left and eventually found a place at a group home. The house deteriorated and was recently torn down.[27]

In the 1980s and 1990s Columbus Neal lived at 2440 Montgall. Longtime residents of the street say that Neal had a heart of gold. He worked at an area grocery store, stocking shelves and doing custodial work, and he used to bring the day-old baked goods to his neighbors and to the homeless at the city's Union Mission. He also looked after the children of some prostitutes who lived down the street. But Neal was a troubled man. Not only did he have a history of domestic violence, he struggled with alcohol, and when his girlfriend, Wanda Ford, left him, his response was violent and had far-reaching effects.

On May 27, 1997, Ford returned home from her job and was sitting in the parking lot of her apartment complex. She had no time to respond when Neal approached her from behind, pulled out his gun, and shot her through the window. She died immediately. The bullets also shattered the lives of her three children who were waiting inside, the youngest of whom was only seven years old.[28]

Columbus Neal is serving a life sentence in a Cameron, Missouri, prison. Not far away is another former Montgall resident, Rocky Jackson (2445), who is serving time in a medium-security facility on a burglary charge and possession of a controlled substance. His single mother worked nights as a nurse and could not keep her son away from the negative influences that had penetrated the neighborhood in the 1990s, when he was a child.[29]

Lucile Bluford suffered a stroke in 1998, and she was no longer able to live alone. She moved in with her friend, Donna Stewart, who became the third editor of the historic *Call* newspaper. Lucile Bluford died in 2003.

Lucile Bluford's family represents the extremes for the Black experience in twentieth-century America. Two years after her brother John was left incapacitated after his run-in with the police, her nephew, Guion, launched into outer space. Just as she had been there for John, she traveled to Florida to celebrate with him.

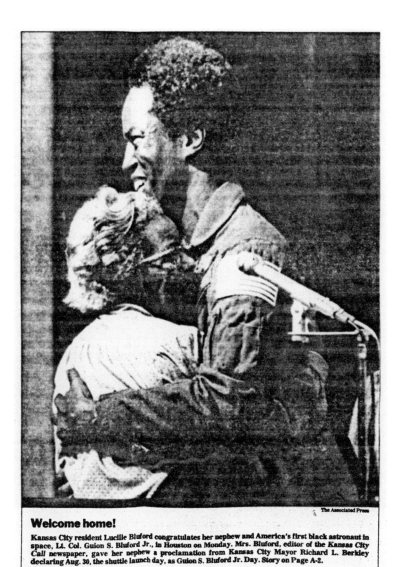

Welcome home!

Kansas City resident Lucille Bluford congratulates her nephew and America's first black astronaut in space, Lt. Col. Guion S. Bluford Jr., in Houston on Monday. Mrs. Bluford, editor of the *Kansas City Call* newspaper, gave her nephew a proclamation from Kansas City Mayor Richard L. Berkley declaring Aug. 30, the shuttle launch day, as Guion S. Bluford Jr. Day. Story on Page A-2.

Lucile and Guion Bluford embrace. Papers of Dorothy Hodge Johnson, Dowdal Davis Jr., and John Hodge, Kansas Collection, RH MS 549, Kenneth Spencer Research Library, University of Kansas.

While Bluford had a remarkably successful career in journalism, she also lived in one of Kansas City's worst neighborhoods, where "crack dealers openly sell retail, women cruise for 'dates,' winos squat in doorways, buildings stand vacant and vandalized, and people fear the night," as the *Kansas City Star* described it in 1993.[30] And it was the scene of a horrible attack on her neighbor.

Today 2444 Montgall stands empty. This nondescript home at the corner of a largely forgotten street in Kansas City has chronicled the changing nature of discrimination, an eyewitness to the progress—and the pitfalls—of the African American experience in twentieth-century America. Montgall Avenue witnessed the quick advance of Jim Crow and its agonizingly slow retreat, and it symbolizes how the attitudes of racist individuals hardened into government policies. This set the stage for the neighborhood's decline, and its residents were the casualties. Montgall Avenue witnessed the quick advance of Jim Crow and its agonizingly slow retreat, and it symbolizes how harmful attitudes of individual leaders hardened into government policies.

Not everything that is faced can be changed. But nothing can be changed until it is faced.
James Baldwin, "As Much Truth as One Can Bear," *New York Times Book Review*, 1962

16

Montgall Avenue's decline did not happen overnight but over time, and it happened because the scales were tipped against its residents. White leaders saw the residents of Montgall Avenue as "the Other," profoundly different from the majority culture. Scholars, politicians, and others in positions of power spoke in ways that convinced their audiences that Black people were less than they were, perhaps even less than human. These strategies breathed prejudice into White Americans and advanced discriminatory government policies.

In 1904, the year that Anna Jones and Hugh Oliver Cook purchased their homes on Montgall, my grandfather, Joseph Anthony Vusich, arrived at Ellis Island from Croatia. Grandpa arrived in the New World by himself when he was fourteen years old. He was poor and worked hard to build a successful life. He took a job in Kansas City's burgeoning meatpacking industry and settled into the Strawberry Hill neighborhood on the Kansas side of the state line. He married Anna Novak in 1920 and had three sons, William, Joseph, and Raymond. Their middle son, Joseph, was my father, born in 1925. By that time, Grandpa was the head butcher for the upscale Wolferman's Grocery Store, a company already known for its iconic English muffins cooked in a tuna can.

In that same year my father was born, 1925, newspaper

editor Chester Franklin married the love of his life, Ada Crogman, and he built a home for her on Montgall Avenue. Hugh Oliver Cook, still living at 2436 Montgall, was leading Lincoln High School, and that year he earned his master's degree from Cornell University. By 1925 the Montgall home originally owned by Anna Jones was occupied by the Bluford family, which included three children: Lucile, John Jr., and Guion. Lucile was a sophomore at Lincoln and editor of the school newspaper. Her neighbors were her teachers and her mentors.

My father graduated from high school and was drafted into the army during World War II. He fought in the Philippines, Guam, and Iwo Jima and earned a bronze star. My uncle, William, received a medical deferment, so after high school he left Kansas City and attended college in Pittsburgh, Pennsylvania. Because Uncle Bill thought "Vusich" sounded too ethnic for the career and the bride he envisioned, he changed his name to Wolfe and never returned to Kansas City. My father did return, and he attended college on the GI Bill.

In 1941, just before the United States entered World War II, Montgall Avenue residents reach the peak of their political influence. Lucile Bluford was in the middle of her fight to attend the University of Missouri. Chester Franklin was in and out of Washington, DC, working to make defense industry jobs available for African Americans. And John Bluford and Fredericka Perry were engaged in a successful campaign to oust Kansas City's chief of police.

My father became an electrical engineer, married Gladyne Louise Johnson, and eventually settled in Fairway, a racially restricted subdivision built by the real estate magnate J. C. Nichols. We didn't have a key to our home. It wasn't necessary because we never locked the door. I grew up around physicians, architects, and businessmen and attended state-of-the-art public schools, which were supported by a healthy tax base. The stay-at-home moms who lived in my neighborhood ran the Great Books program and led Girl Scout troops; it was an idyllic setting. In 1968 I was a kindergartener when a race riot very nearly destroyed the homes on Montgall Avenue.

This book is not about the assimilation of European immigrants like my grandfather, who worked hard for his piece of the American pie, or my uncle who was able to erase his "Otherness," his ethnicity, just by changing his name. Nor is this book strictly about the changing nature of racism over the course of the twentieth century and how the overt became more covert through language, time, and government policy. It is rather a fairly straightforward story of a street in the heart of America and the remarkable men and women who lived there. And what better way to tell the story of a race surviving in twentieth-century America than through the stories of some of the individuals who were part of that history? But there is more to the Black experience in America than what can be gleaned from individual lives. There are policies that informed these lives and impacted these residents, the same policies that devastated a street.

I wrote this book because I care about Montgall Avenue, and I want others to as well. I also wanted to make more concrete the staggering long-term implications of residential segregation and other government policies that isolated the Montgall community, something that managed to escape me for so many years. When my father died in 2001, my four surviving siblings and I inherited a tidy sum from the sale of our childhood home, a direct benefit of the government investments made to my family. Montgall homes have not fared as well. But more than the monetary value of a home, I also had the advantages of growing up in a neighborhood where no one thought of locking the front door. I sat down to dinner with my neighbors and went on vacations with them. In my teen years I took care of their lawns and their children. It was a neighbor who hired me for my first public school teaching job.

After my husband and I married, we were intentional in choosing the home in which we would raise our children, and when they were growing up we lived in an area very much like Fairway. My children experienced the same security and opportunities that I did, earning money by mowing neighbors' lawns and caring for their pets. Each of my children even served as a legislative page for our next-door neighbor, who was a member of the Kansas House of Representatives. These experiences made them more capable and more confident— much like the experiences once available on Montgall Avenue.

I no longer teach in the public schools, and today I work for CASA, Court Appointed Special Advocates, an organization that advocates for children in the foster care system. The children we serve are all races and ethnicities (although the children in state custody are disproportionately people of color), and the vast majority live in poverty. Some of these children's parents have died; other parents struggle with addictions, mental health issues, and legal challenges; and all of the families have experienced trauma. For the vast majority of these families, the traumas are multigenerational. And although earlier scholars concluded that Kansas City's poor Black community—men and women who were only one or two generations removed from slavery—were biologically inferior because of their race, most of today's social scientists are aware of the landmark Adverse Childhood Experiences (ACEs) study that isolated specific factors in childhood, such as parental incarceration, a mental health diagnosis, or a child feeling physically or emotionally insecure. These scientists have linked these factors to impulsive behaviors and adult outcomes such as heart disease and cancer.[1] As early as 1925, Black leaders like Hugh Oliver Cook understood the causal impact of children's environments, so he advocated that schools prioritize health in the curriculum in his master's thesis.

If homeownership represents the best of the American dream, it could be argued that 1904 was the summit year for Kansas City's Black community and that the 2400 block of Montgall Avenue represents this peak. (Coincidentally, that is the same year my grandfather arrived in America.) Montgall's earliest residents were free to move into their new homes, and they willingly devoted themselves to helping the poor in their community, clearly understanding the need to invest in the younger generation. But that is where the outside investment stopped. The city's White leadership had little interest in supporting the Black community, and instead it used its resources to separate and isolate them. The state of Missouri kept Montgall residents from the state's flagship university, and the federal government created housing policies that erased any assets Black homeowners accumulated and robbed them of their ability to transfer that wealth to the next generation. All of these policies occurred at the same time families such as mine were able to take advantage of government investments and supports. Rather than easing any of the damage wrought by America's original sin of slavery, the local, state, and federal governments did all they could to create environments that perpetuated trauma for Black residents. Today, the 2400 block of Montgall Avenue is situated in one of the poorest neighborhoods in Kansas City.

We are accustomed to learning about the history of African Americans through biographies. Uplifting accounts of individuals overcoming adversity leave us all feeling a little more hopeful about the American experiment and the forward progress of African Americans. It's harder to have that same optimism when the focus is on a street. And while it is true that people create neighborhoods, it is also true that neighborhoods and environments create people.

Unlike people, though, streets and neighborhoods don't have endings, only inflection points, and this book covered several of these periods for Montgall. In 1911, after the Black residents on Montgall became targets of dynamite, Anna Jones and Hugh Oliver Cook had a choice: fight the attacks or move. They fought and remained on the street. But rather than continue living on an integrated street, the White residents left.

In 1941 the Kansas City Police Department faced a choice after the death of Harrison Ware, and Chief Reed was fired after mounting pressure that started in the city's Black community. Yet this change in leadership did nothing to stop what happened to John Bluford Jr. forty years later after his tragic encounter with a police officer.

After World War II, editors of *Roget's Thesaurus* announced they would omit the most offensive terms for people of color. Other, more coded language emerged that had devastating consequences for men and women of color. In the 1980s "welfare queens" became a useful term for leaders looking to justify deep cuts in the social safety net for millions of poor Americans, a disproportionate number of whom were Black. A decade later, "superpredators" helped justify the passage of a crime bill and the mass incarceration of millions of African American men and women.

In 1954 the US Supreme Court ruled in *Brown vs. Board of Education* that separate schools are not equal. Lucile Bluford documented the extraordinary efforts the school board took to keep Black and White students apart, and today, segregation in schools continues.[2]

The second decade of the twenty-first century represents another inflection point for Kansas City—and the rest of the country. The murders of George Floyd and Breonna Taylor highlighted the ongoing threat of overpolicing for certain populations in certain neighborhoods. COVID-19 also disproportionately affected people of color and shined the spotlight on unequal access to health care. In 2020 the Kansas City Board of Parks and Recreation Commissioners voted to remove J. C. Nichols's name from a large fountain near the Country Club Plaza. Such a move suggests that Kansas Citians realize the role J. C. Nichols played in redlining the city's streets. Renaming a fountain is a reasonable beginning. The question is whether this gesture is the sum total of the response. If we look to history to answer this question, those interested in social justice may be disappointed.

Montgall Avenue illustrates persistent attitudes among the White population toward communities of color. "The city takes little interest in any of the Negro districts, except to have them well patrolled by policemen," observed Asa Martin in 1913.[3] Fifty-five years later, after the riots in 1968, the local president of the NAACP, Herman Johnson, observed that it felt as if a net had been thrown over the area around Montgall Avenue. "The attitude was: 'Whatever happens within it, so what?'"[4] Thirteen years after the riot, John Bluford Jr. was stopped by a police officer after a minor traffic stop. He never walked again.

In 2014 writer Ta-Nehisi Coates made a case for reparations for African Americans, pointing out the country's tendency to claim one aspect of history but disavow another. "The last slaveholder has been dead for a very long time. The last soldier to endure Valley Forge has been dead much longer. To proudly claim the veteran and disown the slaveholder is patriotism à la carte," he wrote.[5]

Kansas Citians have honored some of the remarkable men and women who built Montgall Avenue by naming school buildings and libraries after them. But other policies isolated the street's later residents and tore at the community's social fabric, the exact support that street's earliest Black residents provided, support that helped the broader community thrive. Perhaps a more fitting way to honor the men and women of Montgall Avenue would be to continue the work to which they devoted their lives, starting with an examination of the policies that led to the divestment of the 2400 block of Montgall Avenue and all those streets like it.

NOTES

Preface

1. Margie Carr, "150-Year-Old Church Integral to City's History: Ninth Street Baptist Dates to Lawrence's Early Days," *Lawrence Journal-World*, March 3, 2013.

2. "Ethel Moore," interview by Curtis Nether, 1977, Lawrence/Douglas County African American Oral History Interviews, http://oralhistory.lplks .org/4ethel_moore.html.

3. All letters referenced in this paragraph are available from the W. E. B. Du Bois Papers at UMass Amherst. Homer Roberts to the *Crisis*, November 10, 1919, http://credo.library.umass.edu/view/full/mums312-b015-i140; W. H. Crogman to W. E. B. Du Bois, February 5, 1926, http://credo.library.umass.edu /view/full/mums312-b033-i021; Anna H. Jones to W. E. B. Du Bois, December 18, 1911, http://credo.library.umass.edu/view/full/mums312-b006-i298.

Introduction

1. *Kansas City Star*, November 5, 2012, July 2, 2012, March 30, 2012.

2. Society page, *Rising Son*, July 20, 1907.

3. Bluford deposition, *Jenkins v. Kansas City Missouri School District*, Arthur A. Benson II Papers (K0250), SHSMO–KC. Other information about Montgall Avenue at the beginning of the twentieth century can be found in Bluford's oral history with the Washington Press Club Foundation's Women in Journalism Oral History Project Records, 1987–1994, folder 15, pp. 12–13. Bluford sat for a series of interviews with Fern Ingersoll, who spoke to her at her *Call* office four times between May and August 1989. A final video interview was held on March 19, 1990. During Bluford's childhood, this block of Montgall sat amid a Jewish community. For more on Black and Jewish neighborhoods, see Beryl Satter's *Family Properties: How the Struggle over Race and Real Estate Transformed Chicago and Urban America* (New York: Picador, 2009).

4. City directories, Missouri Valley Special Collections (MVSC), Kansas City Public Library (KCPL).

5. W. E. B. Du Bois, *The Souls of Black Folk* (Chicago: A. C. McClurg, 1903), retrieved from http://www.norton.com/college/history/give-me-liberty4/do cs/WEBDuBois-Souls_of_Black_Folk-1903.pdf.

Chapter 1. Rufus Montgall: The Man behind the Street

1. David McCullough, *Truman* (New York: Simon & Schuster, 1992), 15–19. According to McCullough, most of the Kentucky migrants arrived by steamboat. Carrie Westlake, however, reported that Rufus and Nancy Montgall arrived by a team of horses and a wagon.

2. Reva Griffith, 1978 interview with Virginia Oldham, folder 82, Penn Valley Meeting of Friends Records (K0077), SHSMO–KC.

3. For more on Kansas City's difficult topography, see James Shortridge, *Kansas City and How It Grew, 1822–2011* (Lawrence: University Press of Kansas, 2012), 2–7.

4. Carrie Westlake Whitney, *Kansas City, Missouri: Its History and Its People*, vol. 2, *1808–1908* (Chicago: S. J. Clarke, 1908), MVSC Q 091 M53, KCPL.

5. Missouri slave schedules are available for Jackson County at sos.mo.gov /records/archives/census/pages/slave.

6. G. S. Griffin, *Racism in Kansas City: A Short History* (Traverse City, MI: Chandler Lake Books, 2015), 9–11.

7. "Slavery in Missouri," chapter 39 of an unpublished manuscript in James M. Greenwood Papers (SC86–1), box 2, folder 17, MVSC, KCPL.

8. A. Theodore Brown and Lyle W. Dorsett, *K.C.: A History of Kansas City, Missouri* (Boulder, CO: Pruett, 1978), 25–29.

9. Montgall was appointed to Company B, Kansas City Station Guards, on August 9, 1864, by the authority of General Schofield. He served until March 12, 1865. Organization_and_status_of_missouri_troops_union_confederate _published_1902.pdf.

10. Whitney, *Kansas City, Missouri*. See also *A Memorial and Biological Record of Kansas City and Jackson County* (Chicago: Lewis, 1896), MVSC, KCPL.

11. Abstract of 2436 Montgall Avenue, courtesy of Gwen Calderon.

12. See Shortridge, *Kansas City and How It Grew*, 35–44.

13. Clifford Naysmith, "History of Kansas City," unpublished dissertation, Andrew Theodore Brown Collection, folder 5, p. 46, SHSMO–KC.

14. Shortridge, *Kansas City and How It Grew*, 62.

15. Sherry Lamb Schirmer, *A City Divided: The Racial Landscape of Kansas City, 1900–1960* (Columbia: University of Missouri Press, 2002), 34.

16. Naysmith, "History of Kansas City," 60.

17. Naysmith, 169–173.

18. Naysmith, 169.

19. For a list of early Jim Crow laws, see, for example, "Jim Crow Laws and Racial Segregation," Virginia Commonwealth, Commonwealth University Libraries Social Welfare History Project, https://socialwelfare.library.vcu.edu /eras/civil-war-reconstruction/jim-crow-laws-andracial-segregation/.

20. Roy Wilkins, *Standing Fast: The Autobiography of Roy Wilkins* (New York: Viking Press, 1982), 60.

Chapter 2. 2436 Montgall Avenue: Hugh Oliver and Myrtle Foster Cook

1. *Thirteenth Census of the United States*, 1910, and city directories available in MVSC, KCPL.

2. In 1983 Lucile Bluford told the story of how Principal Cook and Daisy found themselves on Montgall in her deposition for *Jenkins v. State of Missouri*, available in box 102, Benson Papers, SHSMO–KC.

3. Advertisement, *Rising Son*, June 24, 1904.

4. The diversity of Montgall is especially extraordinary given the tendency of immigrants and ethnic groups to live in their own somewhat segregated communities. For more on this, see Clifford Naysmith, "History of Kansas City," unpublished dissertation, box 001, folders 4–8, Andrew Theodore Brown Collection.

5. Home Seekers Savings and Loan Articles of Incorporation available online at https://bsd.sos.mo.gov/Common/CorrespondenceItemViewHandler .ashx?IsTIFF=true&filedDocumentid=10003627&version=2.

6. African American teachers were paid the same as White teachers in the Kansas City, Missouri, school district. Because it was the only school for Black students in three counties, many had to travel long distances to attend. It was an expense that fell to individual families, according to a book published by the League of Women Voters. See *The Negro in Kansas City*, 1944, p. 1, Ramos Collection, MVSC, KCPL. Available online at https://kchistory.org/book /negro-kansas-city?solr_nav%5Bid%5D=b523f3fa5d266d4cef01&solr_nav %5Bpage%5D=0&solr_nav%5Boffset%5D=16#page/26/mode/2up.

7. Information about Cook's childhood is available in the biography of his older brother. Marva Carter, *Swing Along: The Musical Life of Will Marion Cook* (Oxford: Oxford University Press, 2008).

8. Carter, 110.

9. When Cook retired from Lincoln High School, the *Call* wrote a lengthy piece about him: "The H. O. Cooks to Live in California," December 10, 1943. All references to him in this section are from this article.

10. "Leonard Reed," Performing Arts Databases, https://memory.loc.gov /diglib/ihas/loc.music.tdabio.160/default.html.

11. Missouri death certificates are available online at S1.sos.mo.gov.

12. Howard W. Odum, *Social and Mental Traits of the Negro: Research into the Conditions of the Negro Race in Southern Towns, a Study in Race Traits, Tendencies and Prospects* (New York: Columbia University, 1910), 38, https://arc hive.org/stream/socialmental100odumrich_djvu.txt. It should be noted that

Odum's theories on race evolved over time, and by the end of his life he was committed to civil rights.

13. Odum, *Social and Mental Traits of the Negro*, 41.

14. Frederick Hoffman, *Race Traits and Tendencies of the American Negro* (New York: Macmillan, 1896), 311–312.

15. Odum, *Social and Mental Traits of the Negro*, 50–52.

16. Asa E. Martin, *Our Negro Population: A Sociological Study of the Negroes in Kansas City, Missouri* (Kansas City, MO: Franklin Hudson, 1913), 115.

17. Hugh Oliver Cook, "A Modern High School Plan for the Negro Children of Kansas City, MO" (master's thesis, Cornell University, 1925), 50. Subsequent references will be given parenthetically within the text.

18. Lincoln High School yearbooks for 1904 and 1917, BAMA. Also available online: https://archive.org/details/lincolncolesarchive?sort=titleSorter.

19. Joshua Russell oral history interview by Horace Peterson, April 6, 1983, BAMA.

20. Lincoln High School yearbook for 1925.

21. 1935 graduation ceremony information from Stanley Crouch, *Kansas City Lightning: The Rise and Times of Charlie Parker* (New York: HarperCollins, 2013), 78–79.

22. 1925 Lincoln yearbook.

23. Myrtle F. Cook to W. E. B. Du Bois, February 20, 1925, W. E. B. Du Bois Papers (MS 312), Special Collections and University Archives, University of Massachusetts Amherst, https://credo.library.umass.edu/view/full/mums 312-b170-i464.

24. Lincoln High yearbooks for 1920, 1922, and 1924.

25. Cook's study for the housing department is discussed in Martin, *Our Negro Population*, 102–103.

26. Martin, *Our Negro Population*, 120.

27. H. O. Cook and I. F. Bradley, "Resolutions: To the Honorable Woodrow Wilson, President of the United States," *Topeka and Kansas City Plaindealer*, November 7, 1913.

28. "Prof. Cook Honored," *Kansas City Sun*, March 8, 1919.

29. Letter from Cook to Crews printed in the *Kansas City Sun*, March 23, 1918.

30. "Prof. Cook Welcomed," *Kansas City Sun*, February 22, 1919.

31. 1924 Lincoln High yearbook.

32. Myrtle Foster Cook's obituary is in *Kansas City Call*, September 7, 1951.

33. "H. O. Cooks to Live in California."

34. Home Seekers Articles of Incorporation papers, https://bsd.sos.mo .gov/Common/CorrespondenceItemViewHandler.ashx?IsTIFF=true&filed Documentid=10003627&version=2.

35. "Depression Does Not Handicap Peoples Finance Corporation," *Kansas City and Topeka Plaindealer*, February 17, 1933.

36. "H. O. Cooks to Live in California."

37. C. G. Williams to Arthur Hyde, May 26, 1921, box 7, folder 460, Arthur Mastick Hyde Gubernatorial Papers (C0007), SHSMO–C.

38. Roy Wilkins, "Mammoth Crowd at N.A.A.C.P Meeting Resents Remark of Gov'r's Substitute," *Kansas City Call*, September 7, 1923.

39. "More than 4,000 See 1,000 Lincoln High Students Depict Transformation in Pageant," *Topeka and Kansas City Plaindealer*, April 5, 1935.

40. "J. H. Cook, Song Writer, Dead," *Topeka and Kansas City Plaindealer*, August 18, 1939.

41. 1939 Lincoln High yearbook.

42. "H. O. Cooks to Live in California."

Chapter 3. 2444 Montgall Avenue: Anna Holland Jones

1. Author interview with Renée Cochée, Anna Jones's great-niece, March 14, 2014, Culver City, California.

2. Gwendolyn Robinson and John W. Robinson, *Seek the Truth: A Story of Chatham's Black Community* (self-published, 1989), 32–34.

3. For more on the experience of African Americans in North Carolina, see Jeffrey J. Crow, Paul D. Escott, and Flora J. Hatley, *A History of African Americans in North Carolina* (Raleigh: Office of Archives and History, North Carolina Department of Cultural Resources, 1992).

4. John Hope Franklin, *The Free Negro in North Carolina, 1790–1860* (Chapel Hill: University of North Carolina Press, 1943), 92.

5. William Bigglestone, *They Stopped in Oberlin* (Oberlin, OH: Oberlin College Publishing, 1981), 122–124.

6. Bigglestone, 124.

7. W. E. B. Du Bois, *John Brown* (Philadelphia: George W. Jacobs, 1909; New York: International, 1962), 235.

8. Oswald Garrison Villard, *John Brown, 1800–1859: A Biography Fifty Years After* (Gloucester, MA: Peter Smith, 1965), 327.

9. Steven Lubet, "The Oberlin Fugitive Rescue: A Victory for Higher Law," Faculty Working Paper 22, 2011, http://scholarlycommons.law.northwestern.edu/facultyworkingpapers/22.

10. Du Bois, *John Brown*, 257. Du Bois described the Chatham community this way: "John Brown's choice of Canada as a center of Negro culture was wise. There were nearly 50,000 Negroes there, and the number included many energetic, intelligent and brave men, with some wealth. Settlements had grown up, farms had been bought, schools established and an intricate

social organization begun." Subsequent references to this book are given parenthetically within the text.

11. G. M. Jones to Emily F. Jones, May 14, 1906. Courtesy of Renée Cochée. G. M. Jones wrote (on Oberlin College stationery) to Emily Jones (Anna's mother) to inquire about her children's addresses and occupations, "except of course Miss Anna H. Jones of our College class of '75, who reports to us regularly." At the bottom of the letter, Emily handwrote an update about her children: George lived with Emily and was a carpenter in Ann Arbor, Fredericka Jones was on Bellefontaine Avenue in Kansas City, Missouri, and Emily Jones was working as a teacher in Jacksonville, Florida.

12. "News and Gossip. Locals," *Rising Son*, October 9, 1903.

13. *Detroit Plaindealer*, July 1, 1892.

14. "The Race Question," *Kansas City Times*, May 28, 1890.

15. Schirmer, *City Divided*, 38–42.

16. For more on the history and development of Cliff Drive, see *A Legacy of Design: An Historical Survey of the Kansas City, Missouri, Parks and Boulevards System, 1893–1940*, ed. Janice Lee, David Boutros, Charlotte R. White, and Deon Wolfenbarge (Kansas City, MO: Kansas City Center for Design Education and Research, in cooperation with the Western Historical Manuscript Collection–Kansas City, 1995), 41–52.

17. For more on the early days of the National Association of Colored Women, see Elizabeth L. Davis, ed., *Lifting as They Climb* (Washington, DC: National Association of Colored Women, 1933).

18. Errin Jackson, "Josephine Silone Yates," April 19, 2007, BlackPast, https://Blackpast.org/african-american-history/yates-josephine-silone.

19. Discussion of Kansas City in "Women's League" section, *Woman's Era* 1, no. 1 (1894), edited and published by Josephine St. Ruffin and Florida R. Ridley. Electronic edition is available from Emory University.

20. *Woman's Era*, 1894.

21. Martin, *Our Negro Population*, 123.

22. Odum, *Social and Mental Traits of the Negro*, 40.

23. Eleanor Tayleur, "The Negro Woman: I. Social and Moral Decadence," *Outlook*, January 1904, 270. Available online at https://babel.hathitrust.org/cgi/pt?id=iau.31858033603162&view=1up&seq=304&skin=2021&q1=negro%20women.

24. *Contributions of Black Women to America*, vol. 2, ed. Marianna Davis (Columbia, SC: Kenday Press, 1982), 87.

25. For more, see Tony Horwitz, "The Mammy Washington Almost Had," *Atlantic Monthly*, May 31, 2013.

26. "National Association of Colored Women. Fifth Biennial or Tenth Anniversary of Organized Afro-American Womanhood," *Rising Son*, August 16,

1906. Jones had just returned from the NACWC conference in Detroit, which ran from July 9 to 14.

27. For more on the city's "90-Day Challenge," see Rick Montgomery and Shirl Kasper, *Kansas City: An American Story*, ed. Monroe Dodd (Kansas City, MO: Kansas City Star Books, 1999), 146–150.

28. Wilda Sandy, *Here Lies Kansas City* (Kansas City, MO: Bennett Schneider, 1984).

29. *New York Times*, Paris ed., July 2, 1900, cited in Esedebe Olisanwuche, *Pan-Africanism: The Idea and Movement, 1776–1991*, 2nd ed. (Washington, DC: Howard University Press, 1994).

30. Olisanwuche, *Pan-Africanism*. Further evidence of Jones's commitment to art is from a paper she delivered at an annual gathering of teachers. "The Art Idea: Its Relations to Negro Education," *Professional World*, January 9, 1903.

31. David Levering Lewis, *W. E. B. Du Bois, the Fight for Equality and the American Century, 1919–1963* (New York: Henry Holt, 2000), 156.

32. Mark Sullivan, "Black Like We," *Harvard Gazette*, October 25, 2013, https://news.harvard.edu/gazette/story/2013/10/black-like-we/.

33. 1904 Lincoln High School yearbook. Yearbooks are available at BAMA.

34. Anna Jones, "A Century's Progress for the American Colored Woman," *Voice of the Negro*, October 1905, 632.

35. Wilkins, *Standing Fast*, 60.

36. "If 'Jim Crow' Bill Should Pass," *Rising Son*, February 20, 1903.

37. Jones to Du Bois, December 18, 1911, series IA, General Correspondence, 1877–1965, Du Bois Papers.

38. Anna Jones, "Woman Suffrage and Social Reform," *Crisis*, August 1915, 189–190. Further evidence of her belief in gender equality is evident in the October 10, 1914, issue of the *Kansas City Sun*, "$4,000 More Needed to Furnish Y.M.C.A.," in which she, after contributing money toward the Paseo YMCA, challenged the mostly male audience to support the YWCA.

39. Jones, "Woman Suffrage and Social Reform."

40. Jones, "A Century's Progress," 694.

41. 1904 Lincoln High School yearbook.

Chapter 4. 2442 Montgall Avenue: Hezekiah Walden

1. Corie Washow and Mark Tappan, "Colby College Graduates of Color 1849–1943, a Preliminary Exploration," *Colby Alumnus Report*, class of 1898 (August 2000). *Rising Son* published a short biography of Hezekiah Walden after he was hired by Lincoln. "Prof. Hezekiah Walden," October 18, 1906.

2. Bill Carey, "The Roger Williams' Legacy," *Tennessee Magazine*, July 2012.

3. "Mayor Crittenden Says Negro Should Be Out of Politics," *Kansas City Journal*, November 5, 1908.

4. *Kansas City Journal*, May 28, 1911.

5. C. A. Franklin to Missouri Gov. Hyde, July 5, 1924, box 3, folder 109, Arthur Mastick Hyde Papers.

6. *Kansas City Journal*, May 28, 1911.

7. See Douglas S. Massey and Nancy A. Denton, *American Apartheid: Segregation and the Making of the American Underclass* (Cambridge, MA: Harvard University Press, 1993), 2; Stanley Lieberson, *A Piece of the Pie: Blacks and Immigrants since 1880* (Berkeley: University of California Press, 1981).

8. Massey and Denton, *American Apartheid*, 23–26.

9. Minutes of the Kansas City, Missouri, School Board Meeting, June 13, 1911, MVSC, KCPL.

10. Minutes of the Kansas City, Missouri, School Board Meeting, June 17, 1911, MVSC, KCPL.

11. H. O. Cook to Oswald Garrison Villard, November 21, 1911, series 1A, General Correspondence, 1877–1965, Du Bois Collection, W. E. B. Du Bois Papers, http://credo.library.umass.edu/view/full/mums312-b007-i032.

12. Anna H. Jones to W. E. B. Du Bois, December 18, 1911, series 1A, General Correspondence, 1877–1965, Du Bois Collection, W. E. B. Du Bois Papers, http://credo.library.umass.edu/view/full/mums312-b006-i298.

13. A Black man was arrested for the bombings for supposedly trying to decrease the value of the homes in the neighborhood. Although prosecutors could not prove that he was responsible for the dynamite attacks, he ended up serving three years in prison on a concealed weapon charge.

Chapter 5. 2434 Montgall Avenue: Frances and Charles Jackson, Carolyn Brydie, and Gwendolyn Calderon

1. *Kansas City Sun*, November 6, 1915; Frances Jackson's death certificate, August 28, 1930, https://www.sos.mo.gov/images/archives/deathcerts/1930/1930_00027630.PDF.

2. "Mr. Lewis Wood Severs His Connection with the *Rising Son*," *Rising Son*, December 6, 1906.

3. "Great Prosperity among the Negroes in this Community, Especially in the South End of Town," *Rising Son*, June 29, 1907.

4. "A Reply to the Pitchfork on John Lange and Other Negro Property Owners," *Rising Son*, November 30, 1907.

5. "A Stand for Negro Morality," *Rising Son*, December 22, 1906.

6. Jackson spoke at a local meeting of the NAACP about discrimination and correctional facilities. *Kansas City Sun*, February 7, 1914.

7. "Imposing Exercises at Garrison School," *Rising Son*, April 29, 1904. All quotations from Jackson are from this article.

8. "The Clansman Excites Race Hatred," *Rising Son*, March 8, 1906.

9. Leon F. Litwack, "The Birth of a Nation," in Mark C. Carnes, ed., *Past Imperfect: History According to the Movies* (New York: Henry Holt, 1995), 136–141.

10. A. Scott Berg, *Wilson* (New York: G. P. Putnam's Sons, 2013), 347–350.

11. D. W. Griffith, *Birth of a Nation*, 1915, https://www.youtube.com/watch ?v=nGQaAddwjxg.

12. For more discussion of the film's impact on American society, see Gerald R. Butters Jr., "The Kansas Board of Review of Motion Pictures and Film Censorship (1913–1924)" (master's thesis, University of Missouri, Kansas City, 1989).

13. Butters, "Kansas Board of Review."

14. See *Crisis*, October 1915, 293–296, for a report on local chapters' efforts to limit or ban the film.

15. "The Denver Law," *Kansas City Sun*, October 23, 1915.

16. "N.A.A.C.P. Works Faithfully," *Kansas City Sun*, October 30, 1915.

17. Butters, "Kansas Board of Review."

18. "'The Birth of a Nation' Is a Stupendous Series of Thrills," *Kansas City Star*, October 25, 1915.

19. City directories, MVSC, KCPL.

20. Charles Jackson's death certificate, June 8, 1926, https://www.sos.mo .gov/images/archives/deathcerts/1926/1926_00020608.

21. Kansas City School District records, MVSC, KCPL.

22. William Crogman to his daughter Ada, Chester Franklin's future wife, about safe lodging, June 3, 1917. Franklin Collection, BAMA.

23. "Rites for Carolyn Brydie, Retired School Teacher," *Kansas City Call*, September 27, 1957.

24. Brydie's extracurricular activities at Lincoln are chronicled in various Lincoln High School yearbooks. For example, the 1916 edition documented her role in the dramatic club, including directing *The Merchant of Venice*.

25. Martin, *Our Negro Population*, 172.

26. 1916 Lincoln High School yearbook.

27. 1928 Lincoln High School yearbook.

28. Martin, *Our Negro Population*, 174.

29. The *Kansas City Sun* published a long letter of grievances about the inadequacies at Lincoln High School on March 20, 1920. "A Memorial to the Board of Education of Kansas City, MO. For Improved School Facilities for Negro Children by 1," Letter to the Board of Education by Parent-Teachers Association, Kansas City Branch of the National Association for the

Advancement of Colored People, City Federation of Colored Women's Clubs, Kansas City Medical Society, Civic League, Lincoln High School Alumni Association, Inter-City Lawyers' Club, Negro Business League, and the Inter-Denominational Ministerial Alliance. It was another fifteen years before a new building was completed for Kansas City's Black students.

30. 1922 Lincoln High School yearbook.

31. Gwendolyn Calderon interview by author, October 31, 2015, Kansas City, Missouri.

32. Joshua Russell oral history interview by Horace Peterson, 1983, BAMA.

Chapter 6. 2451 Montgall Avenue: John Edward Perry and Fredericka Douglass Perry

1. Fredericka provided perhaps the most intimate portrayal of her famous grandfather, Frederick Douglass, describing how he would get down on his hands and knees to allow his grandchildren to climb all over him, as reported in David Blight's biography, *Frederick Douglass: Prophet of Freedom* (New York: Simon & Schuster, 2018), 610–611.

2. W. Montague Cobb, "John Edward Perry, M.D., 1870–," *Journal of the National Medical Association* 48, no. 4 (July 1956): 292–296.

3. John Edward Perry, *Forty Cords of Wood: Memoir of a Medical Doctor* (Jefferson City, MO: Lincoln University, 1947), 1–2. Subsequent references to this work will be given parenthetically within the text.

4. J. E. Perry, "The Negro Doctor: His Professional Work and Progress," *Professional World*, November 8, 1901.

5. History of General Hospital #1, Jackson County Medical Society Collection, box 1, folder 6, Health Facilities in the Kansas City Area 1876–1937 A–L, SHSMO–KC.

6. "Negroes Want Old Hospital," *Rising Son*, October 19, 1907.

7. "Deaths from Tuberculosis," *Kansas City Journal*, October 9, 1906, and October 17 and 25, 1909. The newspaper published reports of city leaders' efforts for marginalized communities, such as the establishment of a bathhouse in the North End.

8. History of General Hospital #2 (Colored Division), Jackson County Medical Society Collection, box 1, folder 6, Health Facilities in the Kansas City Area 1876–1937 A–L, SHSMO–KC.

9. "Removal of Negro Interns Sought," *Kansas City Journal*, August 7, 1912; "Hospital Retains Negro Interns," August 12, 1912.

10. Wilma Peebles-Wilkins, "Black Women and American Social Welfare:

The Life of Fredericka Douglass Sprague Perry," *Affilia*, March 1, 1989, 4, 33.

11. Peebles-Wilkins, "Black Women and American Social Welfare."

12. Author phone interview with Danny Herndon, a friend of Perry's grandson, July 6, 2014.

13. Loren Taylor, "The Historic John Brown Statue of Wyandotte County," *Historical Journal of Wyandotte County* 1, no. 6 (2002): 261–262.

14. Peebles-Wilkins, "Black Women and American Social Welfare."

15. December 14, 1941, fundraising letter for Big Sisters Home, courtesy of Gwendolyn Calderon.

16. Fundraising efforts for Wheatley-Provident Hospital are chronicled in numerous issues of the *Kansas City Sun*. The December 8, 1917, edition of the paper has a large photo of the new Wheatley-Provident Hospital when it moved into a large stone building, a former Catholic school, at 1826 Forest Avenue.

17. "Special Help in Treatment of Children," *Kansas City Call*, January 12, 1923. For schedule of outpatient clinics see *Kansas City Sun*, December 21, 1918.

18. History of Wheatley-Provident Hospital, Jackson County Medical Society Collection, box 1, folder 7, Health Facilities in the Kansas City Area 1876–1937 M–Z, SHSMO–KC.

19. Fredericka Perry death certificate, October 23, 1943, available at https// s1.sos.mo.gov/records/archives/archivesdb/deathcertificates/.

20. Subsequent chapters address other Montgall residents' attempts to integrate private and public spaces.

21. Minutes of the Meeting of the Board of Directors of Lincoln University, Jefferson City, MO, June 26, 1939, box 194, folder 6450, Forrest C. Donnell Gubernatorial Papers (C0194), SHSMO–C.

22. Edward T. Clayton, "The Strange Disappearance of Lloyd Gaines," *Ebony*, May 1951, 25–34.

23. DeBoe to Donnell, May 17, 1943, box 194, folder 6474, Donnell Papers.

24. Slaughter to Donnell, May 17, 1943, box 194, folder 6469, Donnell Papers.

25. Scruggs to McKittrick, August 6, 1943, box 194, folder 6470, Donnell Papers.

26. Cobb, "Medical History: John Edward Perry, M.D."

27. While J. E. Perry spelled out his conservative views in his autobiography and other writings, Fredericka's are less well known. However, there is some indication that she could have been less conservative than her husband in her role in the ousting of Chief of Police Lear Reed (see chapter 11).

Chapter 7. 2453 Montgall Avenue: Homer Roberts

1. See, for example, *Kansas City Sun*, September 5, 1914.

2. Information on Roberts's early life is from B. S. Restuccia, with Edward "Sonny" Gibson and Geraldlyn "Geri" Sanders, *Homer B. Roberts, 1882–1952: An Extraordinary Man* (Kansas City, MO: Rustic Enterprises, 2001).

3. Advertisement, *Kansas City Sun*, April 11, 1914.

4. "Colored Chauffeurs to Army Will Form 317th Sanitary Train 92nd Division," *Kansas City Sun*, December 8, 1917.

5. "Colored Chauffeurs to Army."

6. Roberts to Du Bois, November 10, 1919, Du Bois Papers. This is the same letter in which he offers his assistance to the scholar on his history of Black service to the war effort. While Du Bois answered and expressed interest, Roberts responded that he was working on the story on December 4, 1919. Unfortunately, no other letters were found about Roberts's service in World War I. See "Homer B. Roberts, First of Race to Be Commissioned in United States Signal Crops [sic], Commanded Liaison Unit in Fiercest Battle of War," *Kansas City Sun*, March 29, 1919.

7. Advertisement, *Kansas City Sun*, May 31, 1919.

8. The *Kansas City Sun* announced on February 28, 1920, that Roberts had sold an "elegant new coupe" to Dr. Perry.

9. Restuccia, *Homer Roberts*, 27.

10. Appreciation ad published by Roberts in *Kansas City Sun*, May 21, 1921, in which he credited Lincoln High students, under Mr. Massy's supervision, with painting his new facility. Brick and plaster work was also completed by Lincoln High students under the supervision of Mr. Galliard. Cited in Restuccia, *Homer Roberts*, 21.

11. Wilkins, *Standing Fast*, 58. Wilkins was good friends with "the lanky" Joe LaCour, who was also friends with Homer Roberts.

12. "3,000 Attend Opening of New Motor Mart," *Kansas City Call*, August 3, 1923. Restuccia claims that Roberts was the largest employer of African Americans in the city. At its peak, it employed fifty-five African Americans (*Homer Roberts*, 43).

13. "Golf Appeal to High Court," *Kansas City Star*, August 15, 1928. All quotations in this section are from this article unless otherwise noted.

14. Brady McCollough, "Playing Through," *Kansas City Star*, July 17, 2005.

15. *C. A. Franklin v. John B. Gage, Mayor, Kansas City, Missouri*, February 5, 1943, Franklin Collection, BAMA.

16. "Roberts Company Expands and Opens Auto Salesroom in Chicago," *Kansas City Call*, January 11, 1929. See also "Roberts-Campbell Motor Sales Co. to Open on Jan 27," *Chicago Defender*, January 19, 1929.

17. On November 1, 1940, the Hupp Motor Car Company, which manufactured the Hupmobile, declared bankruptcy, as cited in Restuccia, *Homer Roberts*, 82.

18. Roberts was among a group of Black newspaper men in New York City when the Negro Newspaper Publishers gathered there on June 14, 1951. Copies of the speeches given in Dorothy Hodge Johnson Collection (RH MS 549), box 4, folder 10, Kansas Collection, Kenneth Spencer Research Library, University of Kansas. For more on Black newspaper reporters during World War II, see John D. Stevens, "From the Back of the Foxhole: Black Correspondents in World War II," Association for Education in Journalism, 1973. Available at https://files.eric.ed.gov/fulltext/ED096675.pdf.

19. *Kansas City Star*, February 2, 2017.

Chapter 8. 2447 Montgall Avenue: Chester Franklin and Ada Crogman

1. Early history of Franklin's life is from William H. Young and Nathan B. Young Jr., *Your Kansas City and Mine* (Kansas City, MO: Midwest Afro-American Genealogy Interest Coalition at the Bruce R. Watkins Cultural Heritage Center, 1950, rpt. 1997).

2. "Type Carries His Plea: C. A. Franklin, 70 Tomorrow, Fights a Long Battle," *Kansas City Star*, June 6, 1950.

3. Willa Glenn Peebles and Irene Loretta Smith, "Lincoln High School Crowded," *Kansas City Sun*, September 13, 1919.

4. Lucile Bluford's speech at the dedication of the Chester Franklin Elementary School, May 5, 1968, Manuscript Files, Lucile Bluford, "Chester Arthur Franklin" Ramos Collection, MVSC, KCPL.

5. "Type Carries His Plea."

6. Dowdal Davis speech, June 14, 1951, Dorothy Hodge Johnson Collection, box 4, folder 10, Kansas Collection, Kenneth Spencer Research Library, University of Kansas.

7. Lucile Bluford speech, May 5, 1968.

8. Wilkins, *Standing Fast*, 56–58.

9. "Little Jam" and "Sweet Papa" appear in the numerous letters to Ada from her father, William, in Franklin Collection, BAMA.

10. Information about Crogman's early life comes from Charlotte Crogman Wright, *The Story of an American Bishop's Wife in South Africa* (New York: Exposition Press, 1955). Ada's older sister, Charlotte or "Lottie," was a prominent social worker, minister's wife, and scholar in Pennsylvania.

11. Lincoln High School yearbook, 1922. See also society pages in *Kansas City Sun*, July 26, 1919.

12. The musical score of *Milestones*, Franklin Collection.

13. Crogman to, presumably, Franklin (although the first page of the letter is missing), undated correspondence, Franklin Collection.

14. Crogman to Franklin, Franklin Collection.

15. Various newspaper clippings (many undated) about *Milestones* performances in various cities are in the Franklin Collection, including Crogman's quote in the *Houston Informer*, April 23, 1927.

16. *Milestones* Program for Kansas City performance, Franklin Collection.

17. Richardson to Crogman, December 17, 1924, Franklin Collection.

18. Franklin to Crogman, undated correspondence, Franklin Collection.

19. Wilkins, *Standing Fast*, 58.

20. Stewart to Ada Franklin, July 10, 1928, Franklin Collection.

21. No year is given in the letter, but December 11 was a Tuesday in 1923.

22. Fred and Pearl Dabney lived on that block of Montgall. The Mr. Watkins mentioned was a funeral director.

23. Franklin to Crogman, undated.

24. "Lord, as Ministers, Give Us Men!" *Kansas City Call*, October 19, 1923. See also "We Must Practice What We Preach," *Kansas City Call*, July 6, 1923; "Negro's Plea to Pastors," *Kansas City Call*, April 5, 1926.

25. Like her future husband's letters to her, Ada saved correspondence from her father during this time. These letters provide a fascinating look at the Montgall Avenue community during the second half of the 1920s.

26. Crogman to A. Franklin, June 28, 1926, Franklin Collection.

27. Crogman to A. Franklin, May 26, 1926, Franklin Collection.

28. Crogman to A. Franklin, November 11, 1926, Franklin Collection.

29. A. Franklin to Crogman, March 22, 1928, Franklin Collection.

30. Crogman Ninetieth Birthday Program, Franklin Collection.

31. *C.A. Franklin v. John B. Gage, Mayor, Kansas City, Missouri*, February 5, 1943, Franklin Collection.

32. Franklin to Governor Hyde, October 29, 1923, Gubernatorial Series, folder 105, Hyde Papers.

33. Thomas D. Wilson, "Chester A. Franklin and Harry S. Truman: An African American Conservative and the 'Conversion' of the Future President," in *Kansas City, America's Crossroads: Essays from the Missouri Historical Review, 1906–2006*, ed. Diane Mutti Burke and John Herron (Columbia: State Historical Society of Missouri), 220–251.

34. Truman's and others' birthday wishes appeared in the program for Franklin's seventieth birthday celebration, June 7, 1950, courtesy of Gwendolyn Calderon.

35. Bluford oral history, folder 18, p. 97.

Chapter 9. 2444 Montgall Avenue: The Bluford Family

1. John Bluford married his first wife, Viola C. Harris, in 1910, and the couple had three children: Lucile, John Jr., and Guion. After Viola died, he married Addie Alston, who, according to his obituary, "reared the children as her own." Bluford was educated at Howard University, and while in Washington, DC, he lived with Nathan Sprague, Frederick Douglass's son-in-law and the father of his future neighbor, Fredericka Perry. "Last Rites for J. H. Bluford," *Kansas City Call*, March 29, 1946.

2. Author interview by telephone with Guion Bluford, August 13, 2014.

3. Bluford oral history, folder 15, p. 6.

4. Myrtle Cook to Governor Hyde, April 30, 1921, folder 105, Hyde Papers.

5. John F. Williams to Commanding General of Missouri National Guard, April 29, 1923, folder 108, Hyde Papers. See also George Vaughn to Gov. Hyde, April 30, 1923, folder 108, Hyde papers. Five men were indicted, one charged with first-degree murder and the others with obstructing an officer. The man charged with murder, George Barkwell, was acquitted.

6. Franklin to Hyde, April 30, 1923, folder 108, Hyde Papers.

7. John Love and Myrtle Cook from Kansas City's chapter of the NAACP, telegram to Governor, April 29, 1923, folder 109, Hyde Papers.

8. Ida Becks and Dara Harris to Governor Hyde, April 30, 1923, folder 108, Hyde Papers.

9. Poster, folder 109a, Hyde Papers.

10. J. S. Gossom to Gov. Hyde, March 1923, folder 109, Hyde Papers.

11. Copy of Hyde's telegrams to sheriffs in Caruthersville, Kennett, Charleston, and Benton Counties, Missouri, February 28, 1923, folder 367, Hyde Papers.

12. Bluford oral history, folder 15, p. 7.

13. "Last Rites for J. H. Bluford."

14. Wilkins, *Standing Fast*, 56.

15. "We Had Our Own Garbage Left at Our Door, We Soon Shall Have Other People's," *Kansas City Call*; January 5, 1923; "And from Now on We'll Fight!" *Kansas City Call*, January 5, 1923; *Kansas City Call*, November 2, 1923.

16. Bluford oral history, folder 16, p. 20.

17. Bluford oral history, folder 15, p. 9.

18. Wilkins, *Standing Fast*, 56.

19. Roy Wilkins, "Mammoth Crowd at N.A.A.C.P Meeting Resents Remark of Gov'r's Substitute," *Kansas City Call*, September 7, 1923. Quotations from the remainder of this section are also from Wilkins's story.

20. Lincoln High School yearbooks; 1926 Lincoln High School yearbook,

Thatcher Family Collection (RH MS 1250), Kenneth Spencer Research Library, University of Kansas.

21. Bluford oral history, folder 15, p. 17.

22. "To the Board of Education of Kansas City, MO. for Improved School Facilities for Negro Children," *Kansas City Sun*, March 20, 1920.

23. Bluford oral history, folder 16, p. 17.

24. 1928 Lincoln High School yearbook.

25. William M. Tuttle Jr., "Separate but Not Equal: African Americans and the 100-Year Struggle for Equality in Lawrence and at the University of Kansas 1850s–1960," in *Embattled Lawrence* (Lawrence: KU Continuing Education, 2001).

26. Loren Miller, "The Unrest among Negro Students," *Crisis*, August 1927, 187–188.

27. Bluford oral history, folder 16, pp. 20–21.

28. Bluford deposition for *Jenkins vs. State of Missouri*, 1983, box 102, Arthur A. Benson II Papers (KC 250), SHSMO–KC.

29. Bluford oral history, folder 16, p. 27.

30. "Missouri Negro Slayer Burned at Crime Scene," *University Daily Kansan (UDK)*, January 12, 1931; "Let's Lynch Him!" (editorial), *UDK*, September 21, 1931; "Principle," *UDK*, October 20, 1931.

31. "Negroes Granted Right to Sit in Men's Council: Representative Will Have No Voting Power at Meetings," *UDK*, January 21, 1932; "A Negro in the Council" (editorial), January 26, 1932.

32. "Dr. Carter Shows Lowly Peanut Versatile Plant," *UDK*, February 15, 1932.

33. "Hughes, Noted Negro, Will Read Own Poems," and "Langston Hughes" (editorial), *UDK*, March 8, 1932; "Life Is His Inspiration, Says Langston Hughes," *UDK*, March 10, 1932.

34. "Seeing 'Race' through Colored Glasses," *UDK*, October 11, 1931.

35. "The Color Bar," *UDK*, March 1, 1932.

36. Bluford oral history, folder 16, p. 37. She explained that she didn't even apply at the *Star* after graduation because they didn't hire women.

37. Bluford oral history, folder 16, pp. 31–32.

38. Bluford oral history, folder 17, p. 54. Bluford told Franklin that she "wasn't all that anxious to go back to school."

39. Bluford oral history, folder 17, p. 55.

40. Bluford oral history, folder 17, pp. 55–57.

41. Missouri's Supreme Court decision can be found in the digital collection of the Missouri State Historical Society: https://digital.shsmo.org/digital/collection/aaem/id/97/rec/8.

42. Bluford wrote a scathing story about the closing remarks of William Hogsett, the University of Missouri's attorney, printed in the May 1, 1942, edition of the *Call*. See chapter 12.

43. Bluford to Houston, February 1931, Lucile H. Bluford Collection, MS-0219, University of Missouri–Kansas City Special Collections and Archives.

44. Bluford to Houston, September 10, 1941, Bluford Collection.

45. Houston to Bluford, September 15, 1941, Bluford Collection.

46. Bluford to Houston, September 21, 1941, Bluford Collection.

Chapter 10. 2457 Montgall Avenue: Piney Brown

1. "A Stand for Negro Morality," *Rising Son*. December 22, 1906, shortly after Montgall resident Frances Jackson was hired as city editor. Joshua Russell (2424 and 2461) also spoke about the negative impact the clubs had on the Black community in his oral history, available at BAMA. Lucile Bluford hinted at her aversion to the clubs in her oral history, folder 16, p. 36.

2. There is confusion about the two brothers. For example, David Conrads's biography of Felix Payne from a Kansas City Public Library online resource reports that older brother Thomas Brown was Felix Payne's business partner. See https://kchistory.org/document/biography-felix-payne-1884-1962-businessman-and-politician. Restuccia came to the same conclusion in his book on Homer Roberts. He wrote that Thomas "Piney" Brown worked with Roberts during the day and Felix Payne at night. According to my research conducted for this book, this conclusion is inaccurate. Roberts's lawsuit against the city identifies Thomas Jefferson Brown as a co-plaintiff, and a 1928 *Call* story identifies Thomas as remaining in Kansas City to run Roberts Motor Mart, when Homer Roberts left for Chicago that year. In 1939 it was "Walter" Brown who was arrested for gambling, according to the *Topeka Plaindealer*; Walter is named as Felix Payne's partner in William and Nathan Young's *Your Kansas City and Mine*; it was Walter who lived at 2457 Montgall, and it is Walter who was remembered by the musicians and his neighbors, such as Gwendolyn Calderon, as the generous benefactor.

3. Author interview with Gwen Calderon, October 31, 2015.

4. The city's Black population increased from 17,567 in 1900 to 23,566 in 1910 (34.1 percent increase) to 30,719 in 1920 (30.4 percent), and 38,574 by 1930 (25 percent). See Kevin Fox Gotham, *Race, Real Estate, and Uneven Development: The Kansas City Experience, 1900–2000* (Albany: State University of New York Press, 2002), 33.

5. Nathan Pearson Jr., *Goin' to Kansas City* (Chicago: University of Illinois Press, 1987), 97–98.

6. *Kansas City Star*, August 15, 1928.

7. *Kansas City Call*, January 11, 1929.

8. *Kansas City Call*, September 2, 1932, announced Thomas "Piney" Brown's death on August 29, 1932.

9. Ross Russell, *Jazz Style in Kansas City and the Southwest* (New York: Da Capo, 1997), 16.

10. Pearson, *Goin' to Kansas City*, 97.

11. "Notice! Notice! Notice!" (want ad), *Rising Son*, October 4, 1906.

12. Pearson, *Goin' to Kansas City*, 97.

13. Stanley Crouch, *Kansas City Lightning: The Rise and Times of Charlie Parker* (New York: HarperCollins, 2013), 64.

14. Russell, *Jazz Style in Kansas City*, 9.

15. Calderon interview, October 31, 2015.

16. "Walter 'Piney' Brown Arrested at Club," *Topeka Plaindealer*, November 10, 1939.

17. Calderon interview, October 31, 2015.

18. Joshua Russell oral history.

19. David Roediger, *Working toward Whiteness: How America's Immigrants Became White: The Strange Journey from Ellis Island to the Suburbs* (New York: Perseus, 2005), 158. See also Stanley Lieberson, *A Piece of the Pie: Blacks and White Immigrants since 1880* (Berkeley: University of California Press, 1981).

Chapter 11. 2449 Montgall Avenue: The Pittman Family

1. Paul Pittman interview with author, October 23, 2014, Kansas City, Missouri.

2. Kansas City Public Library, "What Is Walt Disney's Connection to Kansas City?" https://kchistory.org/faq/what-walt-disneys-connection-kansas-city; Elizabeth Nix, "7 Things You May Not Know about Walt Disney," History.com, last updated July 18, 2019, https://www.history.com/news/7-things-you-might-not-know-about-walt-disney.

3. Pittman interview; Lucile Bluford also discussed her childhood experiences on Montgall in her oral history, folder 15, pp. 7–9.

4. Gwendolyn Calderon interview with author, October 23, 2014.

5. Bluford oral history, folder 15, pp. 7–8.

6. Calderon interview, October 23, 2014.

7. Notes on teachers at Lincoln High School, box 2, folder 20, 1910, James M. Greenwood Papers (SC86–1), MVSC, KCPL.

8. 1926 Lincoln High School yearbook.

9. 1917 Lincoln High School yearbook.

10. 1920 Lincoln High School yearbook.

11. Quoted in William S. Worley, *J. C. Nichols and the Shaping of Kansas City: Innovation in Planned Residential Communities* (Columbia: University of Missouri Press, 1993), 72.

12. Kevin Fox Gotham, *Race, Real Estate, and Uneven Development: The Kansas City Experience, 1900–2000* (New York: State University of New York Press), 47.

13. Gotham quotes a 1916 speech before the National Conference on City Planning in which real estate developers "absolutely must have municipal control of the surroundings on the adjacent lot" (41). Real estate developers also understand that they cannot work without water and sewer systems and road maintenance.

14. Gotham, *Race, Real Estate, and Uneven Development*, 47.

15. Gwendolyn Calderon interview with author, March 11, 2016.

16. For more on disparate effects of the GI Bill, see Sarah Turner and John Bound, "Closing the Gap or Widening the Divide: The Effects of the G.I. Bill and World War II on the Educational Outcomes of Black Americans," NBER Working Paper no. 9044, July 2002, https://www.nber.org/papers/w9044.

17. Worley, *J. C. Nichols*, 147.

18. Clifford Naysmith, "History of Kansas City," unpublished dissertation, Andrew Theodore Brown Papers, box 1, folder 7, pp. 163–164.

Chapter 12. Residents Reach Pinnacle of Power, 1941

1. "Kansas City Site for a Huge Plant to Assemble Bomber Aircraft," *Kansas City Star*, December 7, 1940. See also "A Negro Defense Plea: Mass Voice for Fair Part in National Program Is Raised," *Kansas City Times*, December 9, 1940.

2. Lucile Bluford oral history, folder 17, p. 72.

3. See, for example, James Gilbert Cassedy, "African Americans and the American Labor Movement," *Federal Records and African American History* 29, no. 2 (Summer 1997). Available at https://www.archives.gov/publications /prologue/1997/summer/american-labor-movement.html.

4. Undated newspaper clipping, BAMA.

5. For more, see Cornelius Bynum, *A. Philip Randolph and the Struggle for Civil Rights* (Champaign: University of Illinois Press, 2010).

6. For more on police brutality and the community's response to it in nineteenth-century Kansas City, see Clifford Naysmith, "History of Kansas City," unpublished dissertation, Andrew Theodore Brown Papers.

7. Bluford oral history, folder 17, pp. 77–78.

8. Johnson to "Gentlemen" at the *Kansas City Star*, February 19, 1941, Donnell Papers.

9. Johnson to "Gentlemen."

10. After Ware's death, Governor Donnell requested an investigation. Most of the information in this section is from the report that followed this investigation. Available in Donnell Papers, folder 6696.

11. "Police Shoot, Then Kick a Dying Man," *Kansas City Call*, August 1, 1941. The issue contained numerous witnesses who told remarkably similar stories.

12. See affidavits submitted to Governor Donnell, specifically one by John Caesar, who claimed that he was assaulted by police officers when he reported what he witnessed. Donnell Papers, folder 7535.

13. "Charles La Baugh Off Police Force Pending Inquiry," *Kansas City Times*, August 7, 1941, included a detailed version of Dewey Ellis's version of events at the bar.

14. "Say Police Officers Beat, Cursed Negroes," *Kansas City Call*, August 1, 1941.

15. Undated newspaper clipping from the *Kansas City Times* in Donnell Papers, folder 7533.

16. Flyer advertising the meeting, Donnell Papers, folder 7537.

17. Franklin to Gov. Donnell, July 31, 1941, Donnell Papers, folder 7533.

18. "Citizens Demand Dismissal of Officers LaBaugh, Ellis," *Kansas City Call*, August 8, 1941.

19. Gov. Donnell to Police Commissioners, August 27, 1941, Donnell Papers, folder 7539.

20. Richard Righter to Gov. Donnell, September 3, 1941, Donnell Papers, folder 7537.

21. Eldridge King to Gov. Donnell, August 30, 1941, Donnell Papers, folder 7537.

22. Reed to Gov. Donnell, August 29, 1941, Donnell Papers, folder 7539.

23. The police board's report answering the allegations of police brutality can be found in Donnell Papers, folder 7540. All quotations come from this report.

24. John Fristoe to Gov. Donnell, August 31, 1941, Donnell Papers, folder 7540.

25. Robinson to Donnell, August 24, 1941, Donnell Papers, folder 7540.

26. One member of the Missouri State Association of Negro Teachers wrote that Chief Reed had become a symbol of hatred "more real, more brutally terrible than Adolf Hitler." August 25, 1941, Donnell Papers, folder 7537.

27. "Chief Gives Ultimatum to Negro Belt," *Kansas City Journal*, August 29, 1941.

28. Gregg to Donnell, September 4, 1941, Donnell Papers, folder 7537.

29. Tracey to Donnell, August 25, 1941, Donnell Papers, folder 7537.

30. Dorothy H. Davis, "All-White Jury Denies K.C. Newspaperwoman Damaged by Registrar," *Kansas City Call*, May 1, 1942.

Chapter 13. Wartime Abroad, Changes at Home, 1942–1954

1. Louis Blue, "Paul Robeson Stops in Middle of Concert to Protest Municipal Auditorium Jim-Crow," *Kansas City Call*, February 20, 1942.

2. Lucile Bluford oral history, folder 16, pp. 44–45.

3. "Famous Baritone Blasts Segregation in Public Building," *Kansas City Call*, February 20, 1942.

4. For more on Wright's lynching, see Dominic Capeci, *The Lynching of Cleo Wright* (Lexington: University Press of Kentucky, 1988).

5. Johnson to Gov. Donnell, February 23, 1942, Donnell Papers. The letter from Frankie Weaver Johnson asserted that Wright and Sturgeon were lovers and that her wounds were self-inflicted so she could keep her affair with him a secret from her sister-in-law, who was staying with her at the time. Weaver went on to assert that Wright wasn't the first Black man with whom Sturgeon had been acquainted, and there were letters that would have proven the affair but the police had "ceased [*sic*] and burned" them. "You would do well to put Mrs. Sturgeon in jail to keep her away from colored youths as she is crazy about them," the writer concluded.

6. Bluford oral history, folder 17, p. 79. See also Lucile Bluford, "Writer's Investigation Shows Officials Could Have Prevented Killing," *Kansas City Call*, January 30, 1942.

7. Biddle to Governor Donnell, February 10, 1942, Donnell Papers.

8. Undated clipping from the *St. Louis Post-Dispatch*, "St. Louis U. Students Asked to Admitting Negroes," folder 6575, Donnell Papers.

9. Gunnar Myrdal, *An American Dilemma: The Negro Problem and American Democracy* (New York: Harper & Row, 1944; rpt. Routledge, 2017).

10. "The Negro Question at the University of Missouri," *Kansas City Star*, January 19, 1944.

11. "'Master Race' Idea Here Too," *Kansas City Call*, October 8, 1943.

12. "Thesaurus Editors to Remove Insults," *Kansas City Call*, April 27, 1945.

13. For more on the treatment of Black soldiers after the First World War, see, for example, "Racial Violence and the Red Summer," National Archives, last reviewed June 28, 2021, https://www.archives.gov/research/african-americans/wwi/red-summer.

14. Bluford oral history, folder 18, p. 81.

15. "Death to Retired Railroad Man, 77," *Kansas City Call*, March 23, 1951.

16. For more on the Black experience with the railroads, see Theodore Kornweibel Jr., *Railroads in the African American Experience: A Photographic Journey* (Baltimore: Johns Hopkins University Press, 2010).

17. "Death to Retired Railroad Man."

18. Calderon interview, October 31, 2015.

19. Danny Herndon, Montgall resident during this period, phone interview with author, July 16, 2014.

20. "Death to William Flynn, Mortician," *Kansas City Call*, July 7, 1950.

21. "Negro Officer Recalls Tough Climb," *Kansas City Times*, January 4, 1969, written when Warren retired from the Kansas City Police Department.

22. "Jordan and Warren Are Detectives," *Kansas City Call*, July 31, 1941.

23. "Negro Officer Recalls Tough Climb," *Kansas City Times*, January 4, 1969.

24. Lee Kniffton and Greig Inglis, "Poverty and Mental Health: Policy, Practice and Research Implications," *BJPsych Bulletin* 44, no. 5 (October 2020): 193–196, https://www.ncbi.nlm.nih.gov/pmc/articles/PMC7525587/.

25. See Robert Farnsworth, *The Life of Leon Jordan and the Shaping Memories of His Father and Grandfather* (Kansas City: University of Missouri, 2015), https://library.umkc.edu/exhibits/jordan.

26. Errol Warren interview with author, May 20, 2016.

27. Joshua Russell interview, conducted by Horace Peterson, April 6, 1983, BAMA.

28. "Mrs. Josie M. Russell Dies; Funeral Saturday," *Kansas City Call*, week of August 26–September 1, 1988.

29. "Death to Retired Railroad Man."

30. Gwen Calderon interview with author, March 11, 2016.

31. "Last Rites for J. H. Bluford," *Kansas City Call*, March 29, 1946. Bluford suffered a cerebral hemorrhage in September 1942, which led to his retirement, but he didn't officially retire from the Kansas City school district until January 1944.

32. Calderon interview, March 11, 2016.

33. For more on the Negro Leagues, see James A. Riley, *The Biographical Encyclopedia of the Negro Baseball Leagues* (New York: Carroll & Graf, 1994). Arthur "Chick" Pullam's entry is on p. 645.

34. Danny Herndon interview with author, July 16, 2016.

35. "Pool Segregation Put KC in Spotlight," *Kansas City Star*, January 15, 2002, September 18, 2005.

36. Jason Roe, "Water Rights," KCPL, https://kchistory.org/week-kansas-city-history/water-rights.

37. Herndon interview. For more on the struggle for integration of public spaces, see Victoria W. Wolcott, *Race, Riots, and Roller Coasters: The Struggle*

over Segregated Recreation in America (Philadelphia: University of Pennsylvania Press, 2012).

38. Calderon interview, October 31, 2015.

39. "Gwendolyn Calderon retires from Southwestern Bell," *Kansas City Call*, week of August 10–17, 1989.

40. "Masons Here in Seventieth Annual Meet," *Kansas City Call*, July 10, 1936.

41. "Big Dedicatory Meeting," *Kansas City Sun*, June 21, 1919. The opening of the bathhouse was a huge event in the Black community and included a parade led by Montgall resident Homer Roberts.

42. Calderon interview, October 31, 2015.

43. Missouri death certificate, https://www.sos.mo.gov/images/archives /deathcerts/1924/1924_00019574.PDF.

44. Brian Burnes, "Former Slave Met Challenges of Freedom Emancipation Provided Chance for Income, Education, Success," *Kansas City Star*, February 11, 1994.

45. Collins Anderson funeral program, February 3, 2016, courtesy of Gwendolyn Calderon. Collins died on January 27, 2016. Herndon transferred from the University of Kansas after his sophomore year and graduated from Pepperdine University with a degree in engineering. Herndon remained in Los Angeles and worked at IBM as an "early computer nerd" and became friends with the well-known attorney Johnnie Cochran. Dr. Perry's grandson, J. E. Perry II, returned to Houston after graduating from Rockhurst High School and became a physician. Herndon interview.

46. Gotham, *Race, Real Estate*, 63.

47. Thomas L. Gillette, "A Study of the Effects of the Negro Invasion on Real Estate Values," *American Journal of Economics and Sociology* 16, no. 2 (January 1957): 151–163.

48. "Last rites for J. H. Bluford."

49. Bluford deposition, *Jenkins vs. State of Missouri*, box 102, Benson Papers.

Chapter 14. The Civil Rights Two-Step, 1955–1967

1. Lucile Bluford speech on May 5, 1968, at dedication of Franklin Elementary. Ramos Vertical File, MVSC, KCPL. She recalled that when the *Brown* decision came down from the US Supreme Court, Franklin went downtown and "bought the biggest type he could find to create the headline." Bluford oral history, folder 18, p. 94.

2. See Gotham, *Race, Real Estate*.

3. "Wrong Way to Integration," *Kansas City Call* editorial, April 20, 1956.

4. Tanner Colby, *Some of My Best Friends Are Black: The Strange Story of Integration in America* (New York: Penguin, 2012), 73–81.

5. Gwendolyn Calderon interview, March 11, 2016.

6. Joshua Russell oral history, BAMA.

7. Errol Warren interview.

8. Rozelia Russell interview with author, April 9, 2016.

9. Retha Lindsay, interview with author, April 9, 2016.

10. Bluford deposition, *Jenkins vs. State of Missouri*, box 102, Benson Papers. See also "Two Schools in One Block?" *Kansas City Call*, April 13, 1956.

11. Gotham, *Race, Real Estate*, 101.

12. Virginia Oldham interview by Reva Griffith, box 3, folder 82, Penn Valley Meeting of Friends Records (K0077), SHSMO-KC.

13. Bluford oral history, folder 17, p. 75.

14. Virginia Oldham—Diligence in Love, 1979, box 3, folder 82, Penn Valley Meeting of Friends Records.

15. Bluford oral history, folder 18, pp. 104–105.

16. A. Scharnihorst, "They Led the Way in Breaking Down Racial Barriers in Kansas City," *Kansas City Star*, January 15, 1995. See also Steve Paul, "Boycott and Rally Pressured KC Department Stores to Open Dining Rooms to Blacks," *Kansas City Star*, February 24, 2004.

17. Dorothy H. Davis, "Changing Discriminatory Practices in Department Store Eating Facilities in Kansas City, Missouri: A Study of a Project in Community Organization as Illustrated by the Community Committee for Social Action of Greater Kansas City" (master's thesis, University of Kansas, 1960), Dorothy Hodge Johnson Collection, box 1, folder 8, Kenneth Spencer Research Library, University of Kansas.

18. Bluford oral history, folder 18, pp. 104–105.

19. "A New Civil Rights Era!" *Kansas City Call*, September 20, 1963.

Chapter 15. Surviving Riot, Attacks, and Decline, 1968–1998

1. Lucile Bluford, "The Black Press," undated speech, Manuscript file, MVSC, KCPL.

2. For a list of Bluford's honors, see Bluford's oral history, appendix 6, folder 21.

3. For more on the riot, see Joel P. Rhodes, "It Finally Happened Here: The 1968 Riot in Kansas City, Missouri," *Missouri Historical Review* 91, no. 3 (April 1997): 103–112.

4. Andy Sullivan, "U.S. Freeways Flattened Black Communities," Reuters,

May 25, 2021, https://www.reuters.com/world/us/us-freeways-flattened -black-neighborhoods-nationwide-2021-05-25/.

5. Donna Stewart, editor of the *Call* after Bluford, was a middle-school student in 1968 and remembered when Lincoln students arrived at her school to collect more students. Author interview, June 13, 2014.

6. Sid Bordman, "Looting and Burning Hit Kansas City Liquor Stores: Retailers, Wholesalers Suffer Substantial Losses, Kansas City Riot and Its Effect on the Alcoholic Beverage Industry," Report by the *Missouri Beverage Journal*, ed. Gary Diamond, Richard Bolling Papers, Civil Disorders, container 57, folder 14, SHSMO-KC.

7. Bluford oral history, folder 19, pp. 120–121.

8. Calderon interview, October 31, 2015.

9. "A City Shaken by Riots Is Offered a Long Look at How? Why? Future?" *Kansas City Star*, May 5, 1968.

10. "Negroes Still Angry at Police," *Kansas City Star*, May 5, 1968.

11. "Editor of the Call Says Police Incited Riot in Kansas City," *Kansas City Call*, April 26, 1968.

12. "Editor of the Call Says Police Incited Riot."

13. Bluford oral history, folder 19, pp. 122–123.

14. Bluford oral history, folder 19, pp. 123–124.

15. See Mike McGraw and Glenn Rice, "Unsolved Killing of Leon Jordan Echoes Civil Rights Era," *Kansas City Star*, July 6, 2021.

16. Bluford oral history, folder 19, pp. 134–136.

17. Bluford oral history, folder 19, p. 136.

18. Kevin Q. Murphy, "Ending Murders Is Goal This Month," *Kansas City Star*, August 1, 1991.

19. Calderon interview, April 7, 2016.

20. Herndon interview, July 16, 2016.

21. After Lucile Bluford's death, Gwendolyn Calderon wrote a letter about some of her memories of the editor, which described her father's habit of checking in on her. "Just Lucile," *Kansas City Call*, June 20, 2003.

22. Bluford to Manfred Maier, February 16, 1982, box 1, folder 10, Lucile Bluford Collection, LaBudde Special Collections, UMKC.

23. Bluford to Caron, May 2, 1981, box 1, folder 10, Bluford Collection.

24. Calderon interview, October 31, 2015.

25. Author interview with Columbus Neal, October 16, 2015.

26. Calderon interview, October 31, 2015. The home was completely renovated and was sold in 2022.

27. Calderon interview, October 31, 2015.

28. Harry Hawkins interview by Detective Ray Staley, May 27, 1997;

interview with Travionn M. J. Wallace by Detectives Marcus Regan and Robert Gibbs, May 28, 1997, case no. 97–054822, Kansas City Police Department records.

29. Calderon interview, October 31, 2015.

30. Glen Rice, "Rising Hope Amid Urban Decline," *Kansas City Star*, April 11, 1993.

Chapter 16. Conclusion

1. See V. J. Felitti, R. F. Anda, D. Nordenberg, D. F. Williamson, A. M. Spitz, V. Edwards, M. P. Edwards, M. P. Koss, and J. S. Marks, "Relationship of Childhood Abuse and Household Dysfunction to Many of the Leading Causes of Death in Adults," *American Journal of Preventative Medicine* 14 (1998): 245–248.

2. Dana Goldstein, "'Threatening the Future': The High Stakes of Deepening School Segregation," *New York Times*, May 10, 2019.

3. Martin, *Our Negro Population*, 120.

4. "Negroes Still Angry at Police," *Kansas City Star*, May 5, 1968.

5. Ta-Nehisi Coates, "The Case for Reparations," *Atlantic*, June 2014.

PRIMARY SOURCES AND SELECT BIBLIOGRAPHY

Abbreviations Used in Notes and References

BAMA	Black Archives of Mid-America, Kansas City, Missouri
KCPL	Kansas City Public Library, Kansas City, Missouri
MVSC	Missouri Valley Special Collections
SHSMO–C	State Historical Society of Missouri Research Center–Columbia
SHSMO–KC	State Historical Society of Missouri Research Center–Kansas City
UMKC	University of Missouri Kansas City

Author Interviews

Bluford, Guion. Phone interview, August 21, 2014.
Calderon, Gwendolyn. August 14, 2014, October 23, 2014, October 31, 2015, March 11, 2016, April 9, 2016. Kansas City, Missouri.
Cochée, Renée. March 14, 2014, Culver City, California.
Herndon, Danny. Phone interview, July 16, 2016.
Lindsey, Retha. April 9, 2016, Kansas City, Missouri.
Neal, Columbus. October 16, 2015, Cameron, Missouri.
Pittman, Paul. August 14, 2014, April 9, 2016. Kansas City, Missouri.
Russell, Rozelia. April 9, 2016, Kansas City, Missouri.
Stewart, Donna. June 13, 2014, Kansas City, Missouri.
Warren, Errol. May 20, 2016, Lee's Summit, Kansas.

Other Oral Histories

Bluford, Lucile. Interview by Fern S. Ingersoll. May 13, May 15, August 26, and August 28, 1989, and March 19, 1990. Washington Press Club Foundation, Women in Journalism Oral History Project Records, 1987–1994 (C3958), SHSMO–C.
Oldham, Virginia. Interview by Reva Griffith. 1978. Penn Valley Meeting of Friends Records (K0077), SHSMO–KC.
Russell, Joshua. Interview by Horace Peterson. 1983. Black Archives of Mid-America.

Archival Collections

Black Archives of Mid-America
    Franklin Collection
    Lincoln High School Yearbook Collection
    Oral History Collection
Missouri Valley Special Collections, Kansas City Public Library, Kansas City,
    Missouri
    City Directories
    James M. Greenwood Papers (SC86–1)
    Kansas City School District Records
    Ramos Special Collections
State Historical Society of Missouri, Columbia (SHSMO–C)
    Arthur Mastick Hyde Gubernatorial Papers (C0007)
    Forrest C. Donnell Gubernatorial Papers (C0194)
    Women in Journalism Oral History Project (C3958)
State Historical Society of Missouri, Kansas City (SHSMO–KC)
    Andrew Theodore Brown (1923–1983) Collection, 1960–1963 (K0011)
    Arthur A. Benson II Papers (K0250)
    Book Lovers' Club Records, 1915–2011 (K0901)
    Fellowship House Association of Greater Kansas City (K094)
    Jackson County Medical Society Collection, 1859–1938 (K0088)
University of Kansas, Kenneth Spencer Research Library
    Papers of Dorothy Hodge Johnson, Dowdal Davis Jr., and John A. Hodge,
    Kansas Collection, RH MS 549
    Thatcher Family Collection (RH MS 1250)
University of Massachusetts Amherst, Special Collections and University
    Archives
    W. E. B. Du Bois Papers (MS 312)
University of Missouri Kansas City, Special Collections and Archives
    Lucile H. Bluford Collection (MS-0219)

Newspapers

Detroit Plaindealer
Kansas City Call
Kansas City Journal
Kansas City Star
Kansas City Sun
Kansas City Times
Lawrence Journal-World

Professional World
Rising Son
Topeka Plaindealer
University Daily Kansan

Secondary Sources

Alexander, Michelle. *The New Jim Crow: Mass Incarceration in the Age of Colorblindness*, revised edition. New York: New Press, 2012.

Blackmon, Douglas A. *Slavery by Another Name: The Re-Enslavement of Black Americans from the Civil War to World War II*. New York: Random House Anchor Books, 2008.

Brooks, Sheila, and Clint C. Wilson II. *Lucile Bluford and the* Kansas City Call: *Activist Voice for Social Justice*. New York: Lexington Books, 2018.

Bynum, Cornelius L. *A. Philip Randolph and the Struggle for Civil Rights*. Champaign: University of Illinois Press, 2010.

Capeci Jr., Dominic J. *The Lynching of Cleo Wright*. Lexington: University Press of Kentucky, 1998.

Colby, Tanner. *Some of My Best Friends Are Black: The Strange Story of Integration in America*. New York: Penguin, 2012.

Coulter, Charles E. *Take Up the Black Man's Burden: Kansas City's African American Communities, 1865–1939*. Columbia: University of Missouri Press, 2006.

Crouch, Stanley. *Kansas City Lightning: The Rise and Times of Charlie Parker*. New York: HarperCollins, 2013.

Davis, Angela J., ed. *Policing the Black Man: Arrest, Prosecution, and Imprisonment*. New York: Penguin Random House, 2018.

Driggs, Frank, and Chuck Haddix. *Kansas City Jazz: From Ragtime to Bebop—A History*. New York: Oxford University Press, 2005.

Du Bois, W. E. B. *John Brown*. Philadelphia: George W. Jacobs, 1909; New York: International Publishers, 1962.

———. *The Souls of Black Folk*. Chicago: A. C. McClurg, 1903.

Esedebe, Olisanwuche P. *Pan-Africanism: The Idea and Movement, 1776–1991*. 2nd ed. Washington, DC: Howard University Press, 1994.

Foner, Eric. *Reconstruction: America's Unfinished Revolution, 1863–1987*. New York: HarperCollins, 1988.

Franklin, John Hope. *The Free Negro in North Carolina, 1790–1860*. Chapel Hill: University of North Carolina Press, 1943.

Gotham, Kevin Fox. *Race, Real Estate, and Uneven Development: The Kansas City Experience, 1900–2000*. Albany: State University of New York Press, 2002.

Griffin, G. S. *Racism in Kansas City: A Short History*. Traverse City, MI: Chandler Lake Books, 2015.

Hayes, Chris. *A Colony in a Nation*. New York: W. W. Norton, 2017.

Hinton, Elizabeth. *From the War on Poverty to the War on Crime: The Making of Mass Incarceration in America*. Cambridge, MA: Harvard University Press, 2016.

Hoffman, Frederick. *Race Traits and Tendencies of the American Negro*. New York: Macmillan, 1896. Available at https://archive.org/details/racetraits tenden00hoff.

Johnson, Kathryn, and Addie Hunton. *Two Colored Women with the American Expeditionary Forces*. New York: Brooklyn Eagle Press, 1920. Available at https://archive.org/details/twocoloredwomenw00huntiala.

Kendi, Ibram X. *Stamped from the Beginning: The Definitive History of Racist Ideas in America*. New York: Perseus Books, 2016.

Kornweibel Jr., Theodore. *Railroads in the African American Experience: A Photographic Journey*. Baltimore: Johns Hopkins University Press, 2010.

Lewis, David Levering. *W. E. B. Du Bois, Biography of a Race, 1868–1919*. New York: Henry Holt, 1993.

——. *W. E. B. Du Bois, the Fight for Equality and the American Century, 1919–1963*. New York: Henry Holt, 2000.

Lieberson, Stanley. *A Piece of the Pie: Blacks and White Immigrants since 1880*. Berkeley: University of California Press, 1980.

Martin, Asa E. *Our Negro Population: A Sociological Study of the Negroes of Kansas City, Missouri*. Kansas City, MO: Franklin HudsonPublishing Co. Available online at https://archive.org/details/ourngropopulati00mart.

Massey, Douglas S., and Nancy A. Denton. *American Apartheid: Segregation and the Making of the American Underclass*. Cambridge, MA: Harvard University Press, 1993.

McGhee, Heather. *The Sum of Us: What Racism Costs Everyone and How We Can Prosper Together*. New York: Penguin Random House, 2021.

Montgomery, Rick, and Shirl Kasper. *Kansas City: An American Story*. Edited by Monroe Dodd. Kansas City, MO: Kansas City Star Books, 1999.

Morrison, Toni. *The Origin of Others*. Cambridge, MA: Harvard University Press, 2017.

Muhammad, Khalil Gibran. *The Condemnation of Blackness: Race, Crime, and the Making of Modern Urban America*. Cambridge, MA: Harvard University Press, 2011.

Myrdal, Gunnar. *An American Dilemma: The Negro Problem and American Democracy*. Originally published in New York: 1944 by Harper and & Row, 1944;. Republished byNew York: Routledge, 2017.

Odum, Howard W. *Social and Mental Traits of the Negro: Research into the Conditions of the Negro Race in Southern Towns, a Study in Race Traits, Tendencies and Prospects.* New York: Columbia University, 1910. Available at https://archive.org/stream/socialmental00odumrich/socialmental00odumrich_djvu.txt.

Painter, Nell Irvin. *The History of White People.* New York: W. W. Norton, 2010.

Pearson Jr., Nathan W. *Goin' to Kansas City.* Chicago: University of Illinois Press, 1987.

Perry, J. E. *Forty Cords of Wood: Memoirs of a Medical Doctor.* Jefferson City, MO: Lincoln University, 1947.

Restuccia, B. S., with Edward "Sonny" Gibson and Geraldlyn "Geri" Sanders. *Homer B. Roberts 1882–1952: An Extraordinary Man.* Kansas City, MO: Rustic Enterprise, 2001.

Robinson, Gwendolyn, and John W. Robinson. *Seek the Truth: A Story of Chatham's Black Community.* Self-published, 1989.

Roediger, David R. *The Wages of Whiteness: Race and the Making of the American Working Class.* New York: Verso, 2007.

——. *Working toward Whiteness: How America's Immigrants Became White: The Strange Journey from Ellis Island to the Suburbs.* New York: Perseus Books, 2005.

Russell, Ross. *Jazz Style in Kansas City and the Southwest.* New York: Da Capo Press, 1997.

Satter, Beryl. *Family Properties: How the Struggle over Race and Real Estate Transformed Chicago and Urban America.* New York: Picador, 2009.

Schirmer, Sherry Lamb. *A City Divided: The Racial Landscape of Kansas City, 1900–1960.* Columbia: University of Missouri Press, 2002.

Shortridge, James R. *Kansas City and How It Grew, 1822–2011.* Lawrence: University Press of Kansas, 2012.

Smith, Jessie Carney, ed. *Notable Black American Women.* Vol. 2. Detroit: Gale,

Sullivan, Patricia. *Lift Every Voice: The NAACP and the Making of the Civil Rights Movement.* New York: New Press, 2009.

Tuttle, William T. *Race Riots: Chicago in the Red Summer of 1919.* New York: Atheneum, 1972.

Villard, Oswald Garrison. *John Brown 1800–1859: A Biography Fifty Years After.* Gloucester, MA: Peter Smith, 1965.

Washington, Booker T., ed. *The Negro Problem.* New York: James Pott, 1903.

Whitney, Carrie Westlake. *Kansas City, Missouri: Its History and Its People*, vol. 2, *1808–1908.* Chicago: S. J. Clarke, 1908.

Wilkerson, Isabel. *Caste: The Origins of Our Discontents.* New York: Random House, 2020.

———. *The Warmth of Other Suns: The Epic Story of America's Great Migration*. New York: Random House, 2010.

Wilkins, Roy. *Standing Fast: The Autobiography of Roy Wilkins*. New York: Viking Press, 1982.

Williams, Doretha. *Kansas Grows the Best Race Women: Black Club Women in Kansas, 1900–1930*. PhD dissertation, University of Kansas, 2011.

Wilson, Clint. *Whither the Black Press? Glorious Past, Uncertain Future*. Bloomington, IN: Xlibris, 2014.

Wolcott, Victoria W. *Race, Riots, and Roller Coasters: The Struggle over Segregated Recreation in America*. Philadelphia: University of Pennsylvania Press, 2012.

Worley, William S. *J. C. Nichols and the Shaping of Kansas City: Innovation in Planned Residential Communities*. Columbia: University of Missouri Press, 1993.

Wright, Charlotte Crogman, *Beneath the Southern Cross: The Story of an American Bishop's Wife in South Africa*. New York: Exposition, 1955.

Young, William, and Nathan Young. *Your Kansas City and Mine*. 1950; reprinted in 1997 by the Midwest Afro-American Genealogy Interest Coalition (MAGIC) at the Bruce R. Watkins Cultural Heritage Center.

INDEX

Page numbers in *italics* refer to photographs.